Developing Reading and Writing in Second-Language Learners

This book is a synthesis of the full volume, *Developing Literacy in Second-Language Learners*, reporting the findings of the National Literacy Panel on language-minority children and youth. The Panel—a distinguished group of expert researchers in reading, language, bilingualism, research methods, and education—was appointed to identify, assess, and synthesize research on the education of language-minority children and youth with respect to their attainment of literacy. In this book, chapters adapted from the original report concisely review the statement of knowledge on the development of literacy in language-minority children and youth, in relation to five specific themes:

- Development of literacy in second-language learners
- Cross-linguistic relationships in second-language learners
- Sociocultural contexts and literacy development
- Educating language-minority students: instruction and professional development
- Student assessment

This more accessible version of the full report is intended for researchers as well as for use in a wide range of teacher preparation courses and in-service/staff development programs that deal with educating English language learners, and as a resource for individual teachers and other school practitioners.

Developing Reading and Writing in Second-Language Learners: Lessons from the report of the National Literacy Panel on language-minority children and youth

A co-publication of Routledge,
the Center for Applied Linguistics,
and
the International Reading Association

Edited by

Diane August
Principal Investigator

Timothy Shanahan
Panel Chair

 Routledge
Taylor & Francis Group
New York   London

 INTERNATIONAL
Reading
Association

 CENTER
FOR APPLIED
LINGUISTICS

First published by
Lawrence Earlbaum Associates
10 Industrial Avenue, Mahway, New Jersey 07430

Reprinted 2008 by Routledege

Taylor & Francis Group
270 Madison Avenue
New York, NY 10016

Taylor & Francis Group
2 Park Square, Milton Park,
Abingdon, Oxon OX14 4RN

Routledge is an imprint of the Taylor & Francis Group, an informa business

© 2008 Taylor & Francis

Co-published by Routledge, the Center for Applied Linguistics, and the
International Reading Association, 800 Barksdale Road, PO Box 8139,
Newark DE 19714-8139, USA. Visit **www.reading.org** for more information
about IRA books, membership, and other services. Visit **www.cal.org** to learn
more about the Center for Applied Linguistics

Typeset in Palatino by
RefineCatch Limited, Bungay, Suffolk
Printed and bound in the United States of America on acid-free paper by
Edwards Brothers, Inc., Ann Arbor, MI.

Library of Congress Cataloging in Publication Data
A catalog record for this book has been requested

ISBN10: 0–8058–6208–0 (hbk)
ISBN10: 0–8058–6209–9 (pbk)
ISBN10: 1–4106–1590–1 (ebk)

ISBN13: 978–0–8058–6208–9 (hbk)
ISBN13: 978–0–8058–6209–6 (pbk)
ISBN13: 978–1–4106–1590–9 (ebk)

Diane August
To Robert Politzer, my dissertation advisor, for his encouragement and support. To the children of Whisman School District, for inspiring me to work on behalf of language-minority children

Timothy Shanahan
To the College of Education at the University of Illinois at Chicago for allowing me the freedom to participate in endeavors such as the National Literacy Panel

Contents

Preface

In the United States, a large and growing number of students come from homes where English is not the primary language. The number of such students has doubled during the past two decades. Language-minority students are not faring well in U.S. schools; most are failing to meet state education standards (Kindler, 2002), and these students are 300% more likely to drop out of high school than other students (National Center for Education Statistics, 2004)

This volume is a summary of the longer report of the National Literacy Panel on Language-Minority Children and Youth entitled *Developing Literacy in Second-Language Learners*, published in 2006. The goal of this volume is to provide a briefer summary version of that report that would be somewhat more accessible to the general reader. The introductory and concluding chapters of the original report remain virtually unchanged from the original report. However, the rest of the volume includes less detail than the original. This shorter, more accessible version of the full report is intended for researchers as well as for use in a wide range of teacher preparation courses and in in-service staff development programs that deal with educating English language learners, and as resource for individual teachers and other school practitioners.

Two events preceded and contributed to the establishment of the National Literacy Panel on Language-Minority Children and Youth. In December 2000, an important document was published, the report of the National Reading Panel (NRP; National Institute of Child Health and Human Development, 2000) that identified five research-based elements that need to be present in any reading approach or program for children whose first language is English to develop the skills necessary to become successful life-long readers (phonics, phonemic awareness, reading fluency, vocabulary, and reading comprehension). The NRP surveyed, analyzed, and reported on the research literature that addressed what had been shown to be effective instruction for those five elements of reading. The NRP, given the enormity of the task before it, made a conscious decision not to include the scientific literature available in the development of language and literacy for those students learning to read in English for whom English was not their first or native language.

In 1999, two federal research agencies published a solicitation for research to address issues of learning and instruction in non-English-speaking children with a stated emphasis on Spanish-speaking children learning to read in English.[1] Researchers enthusiastically responded, and a research network was funded. The new projects took the current information on reading skills and optimal instructional methods for teaching reading as compiled in the report of the NRP and sought to determine whether and how those principles and approaches might apply to English-language learners, specifically Spanish-speaking children.

Shortly after the funding of that research network, a distinguished group of experts—researchers in reading, language, bilingualism, research methods, and education—from the United States and Canada were invited to be part of the new body, the National Literacy Panel on Language-Minority Children and Youth. This Panel, funded by the Institute of Education Sciences with funds from the Department of Education Office of English Language Acquisition and the National Institute of Child Health and Human Development (NICHD), was charged to examine and report on the research literature on the development of literacy in children whose first language is not the societal or majority language—language-minority students. Diane August served as principal investigator of the Panel, and Timothy Shanahan helped guide the work as Panel chair. David Francis and Frederick Erickson provided methodological expertise, and Catherine Snow and Donna Christian served as senior advisors. The Panel employed two research associates who were instrumental in producing several of the chapters: Nonie Lesaux and Cheryl Dressler.

The formal charge to the Panel was to identify, assess, and synthesize research on the education of language-minority children and youth with respect to their attainment of literacy, and to produce a comprehensive report evaluating and synthesizing this literature. This book is the culmination of that effort. Through extensive discussion, the Panel identified five domains to investigate: the development of literacy in language-minority children and youth, cross-linguistic relationships,

---

[1]Request for Applications number RFA-HD-99–012, in the NIH Guide to Grants and Contracts, July 1999. This document can be accessed at http://grants.nih.gov/grants/guide/rfa-files/RFAHD-99–012.html

sociocultural contexts and literacy development, instruction and professional development, and student assessment. Within each research domain, the Panel identified a series of research questions that guided the review of that domain. To address these research questions, the Panel divided into five subcommittees, with each subcommittee responsible for overseeing the synthesis of the research in a particular domain. Over five Panel meetings, many subcommittee meetings, and numerous conference calls, the substantive issues in each of these areas were outlined and discussed, and the relevant literature was reviewed. The Panel also held several open meetings to gain public advice and input from educators, community members, and researchers. The original volume underwent two rounds of external review by anonymous reviewers selected by the U.S. Department of Education.

The volume reviews the state of knowledge on the development of literacy in language-minority children and youth. Each chapter states the research questions for the chapter, provides background information, describes the methodology, summarizes the empirical findings, addresses methodological issues, and makes recommendations for future research.

REFERENCES

August, D., and Shanahan, T. (Eds.) (2006). Developing literacy in second-language learners: Report of the National Literacy Panel on Language-Minority Children and Youth. Mahwah, NJ: Lawrence Erlbaum Associates.

Kindler, A. L. (2002). *Survey of the states' limited English proficient students and available educational programs and services. 2000–2001 summary report*. Washington, DC: National Clearinghouse for English Language Acquisition.

National Institute of Child Health and Human Development. (2000). Report of the National Reading Panel. *Teaching children to read: An evidence-based assessment of the scientific research literature on reading and its implications for instruction. Reports of the subgroup*. (NIH Publication No. 00–4754). Washington, DC: U.S. Government Printing Office. Also available online: http://www.nichd. nih.gov/publications/nrp/report.htm

National Center for Education Statistics. (2004). *The condition of education, 2004*. Retrieved July 16, 2004, from http://nces.ed.gov/programs/coe

Acknowledgments

The Panel wishes to acknowledge the support and assistance of officials from the federal agencies. Our thanks go to Gil Narro García from the Institute of Education Sciences, who served as the Contracting Officer's Representative for the project at the U.S. Department of Education and also served as an advisory committee member for the Panel along with Peggy McCardle from the NICHD, National Institutes of Health; Kathleen Leos from the Office of English Language Acquisition, U.S. Department of Education; and Sandra Baxter from the National Institute for Literacy.

The Panel benefited from the assistance of numerous research assistants, including Daniel Bekele, Gina Biancarosa, Amy Crosson, Jennifer Gray, Natalia Jacobsen, Jennifer Kang, Michael Kieffer, Adele LaFrance, Marjolaine Limbos, Elana Peled, Patrick Proctor, and Barbara Schuster. An editor of an earlier draft of the volume, Rona Briere, greatly improved its readability. Russell Gersten and Jill Fitzgerald reviewed sections of the volume and provided detailed comments to the Panel.

The Panel also benefited from the support of staff at the Center for Applied Linguistics and SRI International. At SRI, Marilyn Gillespie served as project manager, and Regie Stites served as a senior advisor. At the Center for Applied Linguistics, Grace Burkart managed the project, and Christina Card and Leo Vizcarra served as administrative assistants. Special thanks also go to SRI staff who worked on the final production of the volume: Klaus Kraus, SRI senior editor; Stacey Eaton, administrative specialist; and Bonnee Groover, technical administrator.

Most of all, thanks and acknowledgment of extraordinary effort are due to the members of the Panel and the chair. In addition to participating in meetings and numerous conference calls, and reading and reviewing thousands of pages of studies and background materials, members and staff took responsibility for preparing chapters in this volume.

—Diane August Principal Investigator
National Literacy Panel on Language-Minority Children and Youth

1

Introduction and Methodology

Diane August and Timothy Shanahan

CHARGE TO THE PANEL

In 2002, the Institute for Education Sciences of the U.S. Department of Education formed the National Literacy Panel on Language-Minority Children and Youth. The formal charge to the Panel was to identify, assess, and synthesize research on the education of language-minority children and youth with respect to their attainment of literacy, and to produce a comprehensive report evaluating and synthesizing this literature. The Panel's review represents the most comprehensive review of the research to date on the development of literacy in second-language learners. This report provides a summary of the work of the Panel.

Key terms germane to the Panel's charge include literacy skills, oral language proficiency, societal/national language, language minority, English language learners, limited English proficient, and bilingual students and programs. *Literacy skills* are defined in this review as including pre-reading skills, such as concepts of print and alphabetic knowledge; word-level skills, including decoding, word reading, pseudoword reading, and spelling; and text-level skills, including fluency, reading comprehension, and writing skills. For purposes of this review, *oral language proficiency* denotes knowledge or use of specific aspects of oral language, including phonology, vocabulary, morphology, grammar, and discourse domains; it encompasses skills in both comprehension and expression. We also include studies of phonological processes (phonological recoding, phonological memory, and phonological awareness) because it has been hypothesized that these processes mediate the development of written forms of language (Adams, 1990; Ehri, 1998; Metsala & Walley, 1998; Scarborough, 2001). A *societal language* is one, often one of several, of the languages used in a country for public discourse, whether official (that is, recognized by law) or not, while a *national language* is considered to be the chief language of a country.

There are many labels for the students and programs under consideration in this report. The most commonly used term, *language minority*, refers to individuals from homes where a language other than a national language is actively used, who therefore have had an opportunity to develop some level of proficiency in a language other than a national language. A language-minority student may be of limited second-language proficiency, bilingual, or essentially monolingual in the second language (August and Hakuta, 1997). *Second-language learners* come from language backgrounds other than a national language and whose second language proficiency is not yet developed to the point where they can profit fully from instruction solely in the second language. In instances where the students are acquiring English as a second language, they are referred to as *English-language learners*. The term *limited English proficient (LEP)* may be used, however, when we are quoting another source or citing legal requirements. Appendix 1.A includes a list of standard terms used in the report.

Two other terms appear frequently in this volume. The first is *bilingual students* or *bilingual education* programs. Some education programs for second-language learners use the students' native language as the students acquire the second language. Thus, the term bilingual is often used to refer to programs that use students' first languages as well as a national language for instructional purposes. We also use the term bilingual to refer to individuals who have developed proficiency in more than one language.

PROCEDURES USED TO CONDUCT THE REVIEW

Panel Staff

The Panel included scholars with deep expertise in critical components of literacy, language learning, or research methodology, and an effort was made to include language-minority researchers. In addition, five panelists have important cross-cutting expertise: two are methodologists, two are experts in learning disabilities, and one is an expert in the assessment of students from culturally and linguistically diverse backgrounds.

To address the research questions, the Panel was divided into five subcommittees, each of which oversaw syntheses of research relevant to particular issues. The Panel was served by a principal investigator, Diane August, who managed the project; a chairperson, Timothy Shanahan, who helped guide the Panel's work; and two methodologists— David Francis, who provided expertise in quantitative methodology, and Frederick Erickson, who provided guidance in qualitative methodology. Catherine Snow and Donna Christian served as senior advisors to the Panel. In addition, the Panel was served by two senior research associates who were instrumental in preparing several of the chapters: Nonie Lesaux (Chapters 3 and 6) and Cheryl Dressler (Chapter 4). A list of the subcommittees can be found in Appendix 1.B. Biographical sketches of the Panel members and other contributors can be found at the end of this volume. In addition to the reviews by Christian, Snow, Jill Fitzgerald, and Russell Gersten solicited by the Panel, this volume also reflects the input of anonymous reviewers solicited by the funder. These reviewers provided detailed commentary on multiple drafts, and their contributions were an instrumental part of the process leading to this volume.

Identification of Research Questions

The Panel identified five domains to investigate: the development of literacy in language-minority children and youth (Chapter 3), cross-linguistic and cross-modal relationships (Chapter 4), sociocultural contexts and literacy development (Chapter 5), instruction and professional development (Chapter 6), and student assessment (Chapter 7).

Source of Publications and Current Database

On the basis of the research questions, we set review parameters to ensure as complete and unbiased a search of the research literature as possible. For the most part, the review focused on language-minority children ages 3 to 18 acquiring literacy in a national language. However, to answer some questions, we also reviewed research on the acquisition of literacy in a foreign language, if the foreign language were English, and studied the acquisition of French by English speakers in Canada. The review incorporated only research published in peer-reviewed journals dating back to 1980. However, to be consistent with prior reviews on one topic (Chapter 6), we accepted studies of language of instruction that pre-dated 1980. For some chapters, dissertations and technical reports were used if the research in peer-reviewed journals was not sufficient to answer the research questions. Book chapters and literature reviews were used to provide context for the findings presented; these are used in the discussions, but not in establishing the research findings. Appendix 1.C lists the acceptance criteria used across the chapters in this volume.

Rigorous methodological standards were applied in both the selection and analysis of research studies. Studies had to analyze data; no thought pieces or articles detailing personal experiences were included. If language-minority students did not make up at least 50% of the sample, outcome data had to be disaggregated for those students. For experiments or quasi-experiments, the study had to include a control or comparison group and had to use either random assignment to conditions or pre-testing or other matching criteria to ensure initial similarity of the groups prior to treatment; groups had to have more than four subjects to allow for the appropriate statistical analyses (Maxwell and Delaney, 2003). Each subcommittee adopted additional standards to ensure sound findings and these are reported in the individual chapters that follow.

Approximately 1,800 articles were initially identified in the literature search, but these were reduced as panelists examined the studies more carefully. The database now consists of 970 studies (293 of which were used for this report because they are relevant to the research questions and meet our methodological criteria). Most studies were conducted in the United States, followed by the United Kingdom, Canada, and Australia. However, studies from the Netherlands, Finland, and Israel appear as well. Some studies are relevant to more than one question and, thus, are cited in multiple locations in the report.

Search Procedures

To identify studies for use in this review, we conducted seven literature searches. These entailed extensive searches of various electronic databases and hand searches of particular journals. The purpose of these carefully documented searches (for more details see the longer version of this report, August and Shanahan, 2006) was to ensure the most comprehensive, unbiased search possible for relevant studies. The intent was to use search procedures that could be replicated in future reviews.

Coding Instrument

A coding instrument was developed for use by the Panel. The use of this instrument ensured that each study in the database met the selection criteria, and that no studies that met the criteria were excluded from the report. The use of a common coding instrument ensured that the various articles were summarized in the same ways for all studies. A compact disk containing the database is included as part of the full Panel report published in 2006.

Public Advice and Input

To gain public advice and input from educators, community members, and researchers who were not on the Panel, two sets of outreach meetings were held. The first set of meetings, in Washington, DC and Los Angeles in 2002, helped determine what the research, policy, and practitioner communities considered important research questions. The second set of meetings was held to obtain feedback on a draft of the final report. One meeting was held at the National Reading Conference's annual meeting in Scottsdale, Arizona in 2003 and the other at the International Reading Association meeting in Reno, Nevada in 2004.

NATURE OF THE REVIEW

Types of Research Evidence and Breadth of Research Methods

The Panel synthesized a complex body of empirical data drawn from many research methodologies. As has been indicated by the Committee on Scientific Principles for Education Research, "multiple methods, applied over time and tied to evidentiary standards, are essential to establishing a base of scientific knowledge" (Shavelson & Towne, 2002, p. 2). The committee goes on to indicate that one of the hallmarks of scientific inquiry is the application of "appropriate" methodology to the questions being asked.

Accordingly, the Panel relied on controlled experiments and quasi-experimental designs to evaluate the effectiveness of instructional approaches. However, the Panel's charge also required review of the research literature addressing questions about the nature of literacy development, relationships among various language-learning abilities, and the status of particular approaches in the education of language-minority students. These questions are more appropriately answered through descriptive, ethnographic, and correlational studies and for this reason studies that used these methods were included in the Panel's report.

Data Analysis

When at least five group comparison studies addressed the same hypothesis relevant to a research question, meta-analytic techniques were used. For questions for which quantitative techniques were not appropriate, a systematic interpretive procedure (Fitzgerald, 1995a, 1995b; Glaser, 1978) was used to summarize findings across studies. For each research question, studies were categorized by major themes. Studies in each group were reread and classified with regard to similarities, differences, and results to determine cross-cutting themes, as well as to methodological strengths and weaknesses.

SCOPE OF THE VOLUME

This volume is organized partly around the traditional distinction between basic and applied research, but is also structured to reflect specific areas of concern for educational policymakers. Chapters 3 and 4 address basic research questions about bilingualism, second-language acquisition, and relationships between first- and second-language oral proficiency and literacy. Chapter 5, on sociocultural context and literacy development, addresses both basic research about the relationship between sociocultural variables and student outcomes and more applied research related to the influence of sociocultural variables on the contexts in which students acquire second-language literacy. Chapters 6 and 7 are organized around more practical issues: program evaluations that explore the influence of native-language instruction on second-language literacy, effective instruction, schooling, professional development, and assessment. All of these topics represent key areas of concern in discussions of educational reform.

A final contextual parameter for this volume is a set of assumptions shared by the majority of members of this Panel, which echo those of the Committee on Developing a Research Agenda on the Education of Limited-English Proficient and Bilingual Students. They are as follows: (a) all children in the United States should be able to function fully in the English language; (b) English-language learners should be held to the same expectations and have the same opportunities for achievement in academic content areas as other students; and (c) in an increasingly global economic and political world, proficiency in languages other than English and an understanding of different cultures are valuable in their own right and represent a worthwhile goal for schools.

OVERVIEW OF FINDINGS

Developmental Perspective

The studies reviewed in Chapter 3 indicate that certain components of literacy can not fully develop until other, precursor skills are acquired. For efficient word-recognition skills to develop, for example, it is necessary to have good decoding and orthographic skills; without accurate and fast word-recognition skills, learners cannot achieve satisfactory levels of reading comprehension. However, efficient reading comprehension depends not only on efficient word-recognition skills, but also on general language proficiency.

The dynamic nature of development means that the relationships among the components of literacy are not static and may change with the learner's age, levels of second-language oral proficiency, cognitive abilities, and previous learning. For example, certain aspects of language and literacy are related to general cognitive maturity. Adolescent second-language learners (schooled only in their first language) have well-developed phonological awareness skills, but a similar level of development would not be as likely for 6-year-olds, who are cognitively less advanced in this regard. Similarly, older English-language learners notice cognates common to Spanish and English, but primary-level learners are less likely to do so.

An important finding that emerges from the research reviewed in Chapter 3 is that, for most language-minority children, word-level aspects of literacy, such as decoding or spelling, can be and often are developed to levels equal to those of their monolingual peers. However, it is important to note that while language-minority and monolinguals tend to accomplish similar levels of word identification, none of the studies included a measure of speed of word reading. Similarities in development, however, are not the case for text-level skills, like reading comprehension, which rarely approach the levels achieved by monolingual students. Other findings suggest that although the effect of second-language oral proficiency on word-level skills is limited, having well-developed second language oral proficiency is associated with well-developed reading comprehension skills. More specifically, the evidence suggests that vocabulary knowledge, listening comprehension, syntactic skills, and the ability to handle metalinguistic aspects of language (such as providing definitions of words) are associated with reading comprehension.

The Role of First-Language Oral Proficiency and Literacy in Second-Language Literacy Development

One difference between first- and second-language literacy development is that second-language learners have an additional set of intervening influences—those related to first-language literacy and oral proficiency. The studies reviewed in Chapter 4 provide ample research evidence that certain aspects of second-language literacy development are related to performance on similar constructs in the first language; this suggests that common underlying abilities play a significant role in both first- and second-language development; that certain error types can be understood in terms of differences between the first and second languages; that well-developed literacy skills in the first language can facilitate second-language literacy development; and that some cross-language influences are more likely to affect second-language literacy development than others, and to operate during some, but not all, stages of literacy development. There is also evidence for oral-language-to-literacy influences, though first-language oral vocabulary does not appear to predict second-language reading comprehension.

To illustrate the role that first-language oral proficiency and literacy play in second-language learning, it would be useful to consider letter name knowledge, an important precursor to first- and second-language literacy development. It is difficult to achieve reading and writing fluency without achieving automaticity with letters. If the first and second languages are similar, as is the case when Spanish-speaking children learn to read English, we would expect that familiarity with the Spanish alphabet would contribute to the acquisition of spelling in English. At the same time, because of typological differences, Arabic- or Chinese-speaking English-language learners may have greater difficulty with the English alphabet. With learning, these alphabetic differences would be overcome, but others, such as syntactic differences across the languages, may still interfere.

The Influence of Sociocultural Variables

The six sociocultural areas examined for this review were immigration status; discourse/interactional characteristics; other sociocultural factors; parent and family influences; district, state, and federal policies; and language status or prestige. In general, and with some exceptions, the studies reviewed in Chapter 5 indicate that there is surprisingly little evidence for the impact of sociocultural variables on literacy learning. However, the studies of sociocultural influence have usually been descriptive only, and have not explored empirical links between these factors and student literacy outcomes. In fact, one general shortcoming in this area is that relatively few studies have considered student learning outcomes. Even when student outcomes are reported, the study designs did not permit strong inferences about the influence of sociocultural factors on literacy achievement.

Studies reviewed in Chapter 5 suggest that bridging home–school differences in interaction patterns or styles can enhance students' engagement, motivation, and participation in classroom instruction. This finding is certainly not trivial, but it is not the same as finding that bridging home–school differences improves literacy achievement. Culturally meaningful or familiar reading material does appear to facilitate student comprehension. But culturally familiar reading material is a relatively weak predictor of reading comprehension, compared with students' facility in reading in the language of the material; students perform better when they read or use material in the language they know best. Overall, literacy outcomes are more likely to be the result of home (and school) language and literacy learning opportunities, irrespective of sociocultural factors such as immigration circumstances or students' cultural characteristics.

The literature reviewed for this volume supports three sets of conclusions about the role of the home in language-minority children's literacy achievement. First, language-minority parents express willingness and often have the ability to help their children succeed academically. For various reasons, schools underestimate and underutilize parents' potential contributions. Second, more home literacy experiences and opportunities are generally associated with superior literacy outcomes, but findings in this regard are not consistent. Measures of parent and family literacy often predict child literacy attainment, but two studies found that parents' reading behavior was unrelated to children's literacy. Features of family life (e.g., domestic workload, religious activities) appear to influence the value children place on reading and their concepts of themselves as readers. Parent education is associated with literacy outcomes.

Third, the relationship between home language use and language-minority children's literacy outcomes is unclear. Correlational studies point to language-specific effects: home experiences with the first and second languages are positively (but modestly) correlated with children's literacy achievement in the first and second languages, respectively, and negatively (also modestly) correlated with children's literacy achievement in the other language. Four studies, however, yielded findings that tended to counter this generalization. Overall, these studies provide insufficient basis for policy and practice recommendations with regard to home and school language use.

Classroom and School Factors

Unfortunately, because there have been too few experimental studies, research has not yet provided a complete answer to what constitutes high-quality literacy instruction for language-minority students. However, what is evident from the existing research is that, as is true for language-majority students, instruction that provides substantial coverage of key components of literacy has a positive influence on the literacy development of language-minority students. Focusing instruction on components such as phonemic awareness, decoding, oral reading fluency, reading comprehension, vocabulary, and writing, has clear benefits. Some studies show that enhanced teaching of these various elements provide an advantage to second-language learners; the more complex programs that were studied typically tried to teach several of these elements simultaneously and were also usually successful.

Although second-language literacy instruction should focus on the same curricular components as first-language literacy instruction, the differences in the children's second-language proficiency make it important to adjust this instruction to effectively meet their needs. The research has provided a sketchy picture of what some of these adjustments might be. For example, particular phonemes and combinations of phonemes are not present in Spanish, which means that young Spanish-speaking students learning to read in English might benefit more from phonemic awareness work aimed at those particular elements than would be true for first-language learners. Given the large number of shared cognates between some languages and English, it may be wise for teachers to help second language-learners use this knowledge to help interpret English.

Another important finding with regard to instruction is that successful instructional approaches usually do not improve the literacy skills of second-language learners as much as they do for first-language learners. One exception to this is with vocabulary, which seems to provide greater benefits for second-language learners than first-language learners. To learn literacy with maximum success, students need to have command of the various literacy skills and strategies, as well as sufficient knowledge of oral English. It is not enough to teach reading skills, but instruction must teach these skills while fostering extensive oral English-language development. That the oral English development provided in most programs is insufficient can be seen in studies that show that second-language learners with adequate word recognition, spelling, and decoding skills still may lag behind their first-language peers in reading comprehension and vocabulary. The more promising of the complex literacy instruction routines that have been studied (such as instructional conversations) provide instructional support of oral language development in English along with high-quality instruction in literacy skills and strategies.

The patterns of learning revealed by these studies suggest that the basic sequencing of development is likely to be the same for first- and second-language learners—with greater attention to decoding required early in the process and relatively more direct and ambitious attention to comprehension later on. Vocabulary and background knowledge should be targeted intensively throughout the entire sequence (at one time, we might have claimed that this emphasis distinguished second-language literacy from first-language literacy, but recent research again suggests similarity more than difference). The need to develop stronger English-language proficiency as the basis for becoming literate in English argues for an early, ongoing, and intensive effort to develop this proficiency. It also should be apparent, given the transferability of some literacy skills, that teachers should build on these skills for students who have already developed these transferable skills in their home language.

Language-minority students who are literate in their first language are likely to be advantaged in the acquisition of English literacy. The studies in Chapter 6 demonstrate that language-minority students instructed in their native language (primarily Spanish in this report) and English perform, on average, better on English reading measures than language-minority students instructed only in English. This is the case at both the elementary and secondary levels. It also should be noted that recent evaluations of beginning reading programs used to teach non-English-speaking children to read in English are showing promising results. This is an important finding, in that first-language instruction is not an option in many schools where children speak multiple languages or instructional staff cannot provide first-language instruction.

Findings from the effective schools and professional development research suggest that systemic efforts are important; the school change research indicates that outside change agents help the process, but also that change is difficult to achieve.

Assessment

The assessments used in the research to gauge language-minority students' language proficiency are inadequate in many ways. For example, most of these measures are not able to assess appropriately development over time or to predict how well English-language learners perform on reading or content area assessments in English. It may be that low-cost alternative assessments can be developed which could, to guide instruction, measure students' literacy performance. For example, a cloze test based on students' literacy and content area instruction might provide information on students' vocabulary, semantic, syntactic, and discourse knowledge of English.

The few studies that were reviewed on standardized and standards-based tests point to linguistic and cultural issues that should be considered when such tests are used with English-language learners. For example, these students may know different vocabulary items in each of their languages, making it difficult to assess their total vocabulary knowledge with an assessment in only one language, or they may understand text in a second language, but be unable to communicate this understanding in that language.

Several studies reported that tests of letter naming and phonological awareness in English were good predictors of language-minority students' English reading performance, though these studies have not controlled for students' oral English proficiency or considered native-language literacy development. The evidence regarding teacher judgment and the nomination of language-minority students who might be in danger of dropping out or needing intensive reading services was quite limited. The findings suggest, however, that teacher nomination may be more reliable when teachers are asked to respond thoughtfully to specific criteria, rather than express their opinions spontaneously. Because teacher judgment and assessment play a significant role in the education of language-minority students, additional research needs to explore teacher judgment as an assessment tool.

Almost all of the researchers who dealt with the identification of language-minority students eligible for special education, language disorder services, or learning disability instruction recommended that language-minority students should be assessed in both languages. Very little research has focused on identifying older language-minority students with learning difficulties, and this is an important area for future study.

APPENDIX 1.A: STANDARD TERMS USED
IN WRITING THE NLP REPORT

1.   The following terms are used to describe subjects:

Language minority refers to individuals from homes where a language other than the societal language is actively used, who therefore have had an opportunity to develop some level of proficiency in a language other than the societal language. Thus, children in the United States who come from Spanish- or Chinese-speaking homes are referred to as *language minority*. A language-minority student may be limited proficient in their second language, bilingual, or essentially monolingual in their second language (August & Hakuta, 1997).

Individuals who come from language backgrounds other than English and whose English proficiency is not yet developed to the point where they can profit fully from English-only instruction are palled *English-language learners*. We have elected to use this term, first proposed by Rivera (1994) and adopted by the National Research Council's Committee on Developing a Research Agenda on the Education of Limited-English-Proficient and Bilingual Students (August & Hakuta, 1997).

The term *limited English proficient* (LEP) may be used, however, when we are quoting another source or citing legal requirements. Note that we have chosen to forgo the editorially convenient practice of reducing *English-language learners* to an abbreviation.

Children learning an unspecified second language are called *second-language learners*.

However, a child who is learning Dutch as a second language is referred to as a *second-language learner of Dutch*.

Children who speak a language as their first language are called *native speakers*. Thus, a child who speaks English as a first language is a native English speaker, a native speaker of English, or a native-English-speaking student or child. A child who reads English as a first language is referred to as a *native-language reader of English*.

Children who speak only one language are called *monolinguals* or *monolingual children*.

2.   The following terms are used to describe literacy or language components:

First-language vocabulary refers to vocabulary in a child's first language. Thus, for a native English speaker, this would refer to vocabulary in English.

Second-language vocabulary refers to vocabulary in a child's second language. Thus, for a Spanish-speaking child learning English, this would refer to vocabulary in English.

APPENDIX 1.B: NATIONAL LITERACY
PANEL SUBCOMMITTEES

Subcommittee 1: Development of Literacy in Language-Minority
Children and Youth
  Esther Geva
  Keiko Koda
  Nonie Lesaux
  Linda Siegel

Subcommittee 2: Cross-Linguistic Relationships
  Cheryl Dressier
  Fred Genesee
  Esther Geva
  Michael Kamil

Subcommittee 3: Sociocultural Contexts and Literacy Development
  Diane August
  Claude Goldenberg
  Robert Rueda

Subcommittee 4: Instruction and Professional Development
  Diane August
  Isabel Beck
  Margarita Calderón
  Frederick Erickson
  David Francis
  Nonie Lesaux
  Timothy Shanahan

Subcommittee 5: Student Assessment
  Diane August
  Georgia García
  Gail McKoon

Methodologists and Advisors to the Panel
  David Francis
  Frederick Erickson
  Donna Christian
  Catherine Snow

APPENDIX 1.C: ACCEPTANCE CRITERIA

Acceptance/rejection criteria (such as age of subjects, methodological criteria, etc.) are presented in the section of the instrument labeled Acceptance Round 1. Acceptance Round 2 was added to the instrument to give panelists an opportunity to reject articles that were not relevant to their research questions or did not meet the established methodological criteria. Criteria for accepting studies are reported next.

Acceptance Round 1

Year published/produced
    Published after 1979.

Language of publication
    Published in English.

Publication type
    Peer-reviewed journals (all chapters).
    Technical reports (Chapter 5, sociocultural influences on literacy; Chapter 6, language of instruction, effective literacy instruction; Chapter 7).
    Dissertations (Chapter 6, language of instruction, effective literacy instruction).

Research focus
    Literacy (all chapters except Chapter 4, cross-linguistic relationships in working memory, phonological processes, and oral language).
    Oral language related to literacy (Chapter 4, cross-linguistic relationships in working memory, phonological processes, and oral language).

Subjects' age
    3–18 years.

Language context for study
    Subjects are language-minority students (all chapters).
    Target language is English AND English is the societal language (all chapters).
    Target language is a societal language other than English (Chapter 3, development of literacy; Chapter 4, first- and second-language literacy; and Chapter 5).
    Target language is English, but English is NOT the societal language (Chapter 3; Chapter 4).

Duration of Program
The programs included at least a 6-month span between the onset of instruction and post-tests (Chapter 6, language of instruction).

Methodological Rigor
Reports empirical data (all chapters).
Data disaggregated for key study groups, and/or target group is 50% or more of sample (all chapters).

Experiments and Quasi-experiments
Study has control group, comparison group, or normative data (all chapters that include experimental and quasi-experimental studies).
Comparison samples include more than four subjects (all chapters).

Quasi-experiments
Pretesting of outcomes of interest or other matching criteria employed; exception is regression discontinuity design.

Correlational studies
sample size 20 or more (all chapters).

Acceptance Round 2

Studies are rejected if:
Serious confounds exist in the design of the research that prevent effects from being a attributed to variables of interest.
Not relevant to research questions.
Other criteria for rejection noted by panelists and recorded in database.

REFERENCES

Adams, M. J. (1990). *Beginning to read: Thinking and learning about print*. Cambridge, MA: MIT Press.

August, D., & Hakuta, K. (1997). *Improving schooling for language-minority children: A research agenda*. Washington, DC: National Academy Press.

Ehri, L. C. (1998). Grapheme–phoneme knowledge is essential for learning to read words in English. In J. L. Metsala & L. C. Ehri (Eds.), *Word recognition in beginning literacy* (pp. 3–40). Mahwah, NJ: Lawrence Erlbaum Associates.

Fitzgerald, J. (1995a). English-as-a-second-language learners' cognitive reading processes: A review of research in the United States. *Review of Educational Research*, 65(2), 145–190.

Fitzgerald, J. (1995b). English-as-a-second-language reading instruction in the United States: A research review. *Journal of Reading Behavior*, 27(2), 115–152.

Glaser, B. G. (1978). *Theoretical sensitivity: Advances in the methodology of grounded theory*. Mill Valley, CA: Sociology Press.

Maxwell, S. E., & Delaney, H. D. (2003). *Designing experiments and analyzing data: A model comparison perspective* (2nd ed.). Mahwah, NJ: Lawrence Erlbaum Associates.

Metsala, J. L., & Walley, A. C. (1998). Spoken vocabulary growth and the segmental restructuring of lexical representations: Precursors to phonemic awareness and early reading ability. In J. L. Metsala & L. C. Ehri (Eds.), *Word recognition in beginning literacy* (pp. 89–120). Mahwah, NJ: Lawrence Erlbaum Associates.

Rivera, C. (1994) Is it real for all kids? *Harvard Educational Review*, 64(1), 55–75.

Scarborough, H. S. (2001). Connecting early language and literacy to later reading (dis)abilities: Evidence, theory, and practice. In S. Neuman & D. Dickinson (Eds.), *Handbook for research in early literacy* (pp. 97–110). New York: Guilford.

Shavelson, R. J., & Towne, L. (Eds.). (2002). *Scientific research in education*. Washington, DC: National Academy Press.

2

Demographic Overview

Diane August

STUDENTS

As noted in the preface, the proportion of language-minority children and youth speaking a language other than English at home has dramatically increased—from 6% in 1979 to 14% in 1999 (National Center for Education Statistics, 2004, p. 7). In 1979, 6 million children and youth were language-minority. By 1999, that number had more than doubled to 14 million. In 1999, of those who spoke a language other than English at home, Spanish was the most frequent language spoken (72%), followed by Asian languages (21%), and then other European languages (10%) (National Center for Education Statistics, 2004, p. 10). Although Spanish speakers are by far the largest group of language-minority students, Spanish is not the dominant second language in several states. For example (Kindler, 2002), in 2000–2001, states reported that Blackfoot predominated in Montana, French in Maine, Hmong in Minnesota, Ilocano in Hawaii, Lakota in South Dakota, Native American in North Dakota, Serbo-Croatian in Vermont, and Yup'ik in Alaska. Kindler also notes that during this same school year, more than 460 languages were reported to be spoken by limited English proficient (LEP) students in the United States.

In 1999, one-third of 5- to 24-year-old language-minority children and youth reported having difficulty speaking English. Moreover, native-born children who spoke a language other than English at home were more likely than their foreign-born peers to speak English very well (78% vs. 49%). Among native-born children who spoke a language other than English at home, those with native-born parents were more likely than those with foreign-born parents to speak English very well. Among foreign-born children who spoke a language other than English at home, the more recently the child had come to the United States, the more likely that child was to report difficulty speaking English: 74% of those who came between 1996 and 1998 spoke English with difficulty, compared with 49% of those who came between 1990 and 1994. Thus, children who had been in the United States 4 to 9 years had less difficulty speaking English than those who had been in the United States 0 to 3 years.[1] Finally, it should be noted that the prevalence of limited-English proficiency declines across generations to the point where it largely disappears by the third generation, at least in terms of percentage of the population.[2] According to data collected for the annual Survey of State Educational Agencies in the United States, conducted by the Office of English Language Acquisition (Kindler, 2002), in 2000–2001, states reported that English-language learners[3] were enrolled primarily in pre-kindergarten through third-grade classrooms (44%), followed by the middle grades (35%) and high school (19%). California enrolled the largest number of English-language learners in public schools (1,511,646), followed by Puerto Rico (598,063), Texas (570,022), Florida (254,517), New York (239,097), Illinois (140,528), and Arizona (135,248). The Outlying Areas, however, have the highest overall percentages of English-language learners, with the Marshall Islands, Micronesia, the Northern Mariana Islands, Palau, and Puerto Rico each reporting more than 95% of their students having limited-English proficiency.

RANGE OF INSTRUCTIONAL AND ORGANIZATIONAL CONTEXTS

Patterns of segregation of English-language learners in some instances may impede educators' and schools' capacity to meet high new standards. According to the Schools and Staffing Survey, 1999–2000 (National Center for Education and Statistics, 2002b), nationally more than half (53%) of English-language learners attend schools where more than 30% of their fellow students are also English-language learners. In contrast, only 4% of non-English-language learner students go to schools where more than 30% of the student body is English-language learners. These

---

[1]Data come from the U.S. Department of Commerce, Census Bureau, Current Population Surveys and supplemental questions asked in 1979, 1989, 1992, 1995, and 1999.

[2]Source: Tabulations by the Urban Institute from the Census 2000 Supplementary Survey (C2SS); includes Puerto Ricans.

[3]English-language learners are a subset of language-minority students; they are language-minority students who are limited English proficient.

patterns of segregation appear to be reproducing themselves in the 22 "new-growth" states to which many immigrants moved in the 1990s. In the new-growth states, 38% of English-language learners attend schools where more than 30% of the student body is English-language learners. In the six major immigrant destination states (California, Texas, Florida, New York, Illinois, and Arizona), the percentage is much higher—60% of English-language learners are in schools where more than 30% of the students are English-language learners. These patterns of segregation are particularly striking, given the percentages of the population represented by English-language learners. In the six major destination states, only 13% of the students are English-language learners; in the 22 new-growth states, this figure is just 4%. Schools with high concentrations of English-language learners may have more difficulty than others demonstrating annual yearly progress toward standards-based goals.

English-language learners are educated in a variety of settings. Survey data (Development Associates, 2003) indicate that at the time of the survey, across program types, 12% of English-language learners received no services, 36% received some special language services, and 52% received extensive services.[4] The most common service types provided to English-language learners were some services, all English (25%); extensive services, all English (23%); and extensive services, significant native-language use (17%). Since the last survey in 1993,[5] there has been a significant decrease in the number of English-language learners receiving extensive services in the native language and a significant increase in students receiving extensive services in all English. Across all service types, the percentage of English-language learners receiving all-English instruction increased from 37% to 60%, whereas the percentage of English-language learners in predominantly Spanish instruction decreased from 40% to 20%. Native-language use was more prevalent in the elementary grades.

---

[4]"Some services" refers to instructions designed for English-language learners that support regular instructions they are receiving. Included in these service types are pull-out English as a second language (ESL) for less than 10 hours per week or having an aide who speaks the student's native language present in the classroom. "Extensive services" refers to those services in which a substantial portion of the student's instructional experience is specifically designed to address his or her needs, such as 10 or more hours a week of special ESL classes in which at least one subject area is taught using a specially designed curriculum and approach.

[5]The 1993 survey used a different methodology from later surveys to collect the survey data, so some degree of caution should be used in interpreting the data.

TEACHERS

It is estimated that 1,273,420 public school teachers instructed English-language learners, Grades K–12, during 2001–2002. This represents a dramatic increase over the preceding decade—from 15% of all teachers who worked with at least one English-language learner to 43% (Development Associates, 2003). The academic background and certification of teachers who worked with English-language learners were varied. Six percent of these teachers had a master's or doctoral degrees; 23% had certification in bilingual education, English as a second language (ESL), or other relevant specialty; and 10% were working with provisional credentials (Development Associates, 2003). However, the qualifications of teachers who taught three or more English-language learners were better: an estimated 46% of these teachers had at least a master's degree, and 54% held a bachelor's degree; an estimated 98% held one or more relevant certifications, including ESL (18%), and bilingual education (11%). Among those teachers who described their primary responsibility as ESL, 77% held ESL certification. Thus, most teachers who teach at least three English-language learners are certified, but many whose primary responsibility is not ESL have received no training in working with these students.

With regard to professional development, 6 of 10 teachers who worked with at least three English-language learners reported they had received in-service training specifically related to the teaching of these students in the past 5 years; overall, they had received a median of 4 hours of such training. According to *The Condition of Education*, 2002 (National Center for Education Statistics, 2002a),[6] in 1999–2000, only 13% of teachers who taught English-language learners had received 8 or more hours of training during the preceding 3 years.[7] The levels of professional development of teachers who work with English-language learners fall short of what is needed. Although a majority of these teachers have received some professional development, a large proportion (40%) had not, and the amount of training specifically related to English-language learners was limited.

In California, researchers have documented the limited amount of professional development teachers of English-language learners have received. After Californians passed Proposition 227 in 1998, large numbers of bilingual programs were replaced by English-only structured

---

[6]Excepted from U.S. Department of Education National Center for Education Statistics (2002b), Table 1.19, pp. 43–44.

[7]According to the survey, the numbers include both full-time and part-time teachers in traditional public schools in the United States.

immersion programs. Since then, classrooms without bilingual teachers have experienced a sudden influx of English-language learners. Yet, for the most part, they have received "little or no professional development to help them teach these students," according to a study released by the Center for the Future of Teaching and Learning (Gándara, Maxwell-Jolly, & Driscoll, 2005). In a survey of 5,300 California teachers, more than half of those who had up to 50% English-language learners in their classrooms had attended only one in-service training in bilingual or ESL methods—or none at all—over the past 5 years.

LITERACY OUTCOMES

The educational outcomes for English-language learners are discouraging. According to the U.S. Department of Education's *State Education Indicators with a Focus on Title I* (U.S. Department of Education, 2002)[8] in Arizona, 12% of all students at the fourth-grade level fall far below standards in reading and language arts, compared with 35% of English-language learners; at the eighth-grade level, 30% of all students fall far below the standards, compared with 69% of English-language learners. In Florida, 42% of all students at the fourth-grade level are partially proficient, compared with 92% of English-language learners; at the eighth-grade level, 54% of all students are partially proficient, compared with 95% of English-language learners. In Texas, where proportionately more English-language learners are meeting state standards in reading and language arts at both the fourth- and eighth-grade levels (59% and 52%, respectively), only 13% (compared with 31% overall) of these students at the fourth-grade level and 2% (compared with 27% overall) at the eighth-grade level reach advanced proficiency in reading and language arts. In all of these states, the proportions of English-language learners in the public schools are particularly high.

The *Survey of the States' Limited English Proficient Students and Available Educational Programs and Services 2000–2001 Summary Report* (Kindler, 2002) indicates that for the 41 state education agencies (SEAs) reporting on both participation and success of English-language learners in

---

[8]This report is a useful source of state data. The profiles in the report focus on the status of each indicator as of the 1999–2000 school year. States reported student achievement results for the 1999–2000 school year for mathematics and reading/language arts at three grade levels, as specified by Title requirements before the program's reauthorization in 2002: elementary—grade 3, 4, or 5; middle—grade 6, 7, 8, or 9; and high—grade 10, 11, or 12.

English reading comprehension, only 19% of the students met the state standard.[9]

High school dropouts are more likely to be unemployed and to earn less when they are employed than those who complete high school (National Center for Education Statistics, 2003). High school dropouts are more likely to receive public assistance than high school graduates who do not go to college. As defined by National Center for Education Statistics (2004), the dropout rate represents the percentage of an age group that is not enrolled in school and has not earned a high school credential. In 1999, among 18- to 24-year-olds not enrolled in a secondary school, 31% of language-minority students had not completed high school, compared with 10% of students who spoke English at home. Moreover, successful completion of high school is associated with ability to speak English. Among language-minority students, about 51% of language minorities who spoke English with difficulty had not completed high school, compared with about 18% of language minorities who spoke English very well.

These data are particularly troublesome because a fundamental restructuring of the American economy that began in the early 1980s has made postsecondary education or training the threshold requirement for good jobs (Carnevale & Desrochers, 2003). Just since 1973, the share of all jobs that require at least some college has risen from 28% to more than 60%. Postsecondary requirements are most prevalent in technology jobs, education and health care jobs, and white-collar jobs, which now comprise 60% of all jobs. Jobs on the factory floor have been declining, but the share that requires at least some college has increased from 8% to 31%.

IMMIGRATION IN OTHER COUNTRIES

Although the bulk of the studies covered by this report were conducted in the United States, studies from six other countries are also included: the United Kingdom, Canada, Australia, the Netherlands, Finland, and Israel.[10] Among these countries, Israel stands out because 36% of its population of approximately 6.7 million are foreign born. Since 1989, nearly 1

---

[9]Twenty-five states used state-designed tests to assess English reading comprehension. Other commonly used tests include the Language Assessment Scales (LAS) (15 states) and Terra Nova (11 states). Kindler (2002) reports that currently state data do not offer a clear picture of English-language learners' reading achievements because the assessment tools and testing policies differ from state to state, as well as among districts within a state. Other difficulties in data interpretation result because the data are from different grades, and the grade designations were not reported to the Department of Education

[10]Information for these countries that is cited here is found in U.S. Department of State (n.d.) *Background notes and Library of Congress (n.d.) Country studies.*

million immigrants have come to Israel from the former Soviet Union, and in recent years up to 50,000 Ethiopian Jews (14,000 in 1991 alone) have entered the country. Although Hebrew and Arabic are the official languages of Israel, other important languages are Yiddish, Russian, English, and Amharic.

In the other five countries, the net migration rate ranges from a low of. 63 migrants per 1,000 in Finland to a high of 6.01 migrants per 1,000 in Canada. (The rate for the United States is 3.52 per 1,000.) Finland has quite a homogeneous population. By far the majority (93%) are Finnish speaking, with Swedes making up 6% of the population and the remaining 1% comprising a few thousand Sami (Lapps) and others. Canada is certainly more diverse, as indicated in part by the distribution of languages: Anglophone, 28%; Francophone, 23%; other European, 15%; mixed background, 26%; Asian/Arabic/African, 6%; and indigenous Amerindian languages, 2%.

Since World War II, both the United Kingdom and the Netherlands have needed to accommodate large numbers of immigrants from non-European countries. The largest minorities in the United Kingdom (making up 3% of the population) have come from former Commonwealth countries such as India, Pakistan, and the West Indies. The largest minority communities in the Netherlands are the Moroccans, Turks, and Surinamese. Even so, 83% of the population is Dutch.

REFERENCES

Carnevale, A., & Desrochers, D. (2003). *Standards for what? The economic roots of K–16 reform.* Princeton, NJ: Educational Testing Service.

Development Associates. (2003). *Descriptive study of services to LEP students and LEP students with disabilities: Volume IA.* Research report—Text. Retrieved July 16, 2004, from http://www.devassoc. com/pdfs/vol_1_text.pdf

Gándara, P., Maxwell-Jolly, J., & Driscoll, A. (2005). *Listening to teachers of English language learners.* Santa Cruz, CA: Center for the Future of Teaching and Learning.

Kindler, A. L. (2002). *Survey of the states' limited English proficient students and available educational programs and services. 2000–2001 summary report.* Washington, DC: National Clearinghouse for English Language Acquisition.

Library of Congress. (n.d.). *Country studies.* Retrieved July 16, 2004, from http:// lcweb2.loc.gov/frd/cs/cshome.html

National Center for Education Statistics. (2002a). *The condition of education, 2002.* Retrieved July 16, 2004, from http://nces.ed.gov/pubs2002/2002025.pdf

National Center for Education Statistics. (2002b). *Schools and Staffing Survey, 1999–2000.* Retrieved July 16, 2004, from http://nces.ed.gov/pubs2002/2002313.pdf

National Center for Education Statistics. (2003). *The condition of education, 2003.* Retrieved July 16, 2004, from http://search.nces.ed.gov/query.html?charset=iso–8859–1&qt= condition+of+education+2003

National Center for Education Statistics. (2004). *Languages minorities and their educational and labor market indicators—Recent trends.* Retrieved July 16, 2004, from http:// nces.ed.gov/pubs2004/2004009.pdf

U.S. Department of Education. (2002). *State education indicators with a focus on Title I, 1999–2000.* Retrieved July 16, 2004, from http://www.ed.gov/rschstat/eval/disadv/2002indicators/edlite-titlepage.html

U.S. Department of State. (n.d.). *Background notes.* Retrieved July 16, 2004, from http://www.state. gov/r/pa/ei/bgn

3

Development of Literacy in Second-Language Learners

Nonie K. Lesaux and Esther Geva with Keiko Koda, Linda S. Siegel, and Timothy Shanahan

This chapter reviews research focused on the development of literacy skills among language-minority students and, in particular, the course of their literacy development; the predictors of their development, including second-language oral skills; and the profiles of language-minority students with literacy difficulties. Five specific questions guided our review:

1. What are the differences and similarities between language-minority and native speakers in the development of various literacy skills in the national language?
2. Are these differences and similarities similar for students who have been identified as having literacy difficulties?
3. What factors have an impact on the literacy development of language-minority students?
4. What is the relationship between English oral proficiency and English word-level skills?
5. What is the relationship between English oral proficiency and English text-level skills?

Language-minority students enter U.S. schools needing to learn oral language and literacy in English, and they have to learn with enormous efficiency if they are to catch up with their monolingual English classmates. Thus, understanding the basics of these students' literacy development, including how their developmental trajectories may be expected to differ from those of their classmates, is of the utmost importance. Given the overrepresentation of language-minority students among struggling readers, it is important to find ways to identify early those likely to struggle, to prevent them from falling behind. It is imperative that instruction for language-minority students focus on those competencies that are most relevant to their success in reading and writing. It is important to determine how much emphasis should be placed on developing oral proficiency among second-language learners. Only if we examine the relationship between second-language oral proficiency and second-language literacy in language-minority students will we know for sure.

Most research on the development of reading and writing skills— including the underlying cognitive processes (e.g., Adams, 1990; Chall, 1996; Siegel, 1993) and the effects of reading difficulties on children's knowledge and vocabulary (e.g., Stanovich, 1986)—has been conducted with native English speakers. Information about the normal developmental trajectories of literacy for language-minority students, as well as the variables that influence these trajectories, would contribute to evidence-based methods of literacy instruction for language-minority students and the establishment of common expectations for their literacy achievement.

In this chapter, we first present background information that guided our review. Then, following a brief description of the methodology of the review, we present a summary of the empirical findings relevant to the research questions. The final section focuses on directions for future research.

BACKGROUND

Literacy development is a process that is both componential and cumulative; that is influenced by individual, contextual, and instructional factors; and that starts before school entry and continues into adulthood. Early skills that are related to reading and writing typically start developing long before children enter school; these include oral language skills, familiarity with print, an understanding of the concepts of print, an understanding of text structures, and the acquisition of knowledge. Learning how speech is represented in writing requires the capacity to analyze spoken language into smaller units and to learn the rules for representing those units with graphemes. While children are learning to decode and encode, they must attend to the process of reconstructing the writer's meaning. Reading and writing become tools for learning and communicating knowledge and concepts, as well as for developing vocabulary and other skills.

Reading instruction must ensure that children have the opportunity to integrate learning the code (by developing skills in phonological awareness, letter knowledge, phoneme–grapheme relationships, spelling rules, fluency) with learning all that is necessary to read for meaning (by developing skills in vocabulary, world knowledge, discourse structure, comprehension strategies, purposes for reading). Reading research typically differentiates these two aspects of the system, as do we in presenting the theoretical framework here that guided our interpretation of the research results related to language-minority learners.

Oral Language Proficiency

For language-minority learners, oral language proficiency plays an important role in the acquisition of skilled reading. Oral language proficiency is a complex construct that has been conceptualized and operationalized in diverse ways in research on English-language learners. It includes both receptive and expressive skills and can also encompass knowledge or use of specific aspects of oral language, including phonology, vocabulary, morphology, grammar, and discourse features, as well as pragmatic skills.

For the purposes of this review, phonology, part of oral language, includes the ability to recognize and produce the sounds and sound sequences that make up language. Phonology is measured, for example, by speech production tasks and neither entails nor requires the explicit or conscious ability to call up knowledge of the sound system as is required by phonological processing tasks.

Phonological Processing

An important precursor to word reading ability is phonological processing, or the ability to use the sounds of the language to process oral and written language; globally, one's phonological processing abilities have an impact on reading acquisition and comprehension (e.g., Stanovich & Siegel, 1994). Findings from longitudinal, cross-sectional, and intervention studies have converged to demonstrate the crucial role of phonological processing in acquiring reading skills (e.g., Wagner & Torgesen, 1987; Wagner, Torgesen, & Rashotte, 1999).

Research has identified three specific aspects of phonological processing:

- Phonological awareness is the ability to consciously attend to the sounds of language as distinct from its meaning. For first-language learners, phonological awareness skills have been shown to be significantly correlated with beginning reading skills, especially decoding (Adams, 1990). Phonological awareness includes aware-ness of rhymes, syllable segmentation, and phonemic awareness. Phonemic awareness is the "insight that every spoken word can be conceived as a sequence of phonemes. Because phonemes are the units of sound that are represented by the letters of the alphabet, an awareness of phonemes is key to understanding the logic of the alphabetic principle and thus to the learning of phonics and spell-ing" (Snow, Burns, & Griffin, 1998, p. 52). Phonemic awareness includes the ability to segment words into their separate phonemes.

- Phonological recoding refers to the processes required when a nonphonological stimulus, such as a written word or picture, is converted to phonological output. It is typically measured by such tasks as rapid naming of letters, pictures, or numbers. Naming-speed tasks (referred to as rapid automatized naming [RAN]) assess the rate at which verbal labels for high-frequency visual stimuli are produced; these tasks measure linguistic fluency and speed of cognitive processing.

- Phonological memory refers to coding information phonologically for temporary storage in working or short-term memory; it is often measured using digit span or pseudoword repetition tasks. In this report, some studies used phonological short-term memory tasks that require individuals to simply repeat a series of digits, letters, or pseudowords, but do not require any manipulation or additional processing.

Working Memory

Some of the studies reviewed in this report focused on working memory (WM), in addition to short-term memory (STM). Both WM and STM have been shown to be related to word recognition and reading com-prehension performance (Swanson & Siegel, 2001). However it is important to note that they are not terms to be used interchangeably and the two processes are inherently different. Although both require atten-tion to stimuli, the crucial distinction is that WM tasks demand active manipulation of the information presented while simultaneously hold-ing the information in memory (Baddeley, 1986), whereas STM tasks require only the direct recall of information. WM is often measured using tasks such as repeating a string of letters or numbers in reverse order to that presented.

WM is vital to reading comprehension as the reader must simul-taneously decode words, remember, and actively process what has been read (Swanson & Saez, 2003). In the early reading acquisition stage, WM is critical as the grapheme–phoneme conversion rules for each segment of the word are recalled and held in memory as the reader decodes each part of the word (Siegel, 1993). Implicated in WM tasks is the individual's STM ability, in that STM ability has an impact on the amount of phonological information being held in memory for recall. Thus, every measure of verbal working memory necessarily taps one's ability to store or access the sound structure of the language, drawing specifically on phonological processing skills.

Word-Level Skills

While learning to read, skilled learners begin by learning to use letter–sound relationships to decode print. Simultaneously, they build up a sight vocabulary of words encountered frequently in text. Thus, word reading involves a combination of phonological and visual skills. Decoding skills are needed if students are to be effective when they encounter complex and unfamiliar words, especially as the demands and volume of text increase as children progress through school. Similarly, building a sight word vocabulary in long-term memory (LTM) is important for word reading and also contributes to students' fluent, automatic word reading and text comprehension.

For most readers, reading practice results in gains in fluency of word recognition (Kame'enui & Simmons, 2001). Of course, as fluency develops, it is important that children attend to the meaning of text to acquire knowledge and develop vocabulary, as well as skills related to literacy.

Spelling development parallels the process of learning to read and is, in fact, an application of sound–symbol relationships in a written format. Research conducted with native English speakers has shown that reading and spelling draw on common cognitive-linguistic processes, as well as unique orthographic processes (Berninger, Abbott, Abbott, Graham, & Richards, 2002; Fitzgerald & Shanahan, 2000). In the initial stages of learning to read, when children are acquiring an understanding of how to apply sound–symbol relationships to decode, they typically also develop the ability to encode words.

Learning to read and spell involves mastery of the association between printed and spoken forms of language (Adams, 1990; Ehri, 1998; Foorman, Francis, Fletcher, Schatschneider, & Mehta, 1998; Mann, 1993; Moats, 1994; Stanovich & Siegel, 1994). Phonological skills, in particular, have been shown to be essential for learning to read and spell not only alphabetic orthographies (Bradley & Bryant, 1983; Liberman, Shankweiler, Fischer, & Carter, 1974; Lundberg, Olofsson, & Wall, 1980), but also nonalphabetic orthographies, such as Chinese (Perfetti, 1999).

For most readers by the middle elementary years word reading skills are well developed and fluent, and the primary focus of reading instruction shifts from "learning to read" to "reading to learn" (Chall, 1996). Research on reading difficulties has clearly demonstrated the cumulative nature of reading skills; that is, without mastery of decoding, fluency is compromised; if decoding and fluency are not automatic, the reader's ability to extract and construct meaning from text effectively and efficiently is compromised (Perfetti, 1985).

Text-Level Skills

It is typically not until the middle elementary years that readers begin to acquire significant knowledge as a result of reading. If a child is experiencing reading difficulties, the result may be a knowledge base and vocabulary insufficient for the comprehension of the increasingly complex reading material students confront later in their schooling (Stanovich, 1986).

Reading comprehension poses the challenge of translating printed words into sounds in an accurate and efficient manner while constructing meaning out of what is being read. To comprehend text, readers must draw on lexical knowledge (vocabulary), semantic knowledge (meaning), syntactic knowledge (language structure), and background and textual knowledge (Bernhardt, 2000). However, reading comprehension can be undermined by a number of factors, including the reader's knowledge and skills (e.g., reading accuracy and speed, vocabulary, background knowledge), text presentation (e.g., discourse structure, clarity, syntactic complexity), and factors associated with the activity of reading (e.g., motivation; see RAND Reading Study Group, 2002).

Writing is an integrated text-level process that involves word-level skills; cognitive abilities, such as WM, linguistic awareness, and attention; and metacognitive skills, including planning, metacognition, strategy use, and self-regulation (Berninger & Richards, 2002; Wong, 1997). Just as effective reading comprehension is dependent, in part, on fluent, automatic decoding, effective writing development depends, in part, on automatization of low-level transcription skills (Berninger *et al.*, 1992). Specifically, such skills as letter production must be fluent so that cognitive resources, especially WM, can be devoted to integrating all the other processes involved in creating written output.

Cognitive and metacognitive processes contribute to writing development during middle school and high school (Wong, 1997). When writing text, particularly expository text, students must generate discourse in the absence of the social context of oral communication (Berninger & Richards, 2002). As with reading comprehension, writing is influenced by sociocultural practices (Pérez, 1998), and learning the discourse styles specific to a particular culture is part of learning to write and comprehend written texts.

Variation among Individuals

Although these broad principles conceptualize literacy development at the word and text levels, there is considerable variation among individuals in the way in which these processes occur. Many factors influence the speed and trajectory of literacy development. A primary external influence is instruction—both explicit instruction in phonological awareness, letter–sound correspondences, vocabulary, and comprehension strategies, and the incidental instruction associated with providing facilitative language- and literacy-rich environments. Thus, although literacy development is conceptualized as the acquisition of increasingly complex skills and strategies, the effectiveness with which any individual child develops into a proficient reader may depend on exposure to appropriate instruction. For language-minority children and youth, the development of literacy skills in a second language is arguably even more challenging than for native speakers. The same array of word- and text-level skills must be learned, although such learning may begin at a later age, perhaps without the same level of foundation in the cognitive and linguistic precursors to literacy, perhaps with sociocultural presuppositions that differ from those of native speakers, and often by children facing social, fiscal, and familial challenges.

Child factors that have been shown to relate to success in literacy development among monolinguals include literacy-related skills at school entry (Snow et al., 1998); oral language skills, including vocabulary (Stahl, 2003); background knowledge (Afflerbach, 1990); demographic factors (Hart & Risley, 1995; Snow et al., 1998); motivation and engagement (Guthrie & Wigfield, 2000); and the presence of dyslexia, learning disabilities, or language impairment (Lyon, 1995; Shaywitz et al., 1999). Disabilities that interfere with normal reading development are estimated to occur in 5% to 15% of the monolingual population. Presumably, similar percentages of the bilingual population experience such difficulties, although over- and under-identification of English-language learners with learning disabilities have complicated efforts to arrive at reliable estimates.

METHODOLOGY OF THE REVIEW

The studies in the database that address the development of literacy in language-minority students are varied in design, methodology, and the factors hypothesized to influence literacy development. In many ways, this variation reflects the complexity of examining second-language literacy development.[1] The bulk of the studies reviewed in this chapter used correlational designs to examine the relationship between precursor and outcome variables or to investigate the link between second-language oral skills and reading/writing skills in the second language. A number of studies used between-group designs in which language-minority learners and native speakers were compared on indexes of oral language proficiency and literacy.

When it was possible, meta-analytic procedures were used to increase our understanding of some issues. When there were five or more studies that could contribute data to the analysis of a particular issue, then average correlations or average weighted differences between groups were calculated. It would have been preferable to report such effect sizes for all comparisons between second-language learners and monolingual speakers, but often there were not sufficient amounts of data to justify that. There were only two instances where five or more independent studies were available for meta-analysis—studies that investigated differences between language-minority students and monolingual English speakers in word reading and spelling. Even when effect sizes could be calculated, we did not try to provide a thorough analysis of these results given the small numbers of studies and the lack of sampling equivalence even in these comparisons. It is important to bear in mind that studies which report multiple correlations, controlling for differences in particular factors, often provide more nuanced information than can be derived from simple correlations—or even from summaries of simple correlations or differences. Caution should be exercised in interpreting the effect size analysis reported here.

Because of the limited opportunity to synthesize with quantitative techniques, detailed narrative analyses are provided. These narratives rely on the entire collection of studies on a topic or issue, rather than just the subset that could provide effect size estimations.

SUMMARY OF EMPIRICAL FINDINGS

The findings are organized according to the research questions: differences and similarities in the literacy skills development of monolinguals

---

[1]In examining the research on the development of second-language literacy skills, as well as the factors that influence second-language literacy skills, we reviewed a broad range of studies. Given that a large number of studies focus on development, many of the studies reviewed here are also examined in other chapters. In other chapters, however, there is an emphasis on and a more in-depth discussion of other aspects of the studies, such as cross-linguistic literacy transfer (Chapter 4), and the sociocultural context of literacy development (Chapter 5).

and language-minority students; factors influencing development, with a focus primarily on cognitive and linguistic factors; and literacy attainment of language-minority students identified as having literacy difficulties. The last section of the findings reports on studies that examine the relationship between second-language oral proficiency and various second-language reading skills in language-minority students.

The findings are organized by literacy outcomes and findings are reported within a developmental framework, beginning with research on young children in the elementary school years, continuing with middle school students, and finally high school students. Studies in the first three sections were studies conducted with children who were language-minority students acquiring the national language; for the last section of the review—studies that examine the relationship between second-language oral proficiency and various second-language reading skills—children in the samples were language-minority students acquiring English as a national language or as a foreign language. All studies provided empirical outcome measures related to the research questions (for the first section, these outcomes were quantitative; for the second section, they were qualitative or quantitative).

The most salient and consistent finding across these studies is the overall paucity of developmental research, the one exception being those studies that have been conducted to examine the literacy development of elementary school students, mostly children in the primary grades. A second finding is the limited amount of research focused on text-level skills. Thus, the findings reported in this chapter allow us to draw relatively firm conclusions about the word reading development of language-minority children and youth. In contrast, the conclusions to be drawn on the reading comprehension and writing development of language-minority learners as compared with native speakers are much less definitive.

Differences and Similarities between Language-Minority and Native Speakers in the Development of Literacy Skills

With regard to the first and second questions (What are the differences and similarities between language-minority and native speakers in the development of various literacy skills in the national language? Are these differences and similarities similar for students who have been identified as having literacy difficulties?), we reviewed studies that compared (a) literacy-related skills such as phonological processing and print awareness, (b) word-level skills such as word reading and spelling, and (c) text-level skills such as the reading comprehension and writing of language-minority students with those of their monolingual peers. We also report on differences between language-minority students with learning difficulties and native speakers with learning disabilities.

Phonological Processing. Although most studies indicate that second-language learners perform as well as or better than monolinguals on phonological tasks (see Chapter 4), two studies found differences in favor of monolinguals (Cisero & Royer, 1995; Jackson, Holm, & Dodd, 1998). It appears that this relationship is not simple; it depends on a variety of factors, including the age or stage of second-language development of the learner, the child's relative proficiency in each language, the specific combination of languages the child is learning, and other mitigating factors, such as early language and literacy experiences. Nevertheless, studies that have examined the relationship between phonological awareness skills in the first or second language and later reading ability have found that reading readiness, including measures of phonological skills, predicted aspects of language-minority students' later second-language reading development regardless of whether the measures were in the student's first or second language.

In addition to the studies that examined phonological awareness skills in heterogeneous samples of language-minority students, four studies in our database examined the phonological processing skills of language-minority students in the primary grades who were classified as having literacy difficulties. The studies were conducted in Canada (Chiappe & Siegel, 1999; Chiappe, Siegel, & Wade-Woolley, 2002; Wade-Woolley & Siegel, 1997) and the United Kingdom (Everatt, Smythe, Adams, & Ocampo, 2000); the language-minority students were acquiring English. Two of these studies (Chiappe *et al.*, 2002; Wade-Woolley & Siegel, 1997) included mixed samples from diverse linguistic backgrounds; one (Everatt *et al.*, 2000) focused on language-minority students who were Sylheti first-language speakers; and one (Chiappe & Siegel, 1999) focused on language-minority students who were Punjabi speakers. In these studies, as in most studies reviewed in this chapter, only measures of second-language literacy and related skills were included; no information is provided about native language and literacy proficiency.

In each of the four studies, those language-minority students who were classified as having difficulties in spelling (Everatt *et al.*, 2000) or word reading (Chiappe & Siegel, 1999; Chiappe *et al.*, 2002; Wade-Woolley & Siegel, 1997) also demonstrated difficulties in phonological awareness, and these difficulties were very comparable to those of their monolingual peers who were similarly classified.

Some studies examined the rapid-naming skills of language-minority students with literacy difficulties (Chiappe, Siegel, & Wade-Woolley, 2002; Wade-Woolley & Siegel, 1997; Everatt *et al.*, 2000). Rapid naming of letters, numbers, or objects is a task that assesses phonological recoding in lexical access. Given the emphasis on speed, this skill has been linked to reading fluency. These three studies included native English speakers and English-language learners with significant difficulties in reading and spelling. Despite their differing linguistic backgrounds, the children did not differ in their rapid-naming ability. These preliminary findings suggest there is a group of English-language learners with literacy difficulties who, like native English speakers, also demonstrate poor performance on rapid-naming tasks.

Print Awareness.   One study in our database (Bialystok, 1997) examined children's understanding of print awareness and found that bilingual learners were better than monolingual children in their understanding of the general symbolic properties of written English.

Word Reading Skills.   Intensity and length of exposure to the second language appear to be important for the development of word reading skills. With sufficient exposure to second-language reading, word reading skills appear to develop to a level equivalent to those attained by monolingual students. This is the case despite the fact that, in these studies the language-minority students usually performed more poorly on measures of oral language proficiency, such as syntactic awareness and vocabulary. This pattern of findings was evident in studies conducted in different countries (i.e., Canada, England, the Netherlands, the United States), with children of varying ages (kindergarten through eighth grade) and ability levels. The studies included English-language learners who were native speakers of Punjabi (Chiappe & Siegel, 1999), Urdu (Mumtaz & Humphreys, 2001), Arabic (Abu-Rabia & Siegel, 2002), Italian (D'Angiulli, Siegel, & Serra, 2001), and Portuguese (Da Fontoura & Siegel, 1995); who were from various Asian-language backgrounds (Geva, Yaghoub-Zadeh, & Schuster, 2000); and who came from mixed-language backgrounds (Chiappe, Siegel, & Wade-Woolley, 2002; Wade-Woolley & Siegel, 1997). It is important to note that while language-minority and monolinguals tend to accomplish similar levels of word identification, none of the studies included a measure of speed of word reading.

The findings from the meta-analytic work in this area also confirm that there is little or no difference between the performance of language-minority students and their native-speaking peers on measures of word reading accuracy. Meta-analysis based on the data from 10 studies[2]

---

[2]Abu-Rabia & Siegel, 2002; Chiappe, Siegel, & Wade-Woolley, 2002; Chiappe, Siegel, & Gottardo, 2002; Chiappe & Siegel, 1999; D'Angiulli, Siegel, & Serra, 2001; Da Fontoura & Siegel, 1995; Wade-Woolley & Siegel, 1997; Geva, Yaghoub-Zadeh, & Schuster, 2000; Limbos & Geva, 2001; Verhoeven, 2000.

indicated that the first- and second-language speakers were equivalent in word reading accuracy. The effect size (−.09) showed the second-language speakers doing better on word identification, although the difference was not statistically significant. See Table 3.1.

We also examined the prevalence and nature of word reading and spelling difficulties for this group. Several studies show that some English-language learners—as with native speakers—experience difficulties with word reading and spelling. The studies that support this finding included English-language learners in Canada (Abu-Rabia & Siegel, 2002; Chiappe & Siegel, 1999; Chiappe, Siegel, & Wade-Woolley, 2002; D'Angiulli *et al.*, 2001; Da Fontoura & Siegel, 1995; Wade-Woolley & Siegel, 1997), the United States (Miramontes, 1987), and the United Kingdom (Everatt *et al.*, 2000). These studies included primary-grade students (Chiappe & Siegel, 1999; Chiappe, Siegel, & Wade-Woolley, 2002; Wade-Woolley & Siegel, 1997) and students in the middle elementary school years (Abu-Rabia & Siegel, 2002; D'Angiulli *et al.*, 2001; Da Fontoura & Siegel, 1995; Miramontes, 1987). None of these studies looked at secondary school students. Among the English-language learners across the studies, there were first-language speakers of Arabic (Abu-Rabia & Siegel, 2002), Italian (D'Angiulli *et al.*, 2001), Portuguese (Da Fontoura & Siegel, 1995), Punjabi (Chiappe & Siegel, 1999), and Spanish (Miramontes, 1987). Two of the studies (Chiappe, Siegel, &

TABLE 3.1
Comparisons of Word and Pseudoword Reading Skills of First- and Second-Language Students

Study	Weighted Mean Difference	Number of Second-Language Students	Number of First-Language Students
Abu-Rabia & Siegel, 2002	.05	56	65
Chiappe, Siegel, & Wade-Woolley, 2002	−.09	131	727
Chiappe, Siegel, & Gottardo, 2002	.05	59	540
Chiappe & Siegel, 1999	−.22	38	51
D'Angiulli, Siegel, & Serra 2001	−.79*	81	210
Da Fontoura & Siegel, 1995	−.12	37	106
Geva, Yaghoub-Zadeh, & Schuster, 2000	−.02	248	100
Limbos & Geva, 2001	−.04	258	124
Verhoeven, 2000	.05	331	1812
Wade-Woolley & Siegel, 1997	.23	40	33
Total	−.09	1,279	3,768

* Correlation significantly different from 0.

Wade-Woolley, 2002; Wade-Woolley & Siegel, 1997) included mixed samples of children from diverse linguistic backgrounds.

In each of the studies reviewed, the English-language learners showed a range of abilities similar to that of the native English speakers. Furthermore, each of the studies identified a group of English-language learners whose performance was well below average on word and pseudoword reading and related skills, similar to that of native English-speakers who were designated as reading disabled. Interestingly, in all three of the studies with middle school learners (Abu-Rabia & Siegel, 2002; Da Fontoura & Siegel, 1995; D'Angiulli *et al.*, 2001), the reading-disabled English-language learners had better phonological skills than their reading-disabled, native English-speaking peers, which could be due to heightened metalinguistic awareness skills among the bilingual students.

The similarities in reading disability in English first- and second-language groups suggest that teachers should be able to reliably identify disabled readers among second-language learners. However, over-reliance on oral language proficiency may hamper the identification of second-language children at risk for reading disability. Indeed, the research suggests that phonological skills are more closely related to word reading ability than is language-minority status. Limbos and Geva (2001) found that for English-language learners, although teachers noticed students' poor word identification skills, they attributed these poor skills to the children's second-language status rather than recognizing them as specific and addressable reading problems.

Spelling Skills. Studies examining the spelling development of English-language learners have found it to be similar to that of monolingual children (Abu-Rabia & Siegel, 2002; D'Angiulli *et al.*, 2001; Da Fontoura & Siegel, 1995; Fashola, Drum, Mayer, & Kang, 1996; Limbos & Geva, 2001; Tompkins, Abramson, & Pritchard, 1999; Wade-Woolley & Siegel, 1997). Only one study reviewed examined the spelling development of language-minority students acquiring a language other than English (Verhoeven, 2000); the findings from that study diverged from those of the others in that the spelling ability of the language-minority children was not as advanced as that of the monolingual children.

Effect sizes were used to estimate the weighted average differences between groups. Examination of spelling differences between native speakers and second-language learners in nine studies (Table 3.2) revealed a small average difference between groups (effect size: −.05). Second-language learners spelled a bit better than the native speakers, but this difference was not statistically significant. A test of homogeneity showed that there was significant variance in these spelling studies (Q =313.141, df =8, p > .05). See Table 3.2.

TABLE 3.2
Comparison of Spelling Skills of First- and Second-Language Students

Study	Mean Weighted Effect Size	Number of Language Minority Participants	Number of Monolingual Participants
Chiappe, Siegel, & Gottardo, 2002	0.25	59	540
Abu-Rabia & Siegel, 2002	−0.66	56	65
Chiappe, Siegel, & Wade-Woolley, 2002	0.25	131	727
Da Fontoura & Siegel, 1995	−0.68*	37	106
D'Angiulli, Siegel, & Serra, 2001	−1.45*	45	64
Limbos & Geva, 2001	−0.04	258	124
Tompkins Abrahamson, & Pritchard, 1999	−0.07	40	40
Verhoeven, 2000	0.15	331	1812
Wade-Woolley & Siegel, 1997	0.39	40	33
Total	−.13	1,022	3,447

* Significantly different from 0.

In summary, findings from the meta-analysis and narrative review suggest that, over time, English-language learners can accomplish a level of English spelling proficiency equivalent to those of native-language speakers, although in two studies (Fashola et al., 1996; Verhoeven, 2000) the second-language learners demonstrated relatively greater difficulties with spelling.

Each of the five studies discussed previously that examined the word reading skills of English-language learners designated as reading disabled also included measures of spelling in English. These children had lower scores on word and pseudoword spelling tasks than their classmates who were average reading English-language learners (Chiappe, Siegel, & Wade-Woolley, 2002; Da Fontoura & Siegel, 1995; Wade-Woolley & Siegel, 1997). The scores on spelling measures for the native English speakers and the English-language learners designated as poor readers were similar. Also, studies have found that English-language learners designated as poor readers had higher scores on an English spelling test than native English speakers designated as poor readers (Abu-Rabia & Siegel, 2002; Da Fontoura & Siegel, 1995; D'Angiulli et al., 2001).

Reading Comprehension. Five studies conducted in the Netherlands have compared the reading comprehension performance in Dutch of language-minority students and their monolingual, native-speaking peers. Four of the studies (Aarts & Verhoeven, 1999; Droop & Verhoeven,

1998; Verhoeven, 1990, 2000) included samples of children of elementary and middle school age, spanning first through eighth grades, and one (Hacquebord, 1994) considered high-school school students.

Generally, in these studies, language-minority children under-performed their monolingual peers in reading comprehension (Aarts & Verhoeven, 1999; Droop & Verhoeven, 1998; Hacquebord, 1994; Verhoeven, 1990, 2000). The development of reading comprehension, like that of word-level skills, is highly dependent on effective instruction, and we know little about the quality of curriculum and instruction in these studies. Existing large-scale data sets on the school achievement of language-minority students in the United States and abroad suggest that comprehension is a significant area of difficulty for these learners, and the findings on reading comprehension presented in this report certainly suggest this is the case.

Writing. All four studies that examined the writing performance of language-minority students focused on Spanish speakers learning English. Three of the studies focused on late elementary and middle school students (Bermúdez & Prater, 1994; Ferris & Politzer, 1981; Lanauze & Snow, 1989), and one focused on elementary school (Davis, Carlisle, & Beeman, 1999). Two studies examined writing performance in both the first and second languages (Davis *et al.*, 1999; Lanauze & Snow, 1989), and the other two (Bermúdez & Prater, 1994; Ferris & Politzer, 1981) examined writing performance in the second language only.

The four studies varied in the way writing was assessed and examined. Students were asked to compose a genre-specific piece based on a short prompt (Bermúdez & Prater, 1994; Davis *et al.*, 1999) or to write in response to a picture (Lanauze & Snow, 1989) or short film (Ferris & Politzer, 1981). All the studies scored the students' writing on multiple dimensions, including overall quality, linguistic and syntactic complexity, lexical variety, genre-specific features, semantics, productivity, and spelling.

While findings from two of these studies (Davis *et al.*, 1999; Lanauze & Snow, 1989) suggest that cross-linguistic transfer may play an important role in second-language writing, the studies are highly diverse in the tasks and assessment criteria employed. As a result, we cannot use their findings to draw substantive conclusions about the writing development of language-minority students.

Factors That Have an Impact on the Literacy Development
of Language-Minority Children and Youth[3]

Word Reading. Nine studies examined those factors that influenced
word reading-development among children learning to read in their
second language (Arab-Moghaddam & Sénéchal, 2001; Chiappe, Siegel,
& Gottardo, 2002; Chiappe, Siegel, & Wade-Woolley, 2002; Da Fontoura
& Siegel, 1995; Gholamain & Geva, 1999; Gottardo, 2002; Quiroga,
Lemos-Britton, Mostafapour, Abbott, & Berninger, 2002; Verhoeven,
1990, 2000). These studies identify a cluster of competencies underlying
initial word reading development among language-minority students:
second-language phonological awareness, knowledge of second-
language sound–symbol correspondence rules, second-language letter
knowledge, and working memory measured in the second language.
These factors are essentially identical to the known requisites for reading
acquisition among monolingual native English-speaking children (e.g.,
Adams, 1990; Foorman, Francis, Fletcher, & Lynn, 1996; Olson, Wise,
Johnson, & Ring, 1997; Scanlon & Vellutino, 1997; Snow *et al.*, 1998).

Spelling. Nine studies investigated second-language factors that
influence the spelling development of language-minority students (Abu-
Rabia & Siegel, 2002; Arab-Morghaddam & Sénéchal, 2001; Chiappe &
Siegel, 1999; Chiappe, Siegel, & Gottardo, 2002; Cronnell, 1985; Da Fon-
toura & Siegel, 1995; D'Angiulli, Siegel, & Serra, 2001; Verhoeven, 2000;
Wade-Woolley & Siegel, 1997). Five studies (Abu-Rabia & Siegel, 2002;
Arab-Moghaddam & Sénéchal, 2001; Chiappe & Siegel, 1999; Chiappe,
Siegel, & Gottardo, 2002; Da Fontoura & Siegel 1995) focused on second-
language basic literacy skills as predictors of spelling development.
Taken together, their findings suggest that factors associated with spelling performance in a second language are similar to factors that influence word reading (i.e., phonological awareness skills, letter knowledge,
and orthographic knowledge) and that word reading and spelling skills
are, in fact, highly correlated.

In addition to the studies examining the second-language factors that
influence second-language spelling for language-minority students, two
studies (Cronnell, 1985; Fashola *et al.*, 1996) report that spelling errors in
English among Spanish–English bilingual children (second to sixth
grades) reflected their use of Spanish (first language) sound–symbol correspondence rules.

---

[3]Oral language factors that influence literacy development are addressed in the next
section.

Comprehension. In considering variables that influence successful text comprehension, it is essential that the specific demands imposed by the text and task be taken into account (RAND Reading Study Group, 2002). In many studies in our database, however, the measures are not described or represent a global construct of comprehension, and there is no analysis of the different components measured. In many cases, the text type is not specified. Only three of the comprehension studies provided information on specific comprehension subskills measured: coherence building, anaphora resolution, and inference (Verhoeven, 1990); anaphora resolution and explicit/implicit meaning relations (Verhoeven, 2000); and macro- and microlevel text information detection (Hacquebord, 1994). Only two provide specific information about the text type employed (Hacquebord, 1994; Nagy, García, Durgunoglu, & Hancin-Bhatt, 1993).

Factors that influence second-language reading comprehension fall into one of two categories: individual or contextual. Individual factors include such variables as readiness skills, word-level skills, background knowledge, and motivation; contextual factors include such variables as SES and text attributes. Although length of time in the country and instruction are likely to have an influence on reading comprehension for language-minority students, there is little evidence available to examine their influence. In addition, many of these studies include only language-minority students, with no comparative sample of native speakers, so we cannot determine whether the impact of these factors varies according to language status.

Writing. Like reading comprehension, writing is a multidimensional process. It involves word-level skills, cognitive abilities, and higher-order skills. Just as effective reading comprehension is dependent, in part, on fluent, automatic decoding, effective writing development depends, in part, on automatization of low-level transcription skills (Berninger *et al.*, 1992). Specifically, such skills as letter production must be fluent so that cognitive resources, especially working memory, can be devoted to integrating all the other writing skills. As with reading comprehension, writing is influenced by sociocultural practices (Pérez, 1998); discourse styles that are specific to particular cultures may differ from those of the language-minority student (Schierloh, 1991). It is important to note that when creating written text, particularly expository text, students must generate discourse in the absence of the social context of oral communication (Berninger, 1994). This is likely an added challenge for language-minority students.

RELATIONSHIP BETWEEN ENGLISH ORAL PROFICIENCY AND ENGLISH WORD-LEVEL LITERACY SKILLS

Word and Pseudoword Reading. Several studies examined the relationship between English oral proficiency and English word and pseudoword reading skills (Arab-Moghaddam & Sénéchal, 2001; Da Fontoura & Siegel, 1995; Durgunoglu *et al.*, 1993; Geva *et al.*, 2000; Gottardo, 2002; Gottardo, Yan, Siegel, & Wade-Woolley, 2001; Jackson & Lu, 1992; Muter & Diethelm, 2001; Quiroga *et al.*, 2002). Studies that examined the relative contributions of English oral language proficiency and phonological processing skills to English word and pseudoword reading skills found that the measures of oral language proficiency in English explained a small proportion of unique variance (usually 3%–4%) in students' English word and pseudoword-reading scores. At the same time, phonological processing skills (including phonemic awareness and rapid automatized naming) and measures of working memory in English tend to be more consistent predictors of English word and pseudoword reading skills, and they explain a larger proportion of variance than do measures of English oral language proficiency. These conclusions emerged from studies that assessed a variety of oral language proficiency skills (e.g., vocabulary knowledge or grammatical sensitivity); used cross-sectional and longitudinal correlational designs or between-group designs; and involved elementary, middle school, and high school English-language learners who came from different language and instructional backgrounds.

It is important to note that the number of studies examining the relative contributions of oral proficiency and phonological processing skills to word-level reading skills in English-language learners declines as one moves from the lower to the upper grades. Only one study (Abu-Rabia, 1997) was conducted with English-language learners at the high school level; findings indicate positive correlations between oral language proficiency and performance on word reading skills as well as between oral proficiency and phonological awareness. Therefore, these conclusions can be drawn with more certainty for younger than for older English-language learners.

The relationship between English oral proficiency and word reading skills has been found to be influenced by the manner in which oral proficiency is assessed. Some measures of oral language proficiency such as oral cloze tests may additionally be measuring other skills such as working memory and general mental ability. Furthermore, not all measures of English proficiency, such as measures of grammatical sensitivity, are sensitive to the full range of proficiency levels. Thus, in some studies, the lack of relationship between English oral language proficiency and word reading skills may be due, in part, to a restriction in range in the measure of oral language proficiency; this is less likely to be the case for older learners who started their schooling in English at an earlier age and thus display a wider range of proficiency levels. Finally, some oral language skills may be more related to word and pseudoword reading than others. For example, lexical knowledge is more predictive of word reading than is syntactic knowledge. Thus, we must be cautious not to overgeneralize when discussing the relationship between oral proficiency and word-level reading skills.

In assessing the results of correlational studies, it is important to distinguish between the bivariate relation between predictors and outcomes and the unique relations among these same measures. For example, a positive correlation often exists between measures of phonological awareness and measures of oral language proficiency, both of which are also positively related to measures of word-level reading skill. In such cases, some portion of the relation between each of the predictors (i.e., phonological awareness and oral language proficiency) and the outcome (i.e., word-level reading skill) is shared with the other predictor, and some portion of the relation is unshared with the other predictor. The latter represents a unique relation between the predictor and the outcome. If the pair of predictors is used in a regression model to predict outcomes in word-level reading skill, care must be taken not to misinterpret the meaning of the respective regression coefficients, which are measures of the predictors' unique associations with the outcome. In addition, one must be extremely cautious in considering the order in which variables are added to prediction models when such orderings are based on the data rather than theory. Because data-based orders of entry of variables in regression equations are greatly affected by individual sample statistics, such orderings often do not replicate from one sample to another unless sample sizes are large and representative.

Spelling. Only a handful of studies have examined the relationship between English oral language proficiency such as syntactic sensitivity and vocabulary and the English spelling skills of English-language learners in the elementary grades (Everatt, Smythe, Adams, & Ocampo, 2000; Jackson & Lu, 1992; Wade-Woolley & Siegel, 1997). With one exception (Arab-Moghaddam & Sénéchal, 2001), we found that the grammatical skills in English are not strongly related to spelling skills in English-language learners in elementary and middle school. However, this conclusion is tentative given the small number of studies. Little can be said about the relationship between English oral language proficiency and English spelling in higher grades. One study of high school students (Abu-Rabia, 1997) did find a correlation between grammatical skills and spelling recognition. However, the task used to measure oral language proficiency may have been capturing more than oral language proficiency since it was highly related to a measure of math ability and memory. There is some evidence that vocabulary knowledge in English may be correlated with spelling skills in English, but this possibility, based on one study (Arab-Moghaddam & Sénéchal, 2001), requires replication with language-minority and second-language learners.

As was the case for word reading, research suggests that phonological processing skills in English, such as phonological awareness, and working memory play a significant role in the spelling skills of English-language learners. Native English speakers and English-language learners who are poor spellers have similar phonological processing skills despite differences in their oral language proficiency in English. The same is the case for native English speakers and English-language learners who are good spellers. Again, little can be said about the role of phonological processing skills in the spelling ability of older English-language learners; the one study that explored this question was conducted with Hebrew speakers learning English as a foreign language (Abu-Rabia, 1997).

Relationship between English Oral Proficiency and English Text-Level Literacy Skills

Reading Comprehension. Ten studies examined the relationship between English oral proficiency and English reading comprehension (Beech & Keys, 1997; Carlisle, Beeman, & Shah, 1996; Carlisle, Beeman, Davis, & Spharim, 1999; Dufva & Voeten, 1999; Goldstein, Harris, & Klein, 1993; Jiménez, García, & Pearson, 1996; Lee & Schallert, 1997; Peregoy, 1989; Peregoy & Boyle, 1991; Royer & Carlo, 1991). In contrast with its role in spelling and word reading, oral language proficiency in English is associated with reading comprehension skills in English for second-language students. Components of English-language proficiency that are linked to English-reading proficiency include English vocabulary knowledge, listening comprehension, syntactic skills, and the ability to handle metalinguistic aspects of language (such as providing definitions of words). The crucial role of oral vocabulary knowledge in reading comprehension was documented by four studies conducted with elementary or middle school English-language learners (Dufva & Voeten, 1999; Carlisle *et al.*, 1999; Jiménez *et al.*, 1996; Carlisle *et al.*, 1996). Research findings suggest that limited vocabulary knowledge is associated with low levels of reading comprehension in English, and English-language learners with a large repertoire of high-frequency and academically relevant words are better able to process written texts than English-language learners without such a repertoire.

Finally, it is important to note that differences in the reading comprehension abilities of English-language learners relate not only to oral language proficiency, but also to individual factors such as cognitive ability and memory, word reading skills, first-language reading skills and contextual factors, such as SES, home-language use, and literacy practices, as well as to differences in instructional and other educational experiences. The previous section of this chapter as well as Chapters 4, 5 and 6 address these questions more fully.

Writing. Unfortunately, few studies have examined the relationship between English oral language proficiency and English writing (Davis *et al.*, 1999; Dufva & Voeten, 1999; Lanauze & Snow, 1989; Lumme & Lehto, 2002; Yau & Belanger, 1985). Studies of elementary and middle school English-language learners suggest that well-developed oral language skills in English are associated with better writing skills in English. Oral language skills of English-language learners that are related to writing include listening comprehension and vocabulary knowledge. Because phonological memory also plays a role, the research suggests that the link between second-language oral and writing skills is mediated by underlying phonological processing skills.

Limited research also suggests that there are many aspects of oral language proficiency that are important for proficient writing in English as a second language, including decontextualized language skills; grammatical skills; and knowledge of cohesive devices such as anaphora, relativization, temporal reference, and conjunctions, which enable the writer to express ideas not limited to the here and now. In addition, the acquisition of proficient writing skills entails good spelling skills, metacognitive skills such as audience awareness, and familiarity with and opportunities to practice writing different text genres. There is scant evidence in these studies, however, for the role and development of these kinds of skills in English-language learners of any age group.

Quality of writing may also be linked to first-language writing skills. One study conducted with upper elementary age students (Lanauze and Snow, 1989) found that Spanish-speaking English-language learners with relatively better developed writing skills in Spanish were able to use Spanish discourse-level knowledge when writing in English, although their oral language skills in English were less well developed than their skills in Spanish.

METHODOLOGICAL ISSUES

Examining and conducting research on literacy development among language-minority students is a complex undertaking. In interpreting the research, several issues arise. First, it is critical to consider the variables that were not included in the study, but may have played a mediating or moderating role in the results obtained. It is also important to consider that apparent predictors may represent a proxy for another skill or demographic variable that in fact explains the outcome. It is also important to consider the quality and domain of the assessments administered in these studies. Overall, there is a lack of developmentally appropriate and reliable instruments for assessing oral language, literacy, and related skills for this population of students. In the absence of assessments of background knowledge or discourse knowledge, for example, it is not possible to speak to their role in literacy performance. In general, more high-quality assessments and assessments for more domains are needed to better understand the literacy development of language- minority students.

RECOMMENDATIONS FOR FUTURE RESEARCH

Because the population of language-minority students includes a significant number of students who have poor academic achievement as compared with their majority-culture peers (National Center for Education Statistics, 2003), it is imperative that more be learned about the development of literacy skills by this population and the nature of their difficulties.

Reading Readiness Skills of Language-Minority Students

We do not know whether emergent literacy skills vary by first-language background, amount of time in the country (for immigrant populations), or other factors such as preschool attendance. Nor is it clear how early literacy skills might relate to later literacy outcomes given that only one of the longitudinal studies that included kindergarten measures followed the sample past second grade. It is important to look longitudinally to determine long-term outcomes, particularly with respect to reading comprehension. This research would help inform models of early identification and intervention for at-risk second-language learners.

Word-Level Skills of Language-Minority Students

A careful look at the findings of this review reveals many unanswered questions about the word-level skills of language-minority students. First, although it appears that word-level skills can develop to the same extent in language-minority and monolingual children in the primary grades, the extent to which this finding may be contingent on a particular type of literacy instruction provided to children is unclear. Although some studies are explicit about the instructional context, others are not.

Also unclear is the extent to which language-minority students who achieve word-reading accuracy comparable to that of native speakers also achieve a comparable level of fluency. Fluent and automatic word reading is critical for reading comprehension, and only one study in our review looked at the speed and efficiency of word reading. Finally, research is also needed to examine the development of spelling in older second-language learners.

Text-Level Skills of Language-Minority Students

There is a need for more research on the development of text-level skills in language-minority students and how this development compares with that of monolingual students. Only seven studies in our database compared the reading comprehension of language-minority and monolingual children; five of these were conducted in the Netherlands, one in the United States, and one in Canada.

Despite the finding that reading comprehension is an area of weakness for language-minority students, minimal information is available on the nature of their comprehension difficulties and the specific skills having the greatest influence on reading comprehension. For example, more research is needed on how reading fluency in English-language learners influences reading comprehension. Research is also needed to examine precursors to reading fluency and instructional practices that can enhance reading fluency in English-language learners across the school years. Additionally, research is needed on the role of demographic and contextual variables, such as years of second-language instruction, in performance in this area. The research needs to be conducted with similar measures and across various populations of language-minority students.

Finally, as we noted on page 47, minimal research on English-language learners' writing development has been conducted. Studies that focus on the role of spelling skills, decontextualized language skills, cohesive devices and metalinguistic awareness in writing are needed. Equally important is instructional research targeting metacognitive skills (such as audience awareness) and familiarity with and opportunities to practice writing different text genres in the acquisition of proficient writing skills by language-minority students.

Learning Difficulties

Learning disabilities are present in all groups, regardless of age, race, language background, and SES (Lyon, Shaywitz, & Shaywitz, 2003); estimates of the prevalence range from 5% to 15 % of the population (e.g., Lyon, 1995, 1999). While high proportions of language-minority students are failing in school (National Center for Education Statistics, 2003), it is likely that many of them do not have learning disabilities. By and large, the answer to the question of who is an English-language learner with a learning disability is a problem of disentangling the interactions among second-language learning difficulties and such factors as resources in schools, opportunities to learn, the sociocultural context, and the quality of psychometric measures.

For researchers, the issues related to special education and language-minority students emphasize the need to answer related questions about issues such as component skills that influence developmental trajectories, early predictors of difficulties, appropriate intervention, and the role of early screening for literacy difficulties.

The most prevalent criterion for reading disability used in the studies we reviewed was scoring in the 25th percentile or below on a standardized reading measure. Typically, no other information was provided about these children. In addition to the need to collect data on the salient linguistic and literacy variables that influence academic achievement for these learners, there is a need to investigate the sociocultural variables that affect the achievement of English-language learners in the United States (U.S. Department of Education & National Institute of Child Health and Human Development, 2003). Thus, in addition to academic variables, contextual variables, including those related to home-language use and SES, instructional type (bilingual, ESL support, or mainstream), and characteristics of reading instruction (such as quality and language of instruction), should be considered when possible.

The Relationship of Oral Language Proficiency to Second-Language Literacy

It would be important to determine whether the finding that phonological processing skills are better than oral language proficiency as predictors of word reading skills is true of English-language learners at all levels of English oral language development and whether it generalizes to word reading fluency.

It is important to note that there were few upper grade studies examining the contributions of oral language proficiency and phonological processing skills to word recognition skills in English-language learners. Teasing apart the potential contributions of second-language oral proficiency, particularly lexical knowledge, aspects of phonological processing, such as phonological awareness and rapid naming, and orthographic skills in older English-language learners is crucial because the findings of such research could have important implications for instructional and assessment practices.

More research is needed, as well, on the extent to which typological similarities or differences between English and the learner's spoken and written first language mediate the relationships among specific aspects of second-language phonological and orthographic processing skills, and word recognition skills in the second language.

Additional research is needed to understand the developmental foundations of spelling skills in English-language learners and the role played in writing by accurate and fluent spelling skills. Different languages and orthographic systems have different phonological, orthographic, and morphosyntactic features; all of these factors, as well as the age at which English-language learners learn to spell in English, may affect the nature and ease with which specific spelling and orthographic skills develop in English-language learners from different native-language backgrounds.

Given the findings of research conducted with monolinguals that established the strong relationship of oral proficiency to text-level skills, questions concerning the role of second-language proficiency in the domains of reading fluency and comprehension are particularly pertinent in second-language contexts, but there is almost no research in this area. These domains should be studied with English-language learners of different age groups, in different educational programs, and with different first-language backgrounds. Moreover, much more research is needed to identify the specific second-language oral skills that are related to aspects of reading comprehension, such as familiarity with text structure and text genre conventions.

One possible implication of the findings of the review of studies that focus on the relationship of second-language oral proficiency to reading comprehension is that, by focusing instruction on English-language proficiency, particularly academic vocabulary development, it may be possible to enhance English-language learners' reading comprehension skills. Improved reading comprehension, in turn, may expand vocabulary and other academically relevant language skills. This is an area requiring more systematic investigation.

Finally, more research is needed to analyze and achieve consensus on the construct of oral language proficiency. A number of questions deserve more careful examination and study: (a) whether there is an underlying ability or aptitude or a single construct that predisposes the second-language learner to do better on more complex skills, (b) whether language skills are hierarchically nested, and (c) what relationship exists between these oral language constructs and other constructs such as phonological processing as well as specific literacy components at different points in development.

Recommendations for Study Design and Methodology

There is a need for systematic research that carefully examines the development of literacy by language-minority students, including the individual and contextual influences involved. The majority of studies in our review were cross-sectional in nature—that is they compared different samples of students. Although longitudinal research, in which students are followed over time, is the most informative method when studying development in children, this design is especially important for studying the development of literacy in language-minority students. In that population of students, language and literacy skills are undergoing rapid change, development of second-language skills may go hand in hand with decline of first-language skills, growth is likely to be non-linear, and many of our questions can be answered only by tracking development and response to instruction over time.

In the following sections, we provide additional recommendations for designing studies that contribute maximally to our understanding of the development of literacy skills in language-minority students.

Groups Included in the Study. The majority of research on language-minority students has been conducted with children in elementary schools and predominantly in the primary grades. Studies of language-minority students in the middle school and secondary school years are also needed. For example, identifying the potential contributions of second-language oral proficiency and phonological processing in older English-language learners is crucial because the findings of such research would have important implications for instructional and assessment practices, as well as for policy decisions pertaining to the education of these students. Likewise, research with older learners that carefully identifies the components involved in the reading comprehension process would also have important implications for practice and policy decisions.

For certain questions, it is crucial to include samples of both English-language learners and native English speakers. Many of the studies we reviewed would have been more informative had they included a sample of native English speakers and examined whether certain factors have a differential impact on word- or text-level skills for the two groups. As an example, we do not know whether the impact of vocabulary or metacognitive skills on reading comprehension differs for these two groups and, if so, how it might differ. This knowledge would be particularly useful for planning effective instruction and interventions for language-minority students.

Further, language-minority students are a diverse population. More research is needed to examine individual differences in the acquisition of literacy skills in this population. Specifically, research in this area should be designed to examine those factors most related to positive outcomes for these students and those most related to the achievement of children experiencing literacy difficulties.

Demographic Context of the Study.   Given what we know about the demographics of literacy achievement, it is also crucial that studies be explicit about the SES of the participants or at least the schools and neighborhoods in which the research was conducted. Further, if possible, studies comparing the achievement of language-minority students and native speakers should attempt to match the groups on SES; otherwise, this factor is likely to bias the results and confound their accurate interpretation.

Language and Instructional Context.   The research has conceptualized language-minority students primarily as a single, distinct population. Future research must begin to recognize the heterogeneity of this population with respect to language use in the home, school, and community. In particular, information should be provided about the intensity of exposure to the second language for the sample being studied. Children whose native language is the dominant language spoken in their neighborhood and by many other students at school, and who therefore continue to use and develop their first language and perhaps literacy skills in that language, are likely to have a different trajectory of language and literacy development from that of children whose home language is not spoken in their community.

In addition, if we are to interpret findings accurately, the educational context of each study should be described in sufficient detail. As noted, the development of literacy skills is directly dependent on and reflective of instructional practices.

Assessment.   Studies in this area have used a number of standardized and researcher-developed measures (see Chapter 7 for a summary). With regard to the assessment of oral language proficiency among English-language learners, our review of the research indicated that two approaches have been used: (a) a global approach based on general indices of proficiency, teacher ratings, self-ratings, indices of language use at home, and reports of language preferences; and (b) an approach assessing specific aspects of oral language proficiency, including grammatical knowledge, syntactic awareness, vocabulary knowledge, quality of formal definitions provided to nouns, and listening comprehension of sentences or narratives. These two approaches were used in a wide variety of studies, including those that employed different measures of oral language proficiency, involved learners at different ages and with different first languages, and were conducted in different learning settings. Clearly, more research is called for to examine systematically the predictive validity and construct validity of measures of global and specific aspects of oral language proficiency with respect to literacy.

To the extent possible, future research should employ measures that have proved reliable and yielded results related to the questions of interest. It is also important to design studies with the intent of replicating current findings and generating a cohesive body of research; doing so involves employing measures to which other researchers have access. Finally, assessing a range of skills within the language-minority population is essential so we can know whether the difficulties of language-minority students are due to a learning disability, language background, SES, or instructional factors.

Analyses. Some studies in our review examined the literacy achievement of groups of language-minority students spanning several grade levels in school. This is acceptable, but the study results need to be disaggregated by grade level. Moreover, studies focused on literacy difficulties usually compare language-minority students with typical native speakers, when a comparison with struggling native speakers would be more important and informative.

Much research in this area has been conducted with a quantitative approach and analytic techniques that have yielded findings on the average, ignoring individual variability. This is a particular problem in light of the heterogeneity of the language-minority population. To better understand developmental trajectories and individual differences, there is a need for studies that lend themselves to individual growth modeling with samples large enough to identify subgroups of students showing differentiated growth patterns. A multifactorial approach would enable us to disentangle learner, textual, contextual, and instructional factors that may contribute to the development of reading comprehension in language-minority students.

Finally, we need to analyze systematically and reliably the errors that language-minority students coming from different language backgrounds make in reading, spelling, and other literacy skills. It is important to compare these error patterns with those of errors made by native speakers. These error analyses may provide a clue to the specific areas in which language-minority students are having difficulty—errors that reflect more general developmental trajectories, as well as errors that reflect important information about first-language influence.

REFERENCES

Aarts, R., & Verhoeven, L. (1999). Literacy attainment in a second language submersion context. *Applied Psycholinguistics*, 20(3), 377–393.

Abu-Rabia, S. (1997). Verbal and working-memory skills of bilingual Hebrew–English speaking children. *International Journal of Psycholinguistics*, 13(1), 25–40.

Abu-Rabia, S., & Siegel, L. S. (2002). Reading, syntactic, orthographic, and working memory skills of bilingual Arabic–English speaking Canadian children. *Journal of Psycholinguistic Research*, 31(6), 661–678.

Adams, M. J. (1990). *Beginning to read: Thinking and learning about print.* Cambridge, MA: MIT Press.

Afflerbach, P. P. (1990). The influence of prior knowledge on expert readers' main idea construction strategies. *Reading Research Quarterly*, 25(1), 31–46.

Arab-Moghaddam, N., & Sénéchal, M. (2001). Orthographic and phonological processing skills in reading and spelling in Persian/English bilinguals. *International Journal of Behavioral Development*, 25(2), 140–147.

Baddeley, A. D. (1986). *Working memory.* Oxford: Oxford University Press.

Beech, J. R., & Keys, A. (1997). Reading, vocabulary and language preference in 7- to 8-year-old bilingual Asian children. *British Journal of Educational Psychology*, 67(4), 405–414.

Bermúdez, A. B., & Prater, D. L. (1994). Examining the effects of gender and second language proficiency on Hispanic writers' persuasive discourse. *Bilingual Research Journal*, 18(3/4), 47–62.

Bernhardt, E. B. (2000). Second language reading as a case study of reading scholarship in the twentieth century. In M. L. Kamil, P. B. Mosenthal, P. D. Pearson, & R. Barr (Eds.), *Handbook of reading research* (Vol. 3, pp. 791–811). Mahwah, NJ: Lawrence Erlbaum Associates.

Berninger, V. (1994). Intraindividual differences in levels of language in comprehension of written sentences. *Learning and Individual Differences*, 6, 433–457.

Berninger, V. W., Abbot, R. D., Abbot, S. P., Graham, S., & Richards, T. (2002). Writing and reading: Connections between language by hand and language by eye. *Journal of Learning Disabilities*, 35, 39–56.

Berninger, V., & Richards, T. (2002). *Brain literacy for educators and psychologists.* San Diego, CA: Academic Press.

Berninger, V. W., Yates, C., Cartwright, A., Rutberg, J., Remy, E., & Abbott, R. (1992). Lower-level developmental skills in beginning writing. *Reading and Writing: An Interdisciplinary Journal*, 4, 257–280.

Bialystok, E. (1997). Effects of bilingualism and biliteracy on children's emerging concepts of print. *Developmental Psychology*, 33(3), 429–440.

Bradley, L., & Bryant, P. (1983). Categorizing sounds and learning to read: A causal connection. *Nature, 301*, 419–421.

Carlisle, J. F., Beeman, M. M., Davis, L.-H., & Spharim, G. (1999). Relationship of metalinguistic capabilities and reading achievement for children who are becoming bilingual. *Applied Psycholinguistics*, 20(4), 459–478.

Carlisle, J. F, Beeman, M. B., & Shah, P. P. (1996). The metalinguistic capabilities and English literacy of Hispanic high school students: An exploratory study. *Yearbook of the National Reading Conference*, 45, 306–316.

Chall, J. S. (1996). *Stages of reading development* (2nd ed.). Fort Worth, TX: Harcourt Brace College Publishers.

Chiappe, P., & Siegel, L. S. (1999). Phonological awareness and reading acquisition in English- and Punjabi-speaking Canadian children. *Journal of Educational Psychology*, 91(1), 20–28.

Chiappe, P., Siegel, L. S., & Gottardo, A. (2002). Reading-related skills of kindergartners from diverse linguistic backgrounds. *Applied Psycholinguistics*, 23(1), 95–116.

Chiappe, P., Siegel, L. S., & Wade-Woolley, L. (2002). Linguistic diversity and the development of reading skills: A longitudinal study. *Scientific Studies of Reading*, 6(4), 369–400.

Cisero, C. A., & Royer, J. M. (1995). The development and cross-language transfer of phonological awareness. *Contemporary Educational Psychology*, 20(3), 275–303.

Cronnell, B. (1985). Language influences in the English writing of third- and sixth-grade Mexican American students. *Journal of Educational Research*, 78(3), 168–173.

Da Fontoura, H. A., & Siegel, L. S. (1995). Reading, syntactic, and working memory skills of bilingual Portuguese–English Canadian children. *Reading and Writing*, 7(1), 139–153.

D'Angiulli, A., Siegel, L. S., & Serra, E. (2001). The development of reading in English and Italian in bilingual children. *Applied Psycholinguistics*, 22, 479–507.

Davis, L. H., Carlisle, J. F., & Beeman, M. (1999). Hispanic children's writing in English and Spanish when English is the language of instruction. *Yearbook of the National Reading Conference*, 48, 238–248.

Droop, M., & Verhoeven, L. T. (1998). Background knowledge, linguistic complexity, and second language reading comprehension. *Journal of Literacy Research*, 30(2), 253–271.

Dufva, M., & Voeten, M. J. M. (1999). Native language literacy and phonological memory as prerequisites for learning English as a foreign language. *Applied Psycholinguistics*, 20(3), 329–348.

Durgunoglu, A. Y., Nagy, W. E., & Hancin-Bhatt, B. J. (1993). Cross-language transfer of phonological awareness. *Journal of Educational Psychology*, 85(3), 453–465.

Ehri, L. C. (1998). Grapheme–phoneme knowledge is essential for learning to read words in English. In J. Metsala & L. Ehri (Eds.), *Word recognition in beginning reading* (pp. 3–40). Hillsdale, NJ: Lawrence Erlbaum Associates.

Everatt, J., Smythe, I., Adams, E., & Ocampo, D. (2000). Dyslexia screening measures and bilingualism. *Dyslexia*, 6(1), 42–56.

Fashola, O. S., Drum, P. A., Mayer, R. E., & Kang, S.-J. (1996). A cognitive theory of orthographic transitioning: Predictable errors in how Spanish-speaking children spell English words. *American Educational Research Journal*, 33(4), 825–843.

Ferris, M. R., & Politzer, R. L. (1981). Effects of early and delayed second language acquisition: English composition skills of Spanish-speaking junior high school students. *TESOL Quarterly*, 15(3), 263–274.

Fitzgerald, J., & Shanahan, T. (2000). Reading and writing relations and their development. *Educational Psychologist*, 35, 39–50.

Foorman, B. R., Francis, D. J., Fletcher, J. M., & Lynn, A. (1996). Relation of phonological and orthographic processing to early reading: Comparing two approaches to regression-based, reading level-match designs. *Journal of Educational Psychology*, 88, 639–652.

Foorman, B. R., Francis, D. J., Fletcher, J. M., Schatschneider, C., & Mehta, P. (1998). The role of instruction in learning to read: Preventing reading failure in at-risk children. *Journal of Educational Psychology*, 90, 37–55.

Geva, E., Yaghoub-Zadeh, Z., & Schuster, B. (2000). Part IV: Reading and foreign language learning: Understanding individual differences in word recognition skills of ESL children. *Annals of Dyslexia*, 50, 121–154.

Gholamain, M., & Geva, E. (1999). Orthographic and cognitive factors in the concurrent development of basic reading skills in English and Persian. *Language Learning*, 49(2), 183–217.

Goldstein, B. C., Harris, K. C., & Klein, M. D. (1993). Assessment of oral storytelling abilities of Latino junior high school students with learning handicaps. *Journal of Learning Disabilities*, 26(2), 138–143.

Gottardo, A. (2002). The relationship between language and reading skills in bilingual Spanish–English speakers. *Topics in Language Disorders*, 22(5), 46–70.

Gottardo, A., Yan, B., Siegel, L. S., & Wade-Woolley, L. (2001). Factors related to English reading performance in children with Chinese as a first language: More evidence of cross-language transfer of phonological processing. *Journal of Educational Psychology,* 93(3), 530–542.

Guthrie, J., & Wigfield, A. (2000). Engagement and motivation in reading. In M. Kamil, P. B. Mosenthal, P. D. Pearson, & R. Barr (Eds.), *Handbook of reading research* (Vol. 3, pp. 403–422). Mahwah, NJ: Lawrence Erlbaum Associates.

Hacquebord, H. (1994). L2-reading in the content areas: Text comprehension in secondary education in the Netherlands. *Journal of Research in Reading,* 17(2), 83–98.

Hart, B., & Risley, T. (1995). *Meaningful differences in the everyday experience of young American children.* Baltimore, MD: Paul H. Brooks.

Jackson, N., Holm, A., & Dodd, B. (1998). Phonological awareness and spelling abilities of Cantonese–English bilingual children. *Asia Pacific Journal of Speech, Language, and Hearing,* 3(2), 79–96.

Jackson, N. E., & Lu, W.-H. (1992). Bilingual precocious readers of English. *Roeper Review,* 14(3), 115–119.

Jiménez, R. T., García, G. E., & Pearson, D. P. (1996). The reading strategies of bilingual Latina/o students who are successful English readers: Opportunities and obstacles. *Reading Research Quarterly,* 31(1), 90–112.

Kame'enui, E., & Simmons, D. (2001) Introduction to this special issue: The DNA of reading fluency. *Scientific Studies of Reading,* 5(3), 203–210.

Lanauze, M., & Snow, C. E. (1989). The relation between first- and second-language writing skills: Evidence from Puerto Rican elementary school children in bilingual programs. *Linguistics and Education,* 1(4), 323–339.

Lee, J. W., & Schallert, D. L. (1997). The relative contribution of L2 language proficiency and L1 reading ability to L2 reading performance: A test of the threshold hypothesis in an EFL context. *TESOL Quarterly,* 31(4), 713–739.

Liberman, I., Shankweiler, D., Fischer, F., & Carter, B. (1974). Explicit syllable and phoneme segmentation in the young child. *Journal of Experimental Psychology,* 18, 201–212.

Limbos, M., & Geva, E. (2001). Accuracy of teacher assessments of second-language students at risk for reading disability. *Journal of Learning Disabilities,* 34(2), 136–151.

Lumme, K., & Lehto, J. E. (2002). Sixth grade pupils' phonological processing and school achievement in a second and the native language. *Scandinavian Journal of Educational Research,* 46(2), 207–217.

Lundberg, I., Olofsson, A., & Wall, S. (1980). Reading and spelling skills in the first school years predicted from phonemic awareness skills in kindergarten. *Scandinavian Journal of Psychology,* 21, 159–173.

Lyon, G. R. (1995). Research initiatives in learning disabilities: Contributions from scientists supported by the National Institute of Child Health and Human Development. *Journal of Child Neurology,* 10, 120–126.

Lyon, R. (1999). *Education research: Is what we don't know hurting our children?* House Science Committee Subcommittee on Basic Research, U.S. House of Representatives.

Lyon, G. R., Shaywitz, S. E., & Shaywitz, B. A. (2003). A definition of dyslexia. *Annals of Dyslexia,* 53, 1–14.

Mann, V. A. (1993). Phonemic awareness and future reading ability. *Journal of Learning Disabilities,* 26, 259–269.

Miramontes, O. B. (1987). Oral reading miscues of Hispanic students: Implications for assessment of learning disabilities. *Journal of Learning Disabilities,* 20(10), 627–632.

Moats, L. C. (1994). The missing foundation in teacher education: Knowledge of the structure of spoken and written language. *Annals of Dyslexia,* 44, 81–104.

Mumtaz, S., & Humphreys, G. W. (2001). The effects of bilingualism on learning to read English: Evidence from the contrast between Urdu–English bilingual and English monolingual children. *Journal of Research in Reading,* 24(2), 113–134.

Muter, V., & Diethelm, K. (2001). The contribution of phonological skills and letter knowledge to early reading development in a multilingual population. *Language Learning*, 51(2), 187–219.

Nagy, W. E., García, G. E., Durgunoglu, A. Y., & Hancin-Bhatt, B. (1993). Spanish–English bilingual students' use of cognates in English reading. *Journal of Reading Behavior*, 25(3), 241–259.

National Center for Education Statistics. (2003). *National Assessment of Educational Progress, 2003, reading assessments*. Washington, DC: U.S. Department of Education, Institute of Education Sciences.

Olson, R. K., Wise, B., Johnson, M. C., & Ring, J. (1997). The etiology and remediation of phonologically based word recognition and spelling disabilities: Are phonological deficits the "hole" story? In B. Blachman (Ed.), *Foundations of reading acquisition and dyslexia: Implications for early intervention* (pp. 305–326). Mahwah, NJ: Lawrence Erlbaum Associates.

Peregoy, S. F. (1989). Relationships between second language oral proficiency and reading comprehension of bilingual fifth grade students. *NABE: The Journal of the National Association for Bilingual Education*, 13(3), 217–234.

Peregoy, S. F., & Boyle, O. F. (1991). Second language oral proficiency characteristics of low, intermediate and high second language readers. *Hispanic Journal of Behavioral Sciences*, 13(1), 35–47.

Pérez, B. (1998). Language, literacy, and biliteracy. In B. Pérez (Ed.). *Sociocultural contexts of language and literacy*. Mahwah, NJ: Lawrence Erlbaum Associates.

Perfetti, C. A. (1985). Reading ability. In B. Hutson (Ed.), *Advances in reading/language research* (pp. 231–256). London: Oxford University Press.

Perfetti, C. A. (1999). Comprehending written language: A blueprint of the reader. In C. Brown & P. Hagoot (Eds.), *The neurocognition of language* (pp. 167–208). New York: Oxford University Press.

Quiroga, T., Lemos-Britton, Z., Mostafapour, E., Abbott, R. D., & Berninger, V. W. (2002). Phonological awareness and beginning reading in Spanish-speaking ESL first graders: Research into practice. *Journal of School Psychology*, 40(1), 85–111.

RAND Reading Study Group. (2002). *Reading for understanding: Toward an R&D program in reading comprehension*. Washington, DC: Author.

Royer, J. M., & Carlo, M. S. (1991). Transfer of comprehension skills from native to second language. *Journal of Reading*, 34(6), 450–455.

Scanlon, D. M., & Vellutino, F. R. (1997). A comparison of the instructional backgrounds and cognitive profiles of poor, average, and good readers who were initially identified as at risk for reading failure. *Scientific Studies of Reading*, 1(3), 191–215.

Schierloh, J. M. (1991). Teaching standard English usage: A dialect-based approach. *Adult Learning*, 2, 20–22.

Shaywitz, S. E., Fletcher, J. M., Holahan, J. M., Schneider, A. E., Marchione, K. E., Stuebing, K. K., Francis, D. J., Pugh, K. R., & Shaywitz, B. A. (1999). Persistence of dyslexia: The Connecticut Longitudinal Study at adolescence. *Pediatrics*, 104(6), 1351–1359.

Siegel, L. S. (1993). The development of reading. In H. W. Reese (Ed.), *Advances in child development and behavior* (pp. 63–97). San Diego, CA: Academic Press.

Snow, C. E., Burns, M. S., & Griffin, P. (Eds.). (1998). *Preventing reading difficulties in young children*. Washington, DC: National Academy Press.

Stahl, S. S. (2003). Vocabulary and readability: How knowing word meanings affects comprehension. *Topics in Language Disorders*, 23(3), 241–247.

Stanovich, K. E. (1986). Matthew effects in reading: Some consequences of individual differences in the acquisition of literacy. *Reading Research Quarterly*, 21, 360–407.

Stanovich, K. E., & Siegel, L. S. (1994). The phenotype performance profile of reading disabled children: A regression-based test of the phonological-core variable-difference model. *Journal of Educational Psychology*, 86, 24–53.

Swanson, H. L., & Saez, L. (2003). Memory difficulties in children and adults with learning disabilities. In H. L. Swanson, K. Harris, & S. Graham (Eds.), *Handbook of Learning Disabilities* (pp. 182–198). New York: Guilford.

Swanson, H. L., & Siegel, L. S. (2001). Learning disabilities as a working memory deficit. *Issues in Education: Contributions From Educational Psychology, 7*(1), 1–48.

Tompkins, G. E., Abramson, S., & Pritchard, R. H. (1999). A multilingual perspective on spelling development in third and fourth grades. *Multicultural Education, 6*(3), 12–18.

U.S. Department of Education & National Institute of Child Health and Human Development. (2003). *Symposium summary. National Symposium on Learning Disabilities and English Language Learners.* Washington, DC: Author.

Verhoeven, L. T. (1990). Acquisition of reading in a second language. *Reading Research Quarterly, 25*(2), 90–114.

Verhoeven, L. T. (2000). Components in early second language reading and spelling. *Scientific Studies of Reading, 4*(4), 313–330.

Wade-Woolley, L., & Siegel, L. S. (1997). The spelling performance of ESL and native speakers of English as a function of reading skill. *Reading & Writing: An Interdisciplinary Journal, 9*(506), 387–406.

Wagner, R. K., & Torgesen, J. K. (1987). The nature of phonological processing and its causal role in the acquisition of reading skills. *Psychological Bulletin, 101*(2), 192–212.

Wagner, R. K., Torgesen, J. K., & Rashotte, C. A. (1999). *Comprehensive test of phonological processing.* Austin, TX: Pro-Ed.

Wong, B. Y. L. (1997). Research on genre-specific strategies in enhancing writing in adolescents with learning disabilities. *Learning Disability Quarterly, 20*(2), 140–159.

Yau, M. S. S., & Belanger, J. (1985). Syntactic development in the writing of EFL students. *English Quarterly, 18*(2), 107–118.

4

Cross-Linguistic Relationships in Second-Language Learners

Fred Genesee, Esther Geva, Cheryl Dressler, and Michael L. Kamil

This chapter focuses on research that addresses relationships across languages in the development of literacy skills in children and adolescents who are learning to read and write English as a second language. Three general questions guided our review of these studies:

1. What is the relationship between language-minority children's first- and second-language oral development in domains related to literacy?
2. What is the relationship between oral development in the first language and literacy development in the second language, including English as a foreign language?
3. What is the relationship between literacy skills acquired in the first language and literacy skills acquired in the second language, including national languages that are not English?

Answers to these questions are important for theoretical as well as practical reasons. Theoretically speaking, understanding the nature and extent of cross-language effects in the acquisition of literacy skills in a second language is critical for developing a comprehensive theory of second-language literacy development. In contrast to monolingual students, language-minority students bring an additional set of resources or abilities and face an additional set of challenges when learning to read and write in a second language. They bring additional resources that are linked to their first language—both its oral and written forms. They also often bring cultural knowledge and experiences linked to their first language and culture that can influence the development and use of reading and writing skills in a second language. Studies on cross-language/modal effects are important to understand whether and in what ways the additional linguistic resources of language-minority students influence their second-language literacy development and, more specifically, whether the course of acquisition of second-language literacy is different from that of monolingual speakers as a result of these effects. Practically speaking, understanding the nature of these cross-language and cross-modal influences (i.e., between oral and literacy modes) and the conditions that affect their expression is important for designing pedagogical interventions that facilitate the successful acquisition of second-language reading and writing skills

BACKGROUND

Theories related to language and literacy development underlie the research that was reviewed, and we have used these theoretical perspectives to discuss the results of these studies, where appropriate, in the summaries that follow. Some of these theories are concerned with issues relevant to monolingual learners and some with issues relevant to second-language learners. The most salient theoretical frameworks that figure in our discussion of cross-language issues concern transfer, target language influences, interlanguage theories, underlying cognitive abilities, and moderator variables. We also refer to theories of transfer emanating from cognitive psychology (Bransford & Schwartz, 1998).

Transfer

Most studies reviewed in this chapter investigated cross-language relationships on the basis of one of two theoretical orientations: the contrastive analysis hypothesis (Lado, 1964) and the interdependence hypothesis (Cummins, 1978, 1979). Contrastive analysis involves analyzing a learner's first and second languages to identify similarities and differences. According to the contrastive analysis hypothesis, second-language errors will be made when the structures in the second language differ from those in the first language; and facilitation will be apparent when the languages are similar. This hypothesis has undergone considerable refinement since it was first introduced. Contemporary versions of this theory include the possibility that transfer from the first language can facilitate second-language learning when the two languages share features (e.g., phonological forms or cognate vocabulary). In this case, second-language acquisition would be accelerated. Typological similarity is fundamental to the contrastive analysis hypothesis insofar as languages that are typologically similar (e.g., English and Spanish or German) share more structural features than languages that are typologically distant (e.g., English and Chinese or Korean).

Although the theory continues to focus on the comparison of structural features, more recent work has included nonstructural factors (i.e., those not related to grammar) in the comparisons as well. One such factor is psychotypology—learners' perception of the similarity between their first and second languages (Kellerman, 1977). It has been argued that transfer is more likely to occur if learners do not view the two languages as significantly different from each other. For example, the existence of cognates in two languages may not be a sufficient condition for transfer of cognate knowledge to occur; a belief on the part of the learner that the two languages are similar may be necessary (but probably not sufficient) as well.

An additional factor that is thought to constrain transfer derives from the notion of markedness. Linguistically *unmarked* features are those that are universal or present in most of the world's languages, and these are thought to be more susceptible to transfer than typologically unusual features (Eckman, 1977, 1985; Hyltenstam, 1984). In most languages, for example, final consonants are devoiced; thus, the devoicing of final consonants is an unmarked feature. In English, final consonants may be voiced or voiceless. When a learner whose first language is unmarked with respect to this feature (e.g., German) learns English, first-language transfer is predicted when the learner is pronouncing a final consonant in the second language that is voiced. Thus, both *back* and *bag* would be pronounced bæk. It is not predicted, however, that the English speaker will voice final consonants in German because this feature is more marked, or unnatural, in the first language (English), but not in the second (German). More contemporary conceptualizations of the contrastive analysis hypothesis also acknowledge that transfer interacts with a host of additional factors, such as developmental processes and language/literacy proficiency (Ellis, 1994; Odlin, 1989).

The contrastive analysis hypothesis was originally formulated to explain the influence of the first language on the acquisition of subsystems of the second-language *grammar* (e.g., phonological, lexical, morphological, syntactic). Within the current discussion of cross-language relationships in the acquisition of literacy, the hypothesis is most relevant to studies investigating structural domains tied to literacy, such as phonology (e.g., in studies of spelling) and lexical knowledge (e.g., in studies of cognate relationships). However, the contrastive analysis hypothesis cannot account for the existence of cross-language relationships in literacy constructs that are more psychological in nature, such as metacognitive strategies that are used in the first and second languages.

In the second theoretical orientation, the interdependence hypothesis, Cummins (1981, 2000) has postulated that acquisition of first and second languages is interdependent; that is, development of the first language can influence and facilitate development of the second. Not all aspects of first-language development are postulated to be equally facilitative of second-language development.

Cummins distinguishes between language for academic and higher-order cognitive purposes (CALP, Cognitive Academic Language Proficiency) and language for day-to-day interpersonal communication (BICS, Basic Interpersonal Communicative Skills). These constructs are distinguished by the extent of contextual support and the cognitive demands. *Context-embedded communication,* such as talking about a movie with someone who has also seen it, is characteristic of day-to-day social language use, while *context-reduced communication,* such as discussing a movie with someone who has not seen it, requires the provision of more explicit and complete information that will ensure clear communication since the participants cannot draw on shared experiences. This latter form of communication is especially important in school.

The other continuum in Cummins' framework refers to the cognitive demands of communication. *Cognitively undemanding communication* requires language skills that have been overlearned and that require low cognitive involvement on the part of the participants, while *cognitively demanding communication* calls for language skills that have not been fully automatized, such as the explication of the methods and results of a scientific experiment. Cummins (2000) hypothesizes that "academic proficiency transfers across languages such that students who have developed literacy in their first language will tend to make stronger progress in acquiring literacy in their second language" because these academic language skills are developmentally linked to common underlying proficiencies across the languages.

It has been difficult to define with any precision the constructs and developmental relationships proposed in Cummins' hypotheses, and, indeed, they have been the subject of considerable controversy (Edelsky *et al.*, 1983; MacSwan & Rolstad, 2003). In particular, it is not entirely clear what Cummins means by his construct of *common underlying proficiency.* We take it to refer to procedural knowledge that underlies language use for higher-order cognitive purposes and entails the skills involved in defining words or elaborating ideas verbally. We differentiate Cummins' notion of common underlying proficiency from underlying cognitive abilities, which we discuss in later in the background section. We also assume that it does not refer to structural features of the type that figure in the contrastive analysis framework. Despite some uncertainty about the constructs involved, this framework warrants consideration here because of its prevalence in current research on second-language literacy development, especially in research that examines the relationship between literacy skills acquired in the first language and literacy skills acquired in the second language.

Both of these theoretical frameworks assume what Bransford and Schwartz (1998, p. 68) call a "direct application" approach, which "characterizes transfer as the ability to directly apply one's previous learning to a new setting or problem." This is evident in the emphasis on transfer of structures in the contrastive analysis hypothesis and in the emphasis on transfer of language proficiencies in the interdependence hypothesis of Cummins. Empirical tests of transfer using these theoretical frameworks have tended to examine transfer of specific knowledge or skills in isolation from other processes or strategies—what Bransford and Schwartz refer to as "sequestered problem solving." We return later to Bransford and Schwartz's "preparedness for future learning" proposal, which offers a broader framework, to illustrate that alternative frameworks are available for studying cross-linguistic transfer.

Throughout this review, the term *transfer* is used to describe cross-language relationships found in structures that belong exclusively to the linguistic domain (e.g., phonology), as well as skills that involve cognitive and language abilities (e.g., reading comprehension).

Target Language Influences

Some theories include the premise that second-language acquisition, including literacy, can be accounted for primarily by reference to features of the second language (Dulay & Burt, 1974). Such influences result in developmental patterns, including "errors," that resemble those made by first-language learners of the same language and are referred to as *developmental influences*. These effects may be influenced by the nature of the target language itself; for example, English is considered to have a deep orthographic structure, in that the relationship between the orthographic and phonological systems is complex and often obscure (e.g., the "f" sound can be represented in English by each of the following graphemes: "f" as in *fur*, "ph" as in *phenomenon*, and "gh" as in *enough*). In the case of English spelling, then, English influences are expected to emerge relatively late in development owing to the opaqueness of some sound–letter correspondencies. In this case, knowledge of first-language phonology might play a role in early stages of learning to spell, especially if the learner has a first language with a shallow orthographic system, such as Spanish in which the sound–letter relationships are relatively consistent. Even though knowing how to spell in Spanish may enable children to spell certain phonemes common to both languages, learning to spell phonemes in English that have multiple spellings will result in errors that reflect the challenges of the target language.

In contrast to transfer, target language or developmental influences are not cross-linguistic in nature. Yet as was just illustrated, the emergence of developmental errors can be influenced by characteristics of the target language, and this effect, in turn, can indirectly influence the role of first-language transfer.

Interlanguage Theories

Interlanguage theories, developed by researchers working on second-language acquisition in adults, acknowledge the importance of both first- and second-language sources of influence on second-language development. Most notably, Selinker (1972) and Nemser (1971) argue that the mental representations or abstract system of rules of the target language constructed by second-language learners are best described as an interlanguage or "a grammatical system with its own internal organizing principles which may or may not be related to the [first and second languages]" (Towell & Hawkins, 1994, p. 23). Interlanguage theories move theories of second-language acquisition away from an exclusive reliance on first- or second-language influences and postulate that aspects of the internal organization and developmental trajectory of second-language acquisition may be unique.

Underlying Cognitive Abilities

Relationships between first- and second-language acquisition have also been attributed to *underlying cognitive abilities* (Geva & Ryan, 1993), including working memory, phonological short-term memory, phonological awareness, and phonological recoding. Phonological short-term memory is a good example of a common underlying ability that has been investigated. It is thought to be part of one's general cognitive endowment and to be largely independent of specific language experiences or other experiential factors. This does not mean that experience does not influence the development of phonological short-term memory or other abilities in this category, but the abilities apply to the acquisition of any language. These underlying abilities are thought to account for individual differences in the rate and success of language-learning. Phonological awareness, although thought to influence the acquisition of reading in any language, is likely influenced in subtle ways by one's early language and literacy experiences. Nevertheless, awareness that language comprises sounds and sounds have different structural and functional properties is at the core of phonological awareness, and individual differences in such awareness affects literacy learning in the first or second language. The aspects of phonological awareness that are language specific have little effect on cross-language variance.

It is important to distinguish working memory and phonological processing from Cummins' notion of common underlying proficiency. Cummins' notion is clearly language dependent and developmental in nature. In contrast, underlying cognitive abilities are thought to be fundamentally cognitive and nonlinguistic in nature and are part of one's innate endowment—they are not learned. More specifically, Cummins' notion of language for academic purposes is clearly an acquired proficiency that is intimately linked to language experience, in contrast with phonological processing and working memory

Moderator Variables

Finally, cross-language and cross-modal influences on the development of literacy in a second language can be moderated by a broad range of variables. Moderator variables include such factors as level of proficiency in the first and second languages, the extent to which and the ways in which the first language is used in the home, socioeconomic and generational status, instruction, and even personality.

METHODOLOGY OF THE REVIEW

The review of research was conducted as described in the introduction to this report. The findings are summarized with respect to language learning outcomes that are relevant to the main questions posed above. This is a narrative review of evidence. There were not sufficient numbers of studies that addressed the same conceptual hypothesis to warrant quantitative synthesis techniques.

Many of the studies reviewed in this chapter used correlational designs to examine the links between languages. Several others used between-group designs in which English-language learners are divided into high- and low-performing groups which are then compared on measures in the first language. Failure to find differences between the groups suggests a lack of a relationship with the variables in question. For example, if learners who are good English readers also have good first-language vocabulary skills and the poor readers have relatively poor first-language vocabulary skills, then the difference in English reading scores is inferred to be related to first-language vocabulary.

SUMMARY OF EMPIRICAL FINDINGS

Although the studies reviewed in this chapter vary in research designs and language and literacy measures, they all sought to understand how first- and second-language literacy development may be interrelated. The studies reviewed here provide ample evidence for transfer with regard to specific linguistic structure/properties and psycholinguistic processes, although the evidence is not consistently robust in all cases and varies as a function of the construct under study. The empirical evidence for transfer uncovered by research is circumscribed by the researchers' conceptualizations of transfer. Research carried out within contrastive analysis and interdependence theories indicates that certain aspects of second-language oral proficiency and literacy are related in important ways to performance on similar constructs in the first language. There is also evidence for cross-modality influences, although cross-modality transfer has not been observed across the board. For example, first-language vocabulary does not appear to predict second-language reading comprehension.

Despite evidence for transfer, a cross-language framework, especially one that focuses on transfer as the primary influence, is not sufficient for understanding the full complexity of second-language literacy development among diverse English-language learners Transfer is not the sole source of influence in second-language oral proficiency and literacy development. Common underlying abilities (e.g., working memory) also play a significant role in second-language development as they do in first-language development; certain error types can be understood in terms of typological differences between the first and second languages; features of the target language mediate development, especially in advanced stages; and well-developed oral language and literacy skills in the first language can facilitate second-language literacy development to some extent.

Our review indicates that it may be time to move research on second-language literacy development beyond simple frameworks that do not accommodate the complex processes that interact dynamically across grade levels as English-language learners acquire literacy. As an example, a conceptualization of transfer as "preparedness for future learning" might broaden the notion of transfer, and thus expand our understanding of what constitutes cross-linguistic transfer in second-language learning. The concept of preparedness for future learning emanates from current theories of transfer (e.g., Bransford & Schwartz, 1998) that view the learner's use of knowledge from the first language as evidence of resourcefulness. Transfer could entail not only corresponding or analogous skills, but also metalinguistic or metacognitive skills that emerge from competence in the first language. An example would be English-language learners who transfer comprehension monitoring skills from the first to the second language.

The Relationship between Language-Minority Children's First- and Second-Language Oral Development in Domains Related to Literacy

The studies that address the first question examine cross-language relationships in (a) working memory; (b) phonological processes; and (c) oral language, including phonology, vocabulary, grammar, and discourse-level skills.

As explained in Chapter 3, working memory tasks demand *active manipulation* of information presented while concurrently holding the information in memory (Baddeley, 1986). Three studies examined correlations between working memory in English and students' first language (Abu-Rabia, 1997; Da Fontoura & Siegel, 1995; Gholamain & Geva, 1999). All three studies report significant correlations between working memory in the students' first and second languages.

Phonological processes reflect underlying processes related to phonological aspects of language. Phonological processes include phonological awareness, phonological recoding, and phonological short-term memory (Lumme & Lehto, 2002). With respect to phonological processing, there was consistent evidence of cross-language effects for phonological awareness, such that English-language learners with high levels of phonological awareness in the first language also had relatively high levels of phonological awareness when assessed in the second language (Cisero & Royer, 1995; Gottardo, 2002; Gottardo, Yan, Siegel, & Wade-Woolley, 2001; Hsia, 1992; Mumtaz & Humphreys, 2001; Quiroga, Lemos-Britten, Mostafapour, Abbott, & Berninger, 2002). The evidence from studies of phonological recoding and phonological short-term memory, although suggesting that cross-language relationships exist, is inconsistent (Gholamain & Geva, 1999; Gottardo, 2002; Gottardo et al., 2001; Mumtaz & Humphreys, 2001). This inconsistency may be due to the limited research in each of these domains.

There is some limited evidence that cross-language effects in phonological awareness are more likely among younger learners or during early stages of second-language development than later because once students have acquired higher levels of second-language proficiency, phonological awareness is probably less important. In contrast, studies of phonological short-term memory report significant cross-linguistic relationships for students at a wide range of ages. Much more research is needed that systematically examines how age influences the relationships between first- and second-language ability in these three domains.

For purposes of this review, phonology, considered part of oral language, includes the ability to recognize and produce the sound sequences that make up language. A number of studies examined cross-language relationships in phonology: Holm, Dodd, Stow, and Pert (1999) examined speech production, Hsia (1992) examined intraword segmentation, and Kramer and Schell (1982) and Kramer *et al.* (1983) examined phonological (sound) discrimination. These studies are reviewed here because the oral language relationships they examined may be related to second-language reading and writing.

Studies of cross-language effects in the domain of phonology provide evidence for first-language influences on second-language acquisition. More specifically, English-language learners were found to exhibit developmental patterns in sound discrimination and production that were not like those of the target language, but reflected characteristics of the first language. It is impossible to ascertain the generalizability of these effects, however, because these studies varied considerably with respect to both the ages of the students and the specific language domains examined. Moreover, the number of studies in each domain was limited. In all cases, the first-language influences resulted from differences between the first and second languages that resulted in errors or nontargetlike forms (Hsia, 1992; Kramer & Schell, 1982; although see Liow & Poon, 1998, for an example of facilitation with respect to phonological awareness).

There are usually more instances of transfer that result in errors than correct targetlike forms because to document errors in second-language development that may be due to transfer from the first language researchers simply have to show that English-language learners are producing nontargetlike forms that can be linked to first-language forms. Finding evidence of facilitation is harder because it would require researchers to show that English-language learners acquire specific features of English faster than would be the case if they spoke a less facilitative first language. In any case, even examples of errors in the second language should be interpreted as evidence of English-language learners' use of first-language skills to bootstrap English learning (see Bransford & Schwartz, 1989, for a similar argument).

The importance of examining cross-linguistic effects is illustrated by the Holm *et al.* (1999) study, in which first-language influences resulted in second-language patterns of phonological development that resembled those of children with speech impairment. Documenting the influence of the first language on the second is thus additionally important so that we can assist speech and language professionals and educators in properly identifying students with disabilities.

Three studies of cross-language effects on vocabulary development were identified (Carlisle, Beeman, Davis, & Spharim, 1999; Johnson, 1989; Ordóñez, Carlo, Snow, & McLaughlin, 2002). The learners included in these studies were drawn from a wide range of grade levels: from primary grades (Carlisle et al., 1999) to the upper elementary grades (Johnson, 1989; Ordóñez et al., 2002). At issue is whether second-language vocabulary knowledge or skills are influenced by first-language vocabulary knowledge or skills.

The studies showed first-language effects on second-language vocabulary development. Studies of the acquisition of English-as-a-second-language vocabulary revealed that cross-language lexical effects are most likely to occur in higher-order vocabulary skills, such as interpretation of metaphors, paradigmatic associations, and quality of formal definitions (Carlisle et al., 1999; Ordóñez et al., 2002). Studies showing that English-language learners are able to take advantage of cognate relationships also indicated cross-language effects. Clearly, cross-language cognate effects are relevant only when English-language learners have a first language that shares cognate vocabulary with English. It remains to be shown whether these cross-language lexical effects represent transfer of knowledge from one language to another or the influence of language-independent cognitive capacities that make some children better language learners—whether of the first or second language (Johnson, 1989). It is also possible that both influences are at work. In fact, a number of the studies of lexical development suggest that correlations between first and second languages are due to general language-independent influences—metalinguistic abilities that are reflected in quality of formal word definition and conceptual-attentional capacity.

To the extent that future research continues to provide evidence in support of cross-language effects in vocabulary development, it would follow that oral language support for English-language learners' literacy development could be provided in either the first or second language and that this support should focus on language skills that are linked to higher-order cognitive or academic tasks—that is, language for categorizing, reasoning, and abstract thought. At the same time, studies on learners of typologically distinct languages (e.g., Turkish and Dutch) that have few structural and functional similarities were not reviewed in this chapter. Thus, we do not know the extent to which current findings would obtain for learners with other first-language backgrounds. Although one would expect less pronounced cross-language effects in typologically different languages, further research on learners acquiring typologically distinct second languages is needed to examine this issue empirically.

Six studies were identified that examined cross-language effects in the grammatical development of English-language learners (Duncan and Gibbs, 1987; Shin and Milroy, 1999; Morsbach, 1981; Spada and Lightbown, 1999; Flanigan, 1995; Quinn, 2001). Studies of the development of grammar and discourse-level skills in English among English-language learners are inconclusive with respect to cross-language effects because there is little overlap in focus among studies on grammar and there have been no studies on discourse-level skills.

The Relationship between Oral Development in the First Language and Literacy Development in the Second Language

Taken together, findings from studies of elementary and middle school students and one study involving high school students indicate rather consistently that measures of first-language oral proficiency do not correlate with English word reading skills (Abu-Rabia, 1997; Arab-Moghaddam & Sénéchal, 2001; Da Fontoura & Siegel, 1995; Durgunoglu, Nagy, & Hancin-Bhatt, 1993; Gottardo *et al.*, 2001; Quiroga *et al.*, 2002) and do not explain unique variance in English word reading skills. This was true for a wide variety of first languages, including Farsi, Cantonese, Urdu, Hebrew, and Spanish. The only exception is a study by Gholamain and Geva (1999), in which teacher ratings of oral proficiency skills correlated with word-level skills.

The picture is quite different, however, when relationships between first-language phonological processing skills and English word reading skills are examined. The results of several studies of children from different first-language backgrounds and educational settings, conducted in the United States, the United Kingdom, Canada, and Israel, suggest that first-language phonological processing skills are closely related to the development of word reading skills in English. This finding appears across a variety of phonological processing measures, including rhyme detection (Gottardo *et al.*, 2001; Mumtaz & Humphreys, 2002); awareness of grapheme–phoneme correspondences as measured by pseudoword reading (Abu-Rabia, 1997; Arab-Moghaddam & Sénéchal, 2001); phonological awareness involving segmentation, blending, and matching (Durgunoglu *et al.*, 1993; Quiroga *et al.*, 2002); rapid naming of discrete items such as letters or digits (RAN); and working memory (Abu-Rabia, 1997; Da Fontoura & Siegel, 1995; Gholamain & Geva, 1999; Mumtaz & Humphreys, 2002).

Studies indicate that the relationship between first-language oral proficiency and English word-level skills can also vary somewhat as a function of the measures used to assess phonological awareness in each language. For example, it may be that some of the measures used to assess first-language oral proficiency, such as the grammatical sensitivity tasks used by Abu-Rabia (1997), Da Fontoura and Siegel (1995), and Gottardo *et al.* (2001), are not precise enough to capture the aspects of the first-language oral proficiency that are linked to second-language word reading.

Research by Ahern, Dixon, Kimura, Okuna, and Gibson (1980) on

Hawaiian children and by Mumtaz and Humphreys (2002) on Urdu-speaking English-language learners suggest the need for caution to avoid adopting a simplistic view of the relationships between phonological processing skills in children's first language and word reading skills in English. More specifically, these studies indicate that cross-linguistic effects can vary depending on the similarity and differences between first- and second-language orthography. Age is probably yet another factor that influences the relationship between first-language oral proficiency and second-language word reading skills. Finally, students' level of first-language oral proficiency and literacy are likely to influence the results as well.

Correlational designs failed to reveal significant relationships between first-language oral proficiency and English spelling skills. As with word reading skills, it may be that certain oral proficiency measures (e.g., the grammatical sensitivity measures used to assess first-language oral proficiency by Abu-Rabia [1997], Da Fontoura & Siegel [1995], and Gottardo *et al.* [2001]) are not sufficiently sensitive to capture the aspects of first-language oral proficiency that are linked to second-language spelling. However, measures of first-language phonological processing and English spelling skills correlate consistently. Given the small group of studies that examined this relationship, the conclusion that there is a positive relationship between phonological processing in the first language and spelling in English is tentative at this point.

Quasi-experimental studies using error analysis (Cronnell, 1985; Ferroli & Shanahan, 1993) suggest that typological differences between the phonology of the first and second languages influence second-language spelling patterns. Specifically, the evidence suggests that phonological differences between English-language learners' first language and English can hinder or facilitate the acquisition of specific English spelling patterns (e.g., voicing contrasts; see Cronnell, 1985; Ferroli & Shanahan, 1993). Caution is called for in interpreting these results because of the limited number and scope of these studies and because of methodological flaws (e.g., the absence of comparison groups composed of students from a variety of first-language backgrounds) and the possibility that the spelling errors reflect developmental patterns, including errors that resemble those made by first-language learners of the same language (see Chapter 3).

In summary, these studies suggest that the link among first-language oral language proficiency, phonological processes, and spelling achievement in English is not invariant. It is important to consider the measures used and typological similarity between the first and second languages. Thus, multivariate studies are needed to disentangle the relationships between these factors and spelling development in

English-language learners. The virtual absence of relevant studies on high school students is also of concern.

As for text-level aspects of literacy, across the different levels of schooling, the findings from this limited group of studies are complex. On the one hand, most found no relationship between reading comprehension in English and first-language oral proficiency measured through self-ratings of first-language proficiency or language use (Kennedy & Park, 1994; Nguyen, Shin, & Krashen, 2001; Okamura-Bichard, 1985) and through listening comprehension (Royer & Carlo, 1991). However, in the case of students learning English as a foreign language, one study found that listening comprehension in the first language related indirectly to reading comprehension in English. In this study, first-language listening comprehension was directly related to first-language reading comprehension which, in turn, was directly related to second-language reading comprehension. There is also some evidence from research reported in this and other chapters that intervening factors may influence this relationship—more specifically, that phonological memory (Dufva & Voeten, 1999) and sociocultural context (Buriel & Cardoza, 1988) are associated with the development of reading comprehension in English.

Finally, it is difficult to generalize from the available studies about the relationship between first-language oral proficiency and English writing skills in English-language learners because the studies differ in many respects (Cronnell, 1985; Okamura-Bichard, 1985). Nevertheless, they provide suggestive evidence that cross-language/cross-modal effects on the development of second-language writing skills are more likely to occur when discrete rather than general aspects of first-language oral proficiency (e.g., range of vocabulary, rather than overall proficiency) are examined.

The Role of Cross-Linguistic Transfer in Second-Language Literacy Acquisition for Children Who Are Learning English as a Second or Foreign Language

The studies reviewed in this section examined cross-language influences of literacy knowledge, processes, and strategies in students who are learning a second language. These studies differ from those reviewed for the previous two questions, in that they include only students who are literate in their first language, and they employ *written* measures of the constructs investigated. The general approach within these studies was to isolate specific components that underlie reading (e.g., vocabulary, word recognition, reading comprehension, spelling) and test the nature of their relationships across languages. Some studies were guided by the contrastive analysis hypothesis, but the majority of studies looked at transfer within Cummins' hypotheses. As a result of the review, it appears that the contrastive analysis hypothesis works with additional factors (e.g., first-language proficiency and development) to account for transfer in the domains of spelling, vocabulary, and word recognition. Transfer of higher-order literacy skills (such as reading comprehension and strategy use), in contrast, is explained more adequately within Cummins' interdependence hypothesis.

Five studies looked at transfer in word reading. Students in these studies ranged from first graders (Durgunoglu *et al.*, 1993) to fifth graders (Gholamain & Geva, 1999) to children ages 9 to 12 (Da Fontoura & Siegel, 1995) to tenth graders (Abu-Rabia, 1997; Chitiri & Willows, 1997). Findings from four of the five studies supported the interdependence hypothesis (Abu-Rabia, 1997; Chitiri & Willows, 1997; Da Fontoura & Siegel, 1995; Gholamain & Geva, 1999), suggesting that word reading skills acquired in one language transfer to the other. At the same time, differences in orthographic complexity between English and the students' first languages influenced the transfer of word reading skills, revealing a heavier reliance on the phonological than the visual strategy in processing the second language when the first-language orthography is transparent. This suggests that processing strategies applied in word reading are language specific. The Chitiri and Willows study further demonstrates that students with a high level of proficiency in two languages that have significantly different orthographies may develop interlanguages—systems of processing patterns that are different from those used by monolingual students in either language.

Eight studies investigated first-language influences on spelling in English among students in Grades 1 to 6 (Fashola, Drum, Mayer, & Kang, 1996; Ferroli & Shanahan, 1993; James & Klein, 1994; Zutell & Allen, 1988; Davis, Carlisle, & Beeman, 1999; Arab-Moghaddam & Sénéchal, 2001; Nathenson-Mejía, 1989; Edelsky, 1982). Six of these studies involved native speakers of Spanish, one of German, and one of Persian. All of the first languages reported on in this group of studies are relatively more transparent, regular, and consistent with respect to sound–letter correspondences than is English. When students are acquiring a second language with features that are more complex than the corresponding features in the first language, negative transfer is predicted. Thus, the studies described here have largely aimed to account for students' performance in English with reference to differences in orthographic opaqueness between the first and second languages.

Four studies have examined the influence of the first language on second-language spelling at the level of the grapheme (Fashola *et al.*, 1996; Ferroli & Shanahan, 1993; James & Klein, 1994; Zutell & Allen, 1988). These studies typically have employed a combination of correlational and error analyses.

Findings from error analyses and studies of emergent writing indicate that, in the early stages of second-language spelling development, there is an effect both of first-language phonology and first-language graphophonic rules on students' spelling of English words (Edelsky, 1982; Fashola *et al.*, 1996; James & Klein, 1994; Nathansen-Mejía, 1989; Zutell & Allen, 1988).

With the exception of the work of James and Klein, all spelling studies interpreted the first-language influence from a general problem-solving perspective, viewing reliance on first-language phonology and orthography early in second-language acquisition as facilitative—an application of analytic skills and comparable to the phenomenon of invented spelling for emergent first-language spellers. Indeed, the use of first-language knowledge in the absence of second-language knowledge, as in the case of these learners in the initial stages of second-language acquisition, is not considered to represent transfer, but rather a *falling back* on the native language (Odlin, 1989). Several studies demonstrated that, with increased exposure to English print, students progress from heavy reliance on the phonological strategy in spelling (spelling by ear) to use of the visual strategy as well. Such developments point to the dynamic quality of interlanguages (Selinker, 1972), whereby learners may exhibit a mix of linguistic patterns—some typical of the first language (interlingual) and some of the second (intralingual) language.

The single study that looked at reverse transfer (Davis *et al.*, 1999) found it to occur from English to Spanish spelling, despite the fact that students had received no instruction in Spanish literacy.

Finally, the two correlational studies (Arab-Moghaddam & Sénéchal, 2001; Davis *et al.*, 1999) yielded contrasting findings for the transfer of spelling knowledge across languages. The discrepancy between the findings cannot be attributed to the students' ages, which did not differ. Rather, it is possible that the nature of the task (analysis of spelling in a writing task vs. a spelling test) influenced the results. Another possibility lies in the differences between Persian and English relative to Spanish and English orthographies; it is possible, therefore, that spelling knowledge gained in one language will transfer only when the two languages are closely related.

Studies of cross-language relationships in vocabulary knowledge fall into three categories. Several studies have focused on measuring the extent to which students recognize structural and semantic overlap in first- and second-language cognates (i.e., words with common etymological roots and similar forms and meanings). All of these studies (García, 1991, 1998; Hancin-Bhatt & Nagy, 1994; James & Klein, 1994; Jiménez *et al.*, 1996; Nagy, García, Durgunoglu, & Hancin-Bhatt, 1993; Saville-Troike, 1984) provide evidence for cross-language transfer of cognate vocabulary. At the same time, the studies highlight constraints on using cognate knowledge. For example, it appears that certain aspects of word knowledge are understood only through experience with English, the second language (García, 1991; James & Klein, 1994), and in conjunction with other sources of information about a word's meaning (James & Klein, 1994). Further, positive transfer of vocabulary knowledge is most likely to occur when it involves languages that are typologically similar (Saville-Troike, 1984), but even if the languages are similar, vocabulary transfer may not occur if the learners perceive the languages to be distant (Ellis, 1994; García, 1991, 1998; Jiménez et al., 1996; Kellerman, 1977; Nagy et al., 1993). An important criterion for the occurrence of transfer is learners' metalinguistic awareness of cognate relationships, an awareness that appears to be developmentally mediated (Hancin-Bhatt & Nagy, 1994; Nagy et al., 1993). Finally, cognate transfer appears to be influenced by the degree of orthographic overlap between cognate pairs. In summary, transfer between cognates occurs optimally with closely related first and second languages and in learners possessing high levels of reading proficiency, cognitive flexibility, and metalinguistic awareness.

A second group of studies compared the vocabulary produced by students in their first and second languages on several indexes of lexical sophistication and complexity. These studies (Davis, Carlisle, & Beeman, 1999; Francis, 2000; Lanauze & Snow, 1989) yielded conflicting findings. Whereas Francis (2000) found reverse transfer in the use of verbs of cognition, such that students who used such verbs in the language of instruction also used them in the first language, Lanauze and Snow (1989) found transfer of complex vocabulary use to occur only in students with high first-language and low second-language proficiency. Davis et al. (1999) found no relationship between first- and second-language vocabulary knowledge as measured by long words used.

It is likely that a difference in age among the students accounts for the lack of significant findings in the Davis et al. (1999) study. Lanauze and Snow (1989) and Francis (2000) studied students in Grades 3 to 6, whereas Davis et al. looked at students in Grades 1 to 3. It is possible that the nature of word knowledge in subjects in the latter age group is more basic and concrete, so that the students in the Davis et al. study were not cognitively mature enough to demonstrate the kind of higher-order vocabulary knowledge that may transfer across languages.

The discrepant findings of Lanauze and Snow (1989) and Francis (2000), however, cannot be accounted for by age differences and have important implications for transfer on a theoretical level. If positive transfer implicates underlying abilities assessed through tasks that measure the use of decontextualized language, then the finding of Lanauze and Snow—that there was no relationship between enriched vocabulary use in the first and second languages—challenges this theory.

Finally, one study (Nagy, McClure, & Mir, 1997) found that first-language syntactic knowledge influenced guesses about the meanings of unfamiliar words in a second-language context. Further, the rate of transfer errors remained constant across levels of English reading proficiency, suggesting that this specific type of transfer may persist even at high levels of second-language proficiency.

For reading comprehension, which requires the ability to understand complex written language beyond the word level, most studies looked at students above Grade 3. Of the seven studies reviewed here, two tested the threshold hypothesis among middle and high school students of English as a foreign language (Lee & Schallert, 1997; Schoonen, Hulstijn, & Bossers, 1998), and three longitudinal studies investigated the validity of the interdependence hypothesis among language-minority students in elementary school (Royer & Carlo, 1991; Verhoeven, 1994) and elementary and middle school (Reese, Garnier, Gallimore, & Goldenberg, 2000). One study examined cross-lingual transfer in third and fifth graders speaking an indigenous first language (Francis, 2000), and one study investigated relationships between first- and second-language reading comprehension ability in Spanish-speaking English-language learners at the middle school level (Nagy, McClure, & Mir, 1997). Finally, one study examined children's understanding of narrative fables in Spanish and English (Goldman, Reyes, & Varnhagen, 1984).

All these studies provide evidence for the cross-language transfer of reading comprehension ability in bilinguals. This relationship holds (a) across typologically different languages (Korean and English: Lee & Schallert, 1997; and Dutch and Turkish: Verhoeven, 1994); (b) for children in elementary, middle, and high school; (c) for learners of English as a foreign language and English as a second language; (d) over time (Reese *et al.*, 2000; Royer & Carlo, 1991; Verhoeven, 1994); (e) from both first to second language and second to first language (Francis, 2000; Verhoeven, 1994); and (f) within a specific genre (Goldman *et al.*, 1984).

With respect to the influence of second-language proficiency, these studies present conflicting findings. The two studies involving students of English as a foreign language demonstrated that transfer of reading comprehension required proficiency in the second language (Lee & Schallert, 1997; Schoonen *et al.*, 1998). However, the English-language learners in the Goldman *et al.* (1984) study demonstrated comprehension of English text (fables) that was comparable to their understanding of first-language texts despite limited English proficiency. The difference in these findings may be due to differences in tasks and text genres.

Finally, the Royer and Carlo (1991) finding that reading skills, but not listening skills, correlate across the first and second languages counters the notion that the relationship between first- and second-language reading comprehension can be accounted for by language-independent capacities that make some children better language learners. Further, although not specifically examining the threshold hypothesis, Royer and Carlo also found proficiency in the second language (as measured by listening comprehension) to be a significant predictor of second-language reading comprehension. These findings were corroborated by Reese *et al.* (2000)

Strategic reading has been investigated in six studies. Five of these studies looked at transfer between Spanish and English in Grades 3 through 7. One study examined transfer in native-Dutch-speaking sixth, seventh, and tenth graders learning English as a foreign language. Strategy use was generally assessed by the use of (a) checklists or surveys in which students indicated or reported strategies they used while reading in their two languages (Calero-Breckheimer & Goetz, 1993; Schoonen *et al.*, 1998), or (b) think-aloud protocols (García, 1998; Jiménez *et al.*, 1996). It should be noted that both of these methods of measuring strategy use have been criticized. Self-report data collected in first-language reading studies have revealed inconsistencies between what children say they do while reading and what they actually do. Think-alouds, in contrast, permit a more direct investigation of the strategic reasoning processes employed in reading and are designed to reveal the extent to which students' declarative and procedural knowledge converge. However, some researchers have expressed concerns about subjects' (particularly younger children's) ability to describe the processes they perform, as well as the possibility that reporting disrupts the comprehension process (Afflerbach & Johnston, 1984; Jacobs & Paris, 1987).

In summary, with the exception of Hernández (1991), all the studies provide evidence that bilingual children who read strategically in one language also do so in their other language. Further, the extent of strategy use in students' reading correlates positively with reading performance. The two studies that investigated first- and second-language strategic reading processes in students not proficient in the second language yielded conflicting findings. Langer, Bartolome, Vásquez and Lucas (1990) found that it was the use of good meaning-making strategies, and not the degree of second-language proficiency, that distinguished better from poorer readers. In contrast, Schoonen *et al.* (1998) found a greater influence of metacognition on second-language reading performance at higher levels of second-language proficiency and a language proficiency threshold below which no application of strategy use occurred.

Studies employing think-aloud protocols provide valuable insights into the cross-language functioning of reading strategies. Indeed, findings from Jiménez *et al.* (1996) and García (1998) offer a window into the interrelated lexical systems operating in bilinguals. The identification of uniquely bilingual strategies (such as cognate recognition) in these two studies illustrates ways in which the interaction of two languages in a bilingual can give rise to strategies that are available in neither the first nor the second language, but are part of an autonomous system with its own internal organizing principles.

Interestingly, none of Calero-Breckheimer and Goetz's (1993) subjects identified strategies that can be described as unique to bilinguals. This is perhaps a result of the younger ages of her subjects (Grades 3 and 4) or the manner in which strategy use was assessed. The subjects in the Jiménez *et al.* (1996) and García (1998) studies demonstrated strategy use in both procedural and declarative terms through think-alouds, whereas those in the Calero-Breckheimer and Goetz study were given an opportunity to demonstrate only declarative or conscious knowledge of strategies they used in reading. It is possible that explicit knowledge about oneself as a reader is influenced by development (as Schoonen *et al.* [1998] found for sixth-grade students of English as a foreign language).

Alternatively, it may be that an individual's development of bilingual strategies requires a minimal level of metalinguistic knowledge—an awareness of the structural and lexical similarities and differences between the two languages. Increased metalinguistic awareness distinguished better from poorer readers in the Jiménez *et al.* (1996) study, such that the better readers recognized and exploited similarities between English and Spanish; the poorer readers, in contrast, viewed their two languages as more dissimilar than alike. This result again suggests that it is not just typological similarity as defined by linguists that predicts transfer of literacy components, but also the psychological or perceived distance on the part of the learners

Four studies have focused on the relationship between writing ability in the first and second languages (Cummins, 1979; Edelsky, 1982; Francis, 2000; Lanauze & Snow, 1989). All involved language-minority children acquiring a societally dominant language. In three of the studies, the second language was English; in one, it was Spanish. The studies investigated writing performance across Grades 1 to 6. These studies suggest several possibilities about first- and second-language writing relationships. First, for beginning writers, what is known about writing in the first language provides the basis for hypotheses formed in second-language writing (Edelsky, 1982); again, this is not transfer per se, but a falling back on the first language in the absence of second-language knowledge. Second, for young children receiving instruction in the second language exclusively, writing skills may develop first in the second language and subsequently in the first. Third, for older children with varying proficiency in the first and second languages, aspects of writing ability may correlate only for students proficient in the first but not in the second language, suggesting that early in second-language acquisition these children draw on resources available to them in their first language. For older elementary students who are proficient in both languages, these studies present conflicting findings. Lanauze and Snow (1989) found that such students showed no relationship between first- and second-language writing, suggesting that the linguistic systems become independent at more advanced stages of development, whereas Francis (2000) found that writing sophistication and complexity were related in the first and second languages.

METHODOLOGICAL ISSUES

The studies reviewed in this chapter employed a variety of methodologies, the most frequent being error analyses, correlational/regression analyses, and between-and within-group comparisons. Despite these varied methodologies, all of the studies shared a common goal: to identify associations among features, skills, or levels of competence in learners' first and second languages. Our discussion of methodological issues pertaining to the studies revolves around this common goal and focuses on the logic of research designed to elucidate cross-language relationships.

Correlational techniques were used by many of the studies because, obviously, correlations can be used to identify associations between the first and second language in the same or related domains of language development. However, simple correlational analyses between single first- and second-language measures are limited in their ability to elucidate the precise nature of the association between first- and second-language and literacy development because they do not consider alternative theoretically plausible possibilities. For example, evidence for transfer of the type represented in Cummins' developmental interdependence theory often consists of significant positive correlations between academic skills in the first and second languages, such as reading comprehension. Although significant positive correlations between first- and second-language reading comprehension may suggest the transfer of reading skills, they are not sufficient because other factors may also be at work. Pursuing our reading comprehension example, a plausible alternative would be that individual differences in overall cognitive ability underlie, and may even explain, the significant correlation between first- and second-language reading comprehension insofar as English-language learners with superior levels of cognitive ability may also have superior first- and second-language reading skills. Alternatively, cognitive ability along with first-language reading ability may be at work. If research is to provide precise descriptions of first- and second-language relationships, multivariate analyses will be necessary. Alternative conceptualizations of transfer that also include multivariate approaches, such as that proposed by Bransford and Schwartz (1998), will provide more comprehensive conceptualizations of transfer because they consider a broader range of influences in the transfer phenomenon.

Simple correlational techniques are limited in that they can only reveal an association between variables, not the precise causal nature of the relationship. The clearest evidence for the causal role of transfer from the first language to second-language development would come from intervention studies designed to promote acquisition of a particular subcomponent of literacy in the first language, with subsequent testing of the same component in the second language. For example, to establish that knowledge of sound–letter correspondencies in the first language facilitates second-language spelling would require research that provides training of sound–grapheme correspondencies in the first language of an experimental group of English-language learners and no such training for a control English-language learner group. Evidence from subsequent assessment of experimental and control group students' knowledge of sound–grapheme correspondency in the second language that the former outperformed the latter would constitute evidence for transfer. However, no such studies emerged from our search.

Many of the studies conducted within the contrastive analysis framework were based on analyses of how the first- and second-language systems of the learners differed with respect to particular features; analysis of student errors was then undertaken to determine the extent of influence of the first language. This was typically the case with studies of spelling, for example, in which second-language spelling errors could be explained on the basis of differences between first- and second-language phonology and orthography. Although such studies did not necessarily involve formal correlational analyses, they were intended to reveal associations between second-language errors and features of the first language. For example, when attempting to spell words such as *bump*, Spanish-speaking English-language learners might produce *bup*. This could be interpreted as negative transfer from Spanish because words in Spanish do not end in consonant clusters—arguably, *bup* is a simplification of the English form in accordance with Spanish phonological rules. However, such an interpretation would be premature because this particular transfer error is not distinguishable from developmental errors made by native-English-speaking learners. In fact, in initial spelling, children learning English as their first language are unable to spell preconsonantal nasals correctly, and in spelling a word such as *bump*, they may omit the *m*.

Findings based on a sample of second-language learners from a single first-language background do not allow one to attribute the presence of a first-language feature in the second language unambiguously to transfer from the first language because other explanations could account for the same results. Stronger evidence for transfer would come from comparisons with the error patterns of native English speakers, if known, as well as from results for English-language learners with different language backgrounds—some speaking a first language that does not have the target feature and some speaking one that does (double dissociations). If both groups of students made the error predicted on the basis of a contrastive analysis, a source other than transfer, such as developmental factors, might be implicated. Conclusions of cross-language studies on second-language literacy acquisition can be misleading if they do not provide longitudinal results for learners across age/grade levels. In particular, studies that report significant associations between English-language learners' first and second languages in specific domains at one point in development give the impression that these effects are either permanent or characteristic of learners at all ages. Longitudinal data are called for if we are to distinguish negative transfer from the first language that inhibits learning in the second in the long run from negative transfer that reflects a short-term strategy used by novice learners to bootstrap into the second language system. Indeed, the latter possibility enjoys some empirical support from evidence reported earlier that first-language effects on second-language development tended to occur more frequently in novice second-language learners and in the early stages of second-language learning in some domains. In any case, the implications of these alternative interpretations of transfer are theoretically and practically significant. Theoretically, evidence of short-term negative transfer would argue for the bootstrapping hypothesis, whereas evidence of long-term negative transfer would argue for fossilization; that is, acquisition of a target-deviant form that is a part of the learner's stable language system. Practically speaking, short-term transfer would be cause for minimal concern. Indeed, it could be taken as evidence for acquisition. In contrast, evidence of long-term negative transfer would be cause for educational concern.

Strong evidence of relationships and influences between English language learners' first and second languages in second-language literacy development is provided by the studies reviewed here. At the same time, more complex research designs are called for if we are to better understand the precise nature of these relationships, the causal mechanisms they entail, and their long-term developmental impact on second-language learning. In particular, there is a need for more longitudinal intervention studies with multivariate designs that examine learners with different language backgrounds (including native English speakers) across grade levels and take into account the multiple factors that may influence relationships between first and second oral language proficiency and literacy

DIRECTIONS FOR FUTURE RESEARCH

Reading Readiness

The foundations for literacy development are established during the preschool years, both at home and at school. Research on the development of reading readiness skills in second-language learners during the preschool years is sparse. A variety of issues concerning reading readiness in second-language learners' first language and how this facilitates the acquisition of literacy in a second language require empirical investigation, including (a) types of readiness skills that develop in second-language learners in different home environments, (b) factors that influence their development, (c) differences in readiness development among second-language learners who speak typologically diverse languages, (d) interventions that can promote their development in the home and the preschool, and (e) how these factors influence the development of second-language literacy in school.

Despite the importance that has been attached to phonological awareness for early literacy development, additional research is still needed to better understand cross-linguistic aspects of phonological awareness and, in particular, the specific phonological awareness skills in the first language that promote early second-language literacy development and under what circumstances such cross-linguistic facilitation is evident. In a related vein, we need research that examines the influence of phonological awareness in the first language on second-language literacy development at different grade levels, including students who begin schooling in a second language in the primary grades and those who begin in upper elementary, middle, or high school. Research on phonological awareness training in the first language for second-language learners who are at risk for reading difficulty in a second language would also be beneficial.

Relationship between First-Language Literacy and Second-Language Literacy for Academic Achievement

Although the development of reading and writing skills is a goal in itself, reading and writing in school are intimately linked to academic development. Yet cross-language relationships between reading and writing development in specific academic domains (e.g., science) have received scant empirical attention. More specifically, we have virtually no empirical evidence of whether specific first-language reading and writing skills that are linked to mathematics, science, and social studies, influence acquisition of the corresponding reading and writing skills in a second language; how these relationships might change over grade levels; and how they are mitigated by typological similarities in discourse styles of the second-language learners' first and second languages.

Writing

Research on the development of writing skills in second-language learners is extremely sparse, and research on cross-linguistic influences in the acquisition of writing skills by second-language learners is even sparser. Thus, much more research that focuses on the relationship between second-language learners' first- and second-language skills in the context of learning to write for academic purposes is necessary. This should entail studies that investigate the influence of first-language oral as well as first-language reading and writing skills on second-language writing development. The small set of studies that examined the relationship between first-language oral proficiency and second-language writing serves to identify gaps in the extant research base, including studies on the potential role of specific aspects of first-language linguistic knowledge (e.g., cohesion, syntactic complexity, decontextualized oral language skills, range and type of vocabulary, familiarity with various discourse genres); typological similarities and differences among the target language and different first languages; the development of writing skills across grade levels; and the impact of systematic and sustained practice in writing in the first language on second-language writing development.

Proficiency in writing probably requires a host of skills, including good spelling skills; decontexualized language skills that enable the writer to express abstract, complex ideas; metacognitive strategies such as audience awareness; and familiarity with writing different text genres.

Other Groups of Second-Language Learners in the United States

Two characteristics of second-language learners in the United States are deserving of special attention: (a) students with different first languages and sociocultural backgrounds, and (b) students at different grade levels. There is little research on second-language learners whose first language is not Spanish—for example, students who speak Vietnamese, Hmong, Cantonese, and Korean, which are common languages among English-language learners in certain U.S. locations (Kindler, 2002). Research is especially needed that examines cross-linguistic relationships among component skills that underlie literacy in relation to typological similarity with and difference from English. There is also little research at present on middle and high school English-language learners, both those who begin schooling in English at the middle or high school levels and those who have been in schools where English is the language of instruction since primary school and are continuing into middle and high school. Research on most aspects of cross-linguistic influences in the literacy development of middle and high school students is needed.

Similarly, research on cross-linguistic relationships in the literacy development of English-language learners with language delays or impairments is called for if we are to meet the learning needs of all language-minority students, especially in light of the rigorous accountability standards that have been mandated by the No Child Left Behind (NCLB) legislation.

New Conceptual Paradigms

Understanding of cross-linguistic influences in second-language literacy development could be enhanced if additional conceptualizations of transfer were explored. As noted previously, Bransford and Schwartz (1998) have argued that thinking about transfer should be broadened to include the notion of *preparedness for future learning*. Bransford and Schwartz's framework shifts attention away from a search for direct transfer of knowledge and skills to include the ability to learn new language and literacy skills by drawing on all of the learner's resources, including learners' more general knowledge about how to acquire new information.

In a similar vein, Riches and Genesee (2006) have argued that when it comes to literacy development, English-language learners are best conceptualized as having a reservoir of knowledge, skills, and abilities that serve second-language learning and use. Some of these will be the same skills and knowledge possessed by monolinguals, and others will be unique to bilinguals and encompass discrete language skills, related to, for example, phonology and grammar, as well as knowledge and experience acquired through the medium of the first language and first-language learning.

In studying transfer, the relationship among a host of variables needs to be explored. This would include variables that are linked directly to language structures and strategies of the type emphasized by contrastive analysis and interdependence theories. These have been the focus of attention for the most part until now. It would also be useful to include variables that involve cognitive and other problem-solving skills of an entirely different nature from those that have been considered to date.

Both of these conceptualizations would broaden our understanding of cross-linguistic effects in second-language learning and improve the way these effects are studied.

Recommendations for Study Design and Methodology

Longitudinal, Multivariate Research Designs. The issues researched in this chapter are complex and dynamic—complex because there are multiple variables that influence literacy development, multiple components to literacy development (e.g., phonology, vocabulary, grammar), and alternative theoretical frameworks that have influenced the way in which research in the field has been operationalized; and dynamic because the causal relationships that underlie the development of reading and writing and their influence on academic achievement change as second-language learners progress through school. The most common research designs uncovered in our review were correlational and between-group designs.

Greater use of longitudinal designs in the study of cross-linguistic relationships would lead to a clearer understanding of literacy development and its many determinants. In addition, the use of multilevel, longitudinal designs would allow for clearer explication of the student, teacher, family, school, and societal factors that influence students' literacy development and the precise ways in which these factors operate and interact.

Intervention Studies. To advance our understanding of the role of cross-linguistic relationships in literacy development, research is needed that examines the transfer of literacy-related language subskills using intervention studies. In such studies, students would be randomized to either receive first-language training or not. Subsequently, both groups would receive second-language training in the task to which transfer was expected to occur. The first component of the test would be to show that the group that received first-language training developed the first-language skill to a higher level than the group that did not receive first-language training. Next, to test for transfer, the group that received first-language training would be examined to determine whether they learned the second-language skill at a more rapid pace (i.e., acquired new knowledge in the second language more quickly) or otherwise outperformed the group that did not receive the training. Either of these outcomes would be considered evidence of transfer from the first to the second language because the students' acquisition of a second-language skill was enhanced by their acquisition of a first-language skill. Students' differential acquisition of the first-language skill was a result of random assignment, which would allow for a reasonably strong inference that transfer had taken place. To make the study stronger, the group that did not receive the first-language training could receive training in something that is not expected to enhance the first-language skill that transfers to the second language, but instead enhances an unrelated first-language skill that is not expected to transfer.

Such research not only would advance our understanding of cross-language relationships in the development of literacy skills in a second language, but also would provide critical information for the development of home- and school-based interventions.

Standardized Assessment Tools. Synthesizing and generalizing results from the research that has been conducted on cross-linguistic aspects of literacy development in second-language learners is complicated by measurement issues. At present, different tests are used to assess the same underlying construct. In some cases, a problem arises because different tasks are used to assess the same construct without ascertaining how the assessments relate to one another. For example, Abu-Rabia (1997) and Da Fontoura and Siegel (1995) assessed working memory by using a sentence-completion task, while Gholamain and Geva (1999) used an opposites task. In other cases, such as in studies of phonological awareness, complications arise because a construct may actually be composed of different components (such as phoneme-deletion ability vs. rhyme-detection ability) and thus warrant the use of different tests, but only one test is used and the author generalizes to the construct as a whole; this is problematic in that there is insufficient research on the distinctiveness of each component and their developmental relationship to one another. More research on the validity of tests/tasks that are used to assess key constructs in this domain is required. As well, standardization of test instruments used to assess important constructs that have been used in cross-linguistic literacy research (e.g., phonological awareness, working memory, oral language proficiency) would be useful so that it would be possible to compare across studies the cross-linguistic influences in literacy development for learner groups with different first languages (e.g., Spanish vs. Chinese), at different ages/grades, and with different sociocultural backgrounds.

Careful Description of the Learner Group. Our understanding of literacy development in second-language learners could also be enhanced considerably if greater care were taken in the description of study samples. At present, descriptions of learner groups are often sketchy, leaving many unanswered questions about significant characteristics of the learners. To provide better and more detailed descriptions of student samples, researchers would need to agree on what characteristics to describe and what standards to follow when reporting information about these characteristics—that is, what kind of information (and in what detail) is needed about the socioeconomic status, schooling opportunities, language skills, and language and literacy background of second-language learners at the time of testing.

REFERENCES

Abu-Rabia, S. (1997). Verbal and working-memory skills of bilingual Hebrew–English speaking children. *International Journal of Psycholinguistics*, 13(1), 25–40.

Afflerbach, P., & Johnston, P. (1984). On the use of verbal reports in reading research. *Journal of Reading Behavior*, 16(4), 307–322.

Ahern, E. H., Dixon, P. W., Kimura, T., Okuna, J. S., & Gibson, V. L. (1980). Phoneme use and the perception of meaning of written stimuli. *Psychologia: An International Journal of Psychology in the Orient*, 23(4), 206–218.

Arab-Moghaddam, N., & Sénéchal, M. (2001). Orthographic and phonological processing skills in reading and spelling in Persian/English bilinguals. *International Journal of Behavioral Development*, 25(2), 140–147.

Baddeley, A. D. (1986). *Working memory*. Oxford: Oxford University Press.

Bransford, J. D., & Schwartz, D. L. (1998). Rethinking transfer: A simple proposal with multiple implications. *Review of Research in Education*, 24, 61–100.

Buriel, R., & Cardoza, D. (1988). Sociocultural correlates of achievement among three generations of Mexican American high school seniors. *American Educational Research Journal*, 25(2), 177–192.

Calero-Breckheimer, A., & Goetz, E. T. (1993). Reading strategies of biliterate children for English and Spanish texts. *Reading Psychology*, 14(3), 177–204.

Carlisle, J. F., Beeman, M. M., Davis, L.-H., & Spharim, G. (1999). Relationship of metalinguistic capabilities and reading achievement for children who are becoming bilingual. *Applied Psycholinguistics*, 20(4), 459–478.

Carrell, P. L. (1989). Metacognitive awareness and second language reading. *Modern Language Journal*, 73, 121–133.

Chitiri, H. F., & Willows, D. M. (1997). Bilingual word recognition in English and Greek. *Applied Psycholinguistics*, 18(2), 139–156.

Cisero, C. A., & Royer, J. M. (1995). The development and cross-language transfer of phonological awareness. *Contemporary Educational Psychology*, 20(3), 275–303.

Cronnell, B. (1985). Language influences in the English writing of third- and sixth-grade Mexican-American students. *Journal of Educational Research*, 78(3), 168–173.

Cummins, J. (1978). Educational implications of mother tongue maintenance in minority-language groups. *The Canadian Modern Language Review*, 35, 395–416.

Cummins, J. (1979). Linguistic interdependence and the educational development of bilingual children. *Review of Educational Research*, 49(2), 221–251.

Cummins, J. (1981). The role of primary language development in promoting educational success for language minority students. In California State Department of Education (Ed.), *Schooling and language minority students: A theoretical framework*. Los Angeles, CA: National Dissemination and Assessment Center.

Cummins, J. (2000). *Language, power and pedagogy: Bilingual children in the crossfire*. Clevedon, UK: Multilingual Matters.

Da Fontoura, H. A., & Siegel, L. S. (1995). Reading, syntactic, and working memory skills of bilingual Portuguese–English Canadian children. *Reading and Writing*, 7(1), 139–153.

Davis, L. H., Carlisle, J. F., & Beeman, M. (1999). Hispanic children's writing in English and Spanish when English is the language of instruction. *Yearbook of the National Reading Conference*, 48, 238–248.

Dufva, M., & Voeten, M. J. M. (1999). Native language literacy and phonological memory as prerequisites for learning English as a foreign language. *Applied Psycholinguistics,* 20(3), 329–348.

Dulay, H., & Burt, M. (1974). Natural sequences in child second language acquisition. *Language Learning,* 24, 37–53.

Duncan, D. M., & Gibbs, D. A. (1987). Acquisition of Panjabi and English. *British Journal of Disorders of Communication,* 22, 129–144.

Durgunoglu, A. Y., Nagy, W. E., & Hancin-Bhatt, B. J. (1993). Cross-language transfer of phonological awareness. *Journal of Educational Psychology,* 85(3), 453–465.

Eckman, F. R. (1977). Markedness and the contrastive analysis hypothesis. *Language Learning,* 27, 315–330.

Eckman, F. R. (1985). Some theoretical and pedagogical implications of the markedness differential hypothesis. *Studies in Second Language Acquisition,* 7, 289–307.

Edelsky, C. (1982). Writing in a bilingual program: The relation of L1 and L2 texts. *TESOL Quarterly,* 16(2), 211–228.

Edelsky, C., Hudelson, S., Flores, B., Barkin, F., Altweger, J., & Jilbert, K. (1983). Semilingualism and language deficit. *Applied Linguistics,* 4, 1–22.

Ellis, R. (1994). *The study of second language acquisition.* New York: Oxford University Press.

Fashola, O. S., Drum, P. A., Mayer, R. E., & Kang, S.-J. (1996). A cognitive theory of orthographic transitioning: Predictable errors in how Spanish-speaking children spell English words. *American Educational Research Journal,* 33(4), 825–843.

Ferroli, L., & Shanahan, T. (1993). Voicing in Spanish to English knowledge transfer. *Yearbook of the National Reading Conference,* 42, 413–418.

Flanigan, B. O. (1995). Anaphora and relativation in child second language acquisition. *Studies in Second Language Acquisition,* 17(3), 331–351.

Francis, N. (2000). The shared conceptual system and language processing in bilingual children: Findings from literacy assessment in Spanish and Náhuatl. *Applied Linguistics,* 21(2), 170–204.

García, G. E. (1991). Factors influencing the English reading test performance of Spanish-speaking Hispanic children. *Reading Research Quarterly,* 26(4), 371–392.

García, G. E. (1998). Mexican-American bilingual students' metacognitive reading strategies: What's transferred, unique, problematic? *National Reading Conference Yearbook,* 47, 253–263.

Geva, E., & Ryan, B. (1993). Linguistic and cognitive correlates of academic skills in first and second languages. *Language Learning* 43(1), 5–42.

Gholamain, M., & Geva, E. (1999). Orthographic and cognitive factors in the concurrent development of basic reading skills in English and Persian. *Language Learning,* 49(2), 183–217.

Goldman, S. R., Reyes, M., & Varnhagen, C. K. (1984). Understanding fables in first and second languages. *NABE Journal,* 8, 835–866.

Gottardo, A. (2002). The relationship between language and reading skills in bilingual Spanish-English speakers. *Topics in Language Disorders,* 22(5), 46–70.

Gottardo, A., Yan, B., Siegel, L. S., & Wade-Woolley, L. (2001). Factors related to English reading performance in children with Chinese as a first language: More evidence of cross-language transfer of phonological processing. *Journal of Educational Psychology,* 93(3), 530–542.

Hancin-Bhatt, B., & Nagy, W. E. (1994). Lexical transfer and second language morphological development. *Applied Psycholinguistics,* 15(3), 289–310.

Hernández, J. S. (1991). Assisted performance in reading comprehension strategies with non-English proficient students. *Journal of Educational Issues of Language Minority Students,* 8, 91–112.

Holm, A., Dodd, B., Stow, C., & Pert, S. (1999). Identification and differential diagnosis of phonological disorder in bilingual children. *Language Testing,* 16(3), 271–292.

Hsia, S. (1992). Developmental knowledge of inter- and intraword boundaries: Evidence from American and Mandarin Chinese speaking beginning readers. *Applied Psycholinguistics*, 13(3), 341–372.

Hyltenstam, K. (1984). The use of typological markedness conditions as predictors in second language acquisition: The case of pronominal copies in relative clauses. In R. W. Anderson (Ed.), *Second languages: A crosslinguistic perspective*. Rowley, MA: Newbury House.

Jacobs, J. E., & Paris, S. G. (1987). Children's metacognition about reading: Issues in definition, measurement, and instruction. *Educational Psychologist*, 22(3/4), 255–278.

James, C., & Klein, K. (1994). Foreign language learners' spelling and proof-reading strategies. *Papers and Studies in Contrastive Linguistics*, 29, 31–46.

Jiménez, R. T., García, G. E., & Pearson, D. P. (1996). The reading strategies of bilingual Latina/o students who are successful English readers: Opportunities and obstacles. *Reading Research Quarterly*, 31(1), 90–112.

Johnson, J. (1989). Factors related to cross-language transfer and metaphor interpretation of bilingual children. *Applied Psycholinguistics*, 10(2), 157–177.

Kellerman, E. (1977). Toward a characterization of the strategies of transfer in second language learning. *Interlanguage Studies Bulletin*, 2, 58–145.

Kennedy, E., & Park, H.- S. (1994). Home language as a predictor of academic achievement: A comparative study of Mexican- and Asian-American youth. *Journal of Research and Development in Education*, 27(3), 188–194.

Kindler, A. L. (2002). *Summary of the states' limited English proficient students and available educational programs and services. 1999–2000 summary report*. Washington, DC: National Clearinghouse for English Language Acquisition.

Kramer, V. R., & Schell, L. M. (1982). English auditory discrimination skills of Spanish-speaking children. *Alberta Journal of Educational Research*, 28(1), 1–8.

Kramer, V. R., Schell, L. M., & Rubison, R. M. (1983). Auditory discrimination training in English of Spanish-speaking children. *Reading Improvement*, 20(3), 162–168.

Lado, R. (1964). *Language teaching: A scientific approach*. New York: McGraw-Hill.

Lanauze, M., & Snow, C. E. (1989). The relation between first- and second-language writing skills: Evidence from Puerto Rican elementary school children in bilingual programs. *Linguistics and Education*, 1(4), 323–339.

Langer, J. A., Bartolome, L., Vásquez, O., & Lucas, T. (1990). Meaning construction in school literacy tasks: A study of bilingual students. *American Educational Research Journal*, 27(3), 427–471.

Lee, J.W., & Schallert, D. L. (1997). The relative contribution of L2 language proficiency and L1 reading ability to L2 reading performance: A test of the threshold hypothesis in an EFL context. *TESOL Quarterly*, 31(4), 713–739.

Liow, S. J. R., & Poon, K. K. L. (1998). Phonological awareness in multilingual Chinese children. *Applied Psycholinguistics*, 19(3), 339–362.

Lumme, K., & Lehto, J. E. (2002). Sixth grade pupils' phonological processing and school achievement in a second and the native language. *Scandinavian Journal of Educational Research*, 46(2), 207–217.

MacSwan, J., & Rolstad, K. (2003). Linguistic diversity, schooling, and social class: Rethinking our conception of language proficiency in language minority education. In C. B. Paulston & G. R. Tucker (Eds.), *Sociolinguistics: The essential readings* (pp. 329–340). Malden, MA: Blackwell.

Morsbach, G. (1981). Cross-cultural comparison of second language learning: The development of comprehension of English structures by Japanese and German children. *TESOL Quarterly*, 15(2), 183–188.

Mumtaz, S., & Humphreys, G. W. (2001). The effects of bilingualism on learning to read English: Evidence from the contrast between Urdu-English bilingual and English monolingual children. *Journal of Research in Reading*, 24(2), 113–134.

Mumtaz, S. H., & Humphreys, G. W. (2002). The effect of Urdu vocabulary size on the acquisition of single word reading in English. *Educational Psychology*, 22(2), 165–190.

Nagy, W. E., García, G. E., Durgunoglu, A. Y., & Hancin-Bhatt, B. (1993). Spanish–English bilingual students' use of cognates in English reading. *Journal of Reading Behavior*, 25(3), 241–259.

Nagy, W. E., McClure, E. F., & Mir, M. (1997). Linguistic transfer and the use of context by Spanish–English bilinguals. *Applied Psycholinguistics*, 18(4), 431–452.

Nathenson-Mejía, S. (1989). Writing in a second language: Negotiating meaning through invented spelling. *Language Arts*, 66(5), 516–526.

Nemser, W. (1971). Approximative systems of foreign language learners. *International Review of Applied Linguistics*, 9, 115–123.

Nguyen, A., Shin, F., & Krashen, S. (2001). Development of the first language is not a barrier to second-language acquisition: Evidence from Vietnamese immigrants to the United States. *International Journal of Bilingual Education and Bilingualism*, 4(3), 159–164.

Odlin, T. (1989). *Language of transfer: Cross-linguistic influence in language learning*. Cambridge, England: Cambridge University Press.

Okamura-Bichard, F. (1985). Mother tongue maintenance and second language learning: A case of Japanese children. *Language Learning*, 35(1), 63–89.

Ordóñez, C. L., Carlo, M. S., Snow, C. E., & McLaughlin, B. (2002). Depth and breadth of vocabulary in two languages: Which vocabulary skills transfer? *Journal of Educational Psychology*, 94(4), 719–728.

Phifer, S. S., & Glover, J. A. (1982). Don't take students' word for what they do while reading. *Bulletin of the Psychonomic Society*, 19, 194–196.

Quinn, C. (2001). The developmental acquisition of English grammar as an additional language. *International Journal of Language & Communication Disorders*, 36(Suppl.), 309–314.

Quiroga, T., Lemos-Britten, Z., Mostafapour, E., Abbott, R. D., & Berninger, V. W. (2002). Phonological awareness and beginning reading in Spanish-speaking ESL first graders: Research into practice. *Journal of School Psychology*, 40(1), 85–111.

Reese, L., Garnier, H., Gallimore, R., & Goldenberg, C. (2000). Longitudinal analysis of the antecedents of emergent Spanish literacy and middle-school English reading achievement of Spanish-speaking students. *American Educational Research Journal*, 37(3), 633–662.

Riches, C., & Genesee, F. (2006). Crosslanguage and crossmodal influences. In F. Genesee, K. Lindholm-Leary, W. Saunders, & D. Christian (Eds.), *Educating English language learners: A synthesis of research evidence* (pp. 64–108). New York: Cambridge University Press.

Royer, J. M., & Carlo, M. S. (1991). Transfer of comprehension skills from native to second language. *Journal of Reading*, 34(6), 450–455.

Saville-Troike, M. (1984). What really matters in second language learning for academic achievement? *TESOL Quarterly*, 18(2), 199–219.

Schoonen, R., Hulstijn, J., & Bossers, B. (1998). Metacognitive and language-specific knowledge in native and foreign language reading comprehension: An empirical study among Dutch students in grades 6, 8 and 10. *Language Learning*, 48(1), 71–106.

Selinker, L. (1972). Interlanguage. *International Review of Applied Linguistics*, 10(3), 209–231.

Shin, S. J., & Milroy, L. (1999). Bilingual language acquisition by Korean schoolchildren in New York City. *Bilingualism*, 2(2), 147–167.

Spada, N., & Lightbown, P. M. (1999). Instruction, first language influence, and developmental readiness in second language acquisition. *Modern Language Journal*, 83(1), 1–22.

Towell, R., & Hawkins, R. (1994). *Approaches to second language acquisition*. Bristol, GB: Longdunn Press.

Verhoeven, L. T. (1994). Transfer in bilingual development: The linguistic interdependence hypothesis revisited. *Language Learning, 44*(3), 381–415.

Zutell, J., & Allen, V. (1988). The English spelling strategies of Spanish-speaking bilingual children. *TESOL Quarterly, 22*(2), 333–340.

5

Sociocultural Contexts and Literacy Development

Claude Goldenberg, Robert S. Rueda, and Diane August

Chapter 5 discusses *sociocultural influences,* factors that go beyond the individual variations discussed in the previous chapters. This chapter reviews and evaluates the empirical evidence on the role of these sociocultural factors in the literacy development of language-minority children and youth. The studies included in this chapter address the following questions:

1. What is the influence of immigration (generation status and immigration circumstances) on literacy development, defined broadly?
2. What is the influence of differences in discourse and interaction characteristics between children's homes and classrooms?
3. What is the influence of other sociocultural characteristics of students and teachers?
4. What is the influence of parents and families?
5. What is the influence of policies at the district, state, and federal levels?
6. What is the influence of language status or prestige?

For each research question posed in this chapter, we first address the influence of each of these sets of factors on first- or second-language literacy outcomes, defined broadly. We then examine the nature of these factors in settings where language-minority children are acquiring literacy. The principal difference between these two categories of studies is that the studies reviewed first, report data on some aspect of student literacy outcomes, such as measured achievement, behavioral, or attitudinal indicators. Studies reviewed next report no such outcome data. Studies in this second category are more often descriptive accounts of sociocultural factors in literacy settings, although they typically make claims about the effects of sociocultural factors on literacy outcomes.

As we discuss below, socio-economic status (SES) can also be considered a "sociocultural" factor. However, we elected not to do a separate analysis for SES since its relationship to cognitive and academic outcomes has long been widely recognized, even though its influence depends upon how and at what level it is measured (Sirin, 2005). In numerous studies reviewed here, in fact, SES is a serious confound that precludes straightforward interpretation of a study's findings. The better-designed studies control for SES effects, therefore permtting interpretation of the effects of other sociocultural factors not directly related to family income or parents' education levels, typically the two principal components of SES.

The justification for addressing sociocultural factors is straightforward, even if the topic is not: there are well-documented differences between the literacy attainment of language-minority and language-majority students (see Chapter 2 for further discussion of educational outcomes). There are also differences in the literacy attainment of language-minority students from different backgrounds. Language-minority students typically come from different sociocultural backgrounds than mainstream English-speaking students, with variation within and across language-minority groups as well, and various sociocultural characteristics may influence language-minority students' literacy outcomes.

We begin this chapter by presenting pertinent background information. We then describe the methodology of our review. Next, we summarize the findings of the literature on the six research questions addressed by our review. After identifying methodological issues found in the studies reviewed, we recommend directions for future research.

BACKGROUND

There are many ways to characterize or define sociocultural influences; many publications have attempted to do so (e.g., California State Department of Education, 1986; Cole, 1995; Durán, 1983; Forman, Minick, & Stone, 1993; Jacob & Jordan, 1987; Tharp, 1989). While there is overlap among these different perspectives, there is no one widely accepted definition. In a non-trivial sense, "social and cultural" can mean anything that is not obviously biological or physical.

Psychological processes, language and literacy development, instruction, curriculum, intervention programs, assessment strategies—the topics of the other chapters—are social and cultural processes that are influenced by and in turn influence yet other social and cultural processes.

However, the Panel felt it was important to dedicate a chapter to factors that do not explicitly or easily fall within the scope of the other chapters but that educators and researchers have considered important for understanding and improving literacy outcomes for English-language learners. These factors fall under the very broad heading of "social and cultural influences." Generally, we define *sociocultural influences* as factors that make up the broad social context in which children and youth live and go to school. These factors include a wide range of influences related to beliefs, attitudes, behaviors, routine practices, social and political relations, and material resources associated with groups of people sharing some nominal characteristics, such as economic or educational status; cultural, ethnic, or national origin; and linguistic group. The various and complex contexts created by these factors may directly influence learning outcomes by providing more/better or fewer/worse opportunities or motivation to learn, or by providing different types of opportunities that are somehow incongruent with school expectations. As mentioned earlier, these factors can also indirectly affect learning through their role in psychological and linguistic processes, such as transfer (addressed in Chapter 4), or classroom processes, such as teaching and learning (reviewed in Chapter 6).

Classification of Students into Sociocultural Groups

Why should sociocultural factors matter for explaining differences among language-minority children's literacy outcomes? The fundamental premise in this literature is that membership in a socially defined group influences cultural practices, cognitions, motivational attributes, values, beliefs, and assumptions that then influence the learning process and, ultimately, learning outcomes. Children and youth from different sociocultural groups bring with them different experiences that may shape their classroom experiences. A related premise in this literature is that schools are unique cultural settings that reflect a potentially different set of values, practices, and reward structures. Although sociocultural factors can be conceived as individual-difference variables, the emphasis in the studies reviewed here tends to be on characteristics of children and youth as members of particular sociocultural groups. A key assumption is that educational outcomes for language-minority students can be enhanced if educators better understand these groups and how to design optimal learning environments for them.

There are many ways to classify how students from various socio-cultural groups differ, and how (and whether) these differences are associated with differences in literacy or other cognitive or academic outcomes. The major classifications most often reflected in the literature are by socio-economic status (SES), race, ethnicity, and culture.

SES, a cluster of variables having to do with a person's or family's material (economic) circumstances, level of formal schooling, and occupational status, has consistently been shown to predict cognitive and academic outcomes (see e.g., Lara-Cinisomo et al., 2004). These effects are strongest when measured in the aggregate rather than at the individual level. In other words, there is a much stronger relationship to student outcomes when we consider the schools students attend or the neighborhoods in which they live, rather than the status of the students or families themselves (Sirin, 2005; White, 1982). Many studies in this area confound language-minority status, race, or ethnicity with SES. It is usually impossible to determine whether the findings (e.g., low reading achievement or an association between language-minority status and reading achievement) are actually a result of language-minority status or SES.

Geographic origin, race, and ethnicity are different but complexly related categories for differentiating students. Voluntary and involuntary immigrants have had distinct experiences as a result of dramatically different immigration circumstances (Ogbu & Matute-Bianchi, 1986); Africans, Asians, and Europeans have all arrived as newcomers, but under different circumstances in different historical periods. Their experiences in this country can vary because of different racial or ethnic group membership. There are also indigenous populations that cannot be considered newcomers—Native Americans and U.S.-born Latinos—but, if they speak a language other than English in the home, are considered part of the language-minority population. Mexicans and other Latin Americans not of European descent (primarily from Central America) are now seen as part of the large U.S. immigrant population, although many were born in this country. Their experiences can be influenced by both immigration status and ethno-cultural factors.

A third way to distinguish among students is with reference to culture, perhaps the most complex of the variables. Many definitions of culture exist, but they all generally have to do with the behaviors, beliefs, attitudes, and practices of a group of people. Although cultures vary along many dimensions, Tharp (1989) suggests four classes of psychocultural variables that influence how students respond to classroom experiences:

• Social organization—how people organize themselves in groups or as individuals; for example, whether they have an individualistic or group-oriented approach to accomplishing tasks.

- Sociolinguistics—the conventions of interpersonal communication, such as wait-time, proximity, rhythm and flow of conversation, and how turn-taking is organized.
- Cognition—patterns of thought that can influence the learning of new skills and knowledge, such as specific cognitive abilities or cognitive styles.
- Motivation—values, beliefs, expectations, and aspirations that influence how, whether, and why individuals approach and persist in specific goals or tasks.

Tharp also identifies two constants—conditions that do not vary across cultures and are required for optimal educational outcomes: (a) a focus on language development, and (b) contextualized instruction. Tharp's thesis is that classrooms are productive teaching and learning environments to the extent that they follow the *prescriptions* (Tharp's term) of the constants and are compatible with home cultures as characterized by the four psychocultural variables. Tharp posits that for some groups of students—those who are currently reasonably successful in U.S. schools—such compatibility already exists. But for others, compatibility must be created for these students to receive equitable educational opportunities.

Although research in the field has not necessarily adopted Tharp's analytical scheme, the cultural compatibility framework is a common feature in this literature. Regardless of how researchers have conceptualized sociocultural factors (and, as the following sections of the chapter demonstrate, they generally have not been explicit about their conceptions), there appears to be consensus that students' sociocultural characteristics play an important role in their literacy (and general academic) development and that schools, therefore, should tailor curriculum and instruction to make children's school experiences more compatible with their natal cultures. This notion sometimes leads to observations such as the following:

> Competition will probably not motivate a class composed primarily of Native American children, for example, because their culture values cooperation.
>
> (Cole, 1995, p. 14)

More generally, the idea that classroom instruction and students' sociocultural characteristics should be brought into close alignment—and that doing so improves student learning—has become a prominent theme in this literature, as shown by the following example:

> Research has shown that students learn more when their classrooms
> are compatible with their own cultural and linguistic experience . . .
> [Students' learning is disrupted] when the norms of interaction and
> communication in a classroom are very different from those to which
> the student has been accustomed . . . The aspects of culture that influ-
> ence classroom life most powerfully are those that affect the social
> organization of learning and the social expectations concerning
> communication.
>
> (Saravia-Shore & García, 1995, p. 57)

This perspective has had an impact at the policy level as well. Socio-
cultural factors are thought to be important enough to the education of
English-language learners that the subject is a required part of some
teacher certification preparation. In California, for example, the Com-
mission on Teacher Credentialing certifies bilingual teachers in either
Cross-Cultural Language and Academic Development (CLAD) or
Bilingual Cross-Cultural Language and Academic Development
(BCLAD). One of the three modules that teachers must master in the
CLAD certification is "culture and cultural diversity." In the BCLAD
certification, teachers must master a module on "culture of emphasis."

The review that follows may appear to reflect skepticism about the
influence of sociocultural factors on educational outcomes for language-
minority students. This skepticism is in reality aimed at claims that are
made but not yet justified by existing research. We argue later in this
chapter that better-designed studies are critical for examining the
relationships between sociocultural factors and student outcomes, as
well as for providing robust portraits of how these factors play out in
educational settings. We wish to make clear, however, that we consider
sociocultural awareness on the part of educators and students alike to be
a desirable end in and of itself, just as are high levels of literacy, numeracy, critical thinking, general knowledge, pro-social behavior, and other
educational goals. Indeed, such awareness is part of what it means to be
educated.

School Achievement among Diverse Ethnolinguistic Groups

As discussed in Chapter 2, there are differences between language-
minority children and other children with respect to literacy outcomes,
with language-minority children often, although not always, achieving
at lower levels than the others. There are also clear differences in the
literacy achievement of various sociocultural groups of students.
Kennedy and Park (1994), for example, found that Asian Americans had
higher reading scores than Mexican Americans in a nationally representative sample of eighth graders (Kauffman, Chávez, & Laven, 1998),
despite the fact that both groups of students had similar rates of

speaking a language other than English at home. Ima and Rumbaut (1989) found differences in reading achievement among different subgroups of language-minority Asian students, and similar patterns of achievement differences among diverse ethnolinguistic groups exist in other countries. Leseman and de Jong (1998) found that in the Netherlands, Dutch children have greater vocabulary attainment and literacy achievement than do language-minority Surinamese and Turkish children.

Explanations for such outcome differences among diverse language-minority groups have not been satisfactory. One reason is that these differences are confounded with SES and other dimensions of family life. Ima and Rumbaut's (1989) report on the reading achievement of diverse language-minority groups provides a case in point. The relatively high scores among East Asians are attributable at least partly to family SES, particularly with respect to parent education. Ima and Rumbaut report that the East Asian group "frequently includes children from 'brain drain' immigrant families (such as those headed by a Taiwanese engineer)" (p. 64). Thus, the high grade point average (GPA) of East Asian children and children in the *other immigrants* category may reflect the selective migration pattern of families with highly educated parents.

METHODOLOGY OF THE REVIEW

The studies included in this chapter employ correlational, experimental, comparative, ethnographic, observational, or case study designs, and they use quantitative or qualitative methods. To be eligible for inclusion in the analysis that examines the impact of sociocultural influences, a study had to report data on (a) factors in one or more of the six research questions identified earlier, and (b) student outcomes (cognitive, affective, or behavioral) presumably influenced by one or more of these factors. For studies that report data on the nature of the sociocultural factors in one or more of the six areas, there was no requirement that a study report data pertaining to student outcomes.

Student outcomes are defined in this chapter as changes in students' literacy-related cognitive or affective characteristics or behaviors that may be explained by one or more sociocultural factors. We purposely chose a broad definition of student outcomes. Studies used standardized and researcher-constructed achievement tests, but they also used many other outcome indicators, including engagement and participation during instruction, analysis of writing, and story retelling. Outcomes could be gauged in the first language, second language, or both. They could also consist of qualitative data, such as detailed reports of student behavior or engagement or analysis of work products. However, in the absence of corroborating data, author claims *alone* about the impact of one or more sociocultural factors did not meet our outcome criterion. Statements such as "reading improved over the course of the study" or "students more engaged in setting X as opposed to setting Y" were considered insufficient evidence of an outcome.

Most studies that examined sociocultural influence make either explicit or implicit claims about sociocultural factors and how they affect student learning opportunities and learning outcomes. A large part of our task, therefore, was to evaluate the empirical basis for these claims. However, few of the studies reviewed here actually set out to study effectiveness. Instead, investigators have sought only to identify sociocultural factors that may shape students' literacy development in school, home, and community and to describe how these operate in specific settings. Nevertheless, it is still reasonable to ask whether sociocultural factors do influence literacy outcomes for language-minority children and youth. These criteria yielded a corpus of 50 studies for inclusion that we used to assess the influence of various factors on literacy-related outcomes.

In addition, a body of descriptive work related to sociocultural factors in settings where language-minority children are acquiring literacy has accumulated. The most relevant of these additional 25 studies that address the nature of various sociocultural factors are included within each section of the chapter. This work, even though it does not contain outcome measures, could help form the foundation for more systematic research linking sociocultural factors to student outcomes, thereby informing policy and practice decisions.

Only narrative review methods were used in this part of the volume because there were insufficient studies addressing the same conceptual hypothesis relevant to a given research question to conduct a meta-analysis.

SUMMARY OF EMPIRICAL FINDINGS

Immigration Circumstances

Language-minority children differ with respect to how long they and their families have been in the host country and to their generation status. They may be immigrants themselves, near-descendants of immigrants (first to third generation in the host country), or descendants of peoples who lived within the current borders of a country, but whose native language is not the national language (e.g., Native Americans and Mexicans in the United States). Some scholars have suggested that generation status has an impact on language-minority children's academic achievement, in that the immigrants arrive with high expectations for educational and economic success, but some of these groups (e.g., Latinos in the United States) subsequently become disillusioned as they confront discrimination and limited opportunities (Ogbu & Matute-Bianchi, 1986; Rumbaut, 1995; Suárez-Orozco & Suárez-Orozco, 1996),

Educators have also speculated that the persistent underachievement of many language-minority groups around the world may be the result of immigration circumstances that work against literacy attainment. For example, parents' and children's undocumented immigration status can adversely influence children's literacy opportunities, experiences, and development.

The Influence of Immigration Circumstances. Studies addressing issues of immigration's effects on students' literacy development can generally be grouped into two categories: those focusing on circumstances of immigration, and those focusing on generation status. With respect to immigration circumstances, the studies did not reveal strong influences on literacy outcomes (Goldenberg, 1987; Ima & Rumbaut, 1989; Monzó & Rueda, 2001). Although undocumented immigration and refugee experiences can create traumatic situations, there is no evidence that these experiences impede literacy achievement. Given the current research, it is plausible to hypothesize that literacy outcomes are more likely to be the result of home (and school) language and literacy learning opportunities, irrespective of immigration circumstances. Buriel and Cardoza (1988) is the only study located for this review that examined generation status; it compared literacy outcomes among successive generations of language-minority students. Although Buriel and Cardoza found a shift from Spanish to English use across three generations of Mexican American high school seniors who reported at least some Spanish use in the home, generation status did not appear to influence English reading and vocabulary skills.

The Nature of Immigration Circumstances. No studies were located that examined the nature of immigration circumstances independent of the effects of these circumstances.

Differences in Discourse and Interaction Characteristics between Children's Homes and Classrooms

Many educators have suggested that minority children are socialized to interact with others at home and in their community in ways that may be at variance with expectations for interaction in school. These interaction or discourse differences may interfere with school achievement, as children are required to interact with other children and the teacher in ways that are strange for them. By extension, minimizing the interaction differences between home and school could help promote higher levels of literacy attainment by making the classroom more familiar and comfortable.

The Influence of Differences in Discourse and Interaction Characteristics between Children's Homes and Classrooms.   The consequences of these differences for students' literacy attainment and the effects of attempts to address these differences in the classroom are not clear. One highly influential study (Au & Mason, 1981) found that culturally compatible instruction had positive effects on native Hawaiian speakers' level of engagement and participation during reading lessons. But this study did not measure literacy achievement or comprehension of the stories being discussed, so we do not know whether the higher participation led to higher achievement or greater learning. Other studies with Navajo- and Spanish-speaking students (Huerta-Macías & Quintero, 1992; Wilkinson, Milosky, & Genishi, 1986; Kucer & Silva, 1999; McCarty, Wallace, Lynch, & Benally, 1991) also make claims about the effects on literacy of home–school difference in interaction patterns. In each case, however, data or design problems preclude straightforward interpretation.

Thus, the most we can say given the available research is that bridging home–school differences in interaction can enhance students' engagement and level of participation in classroom instruction. This outcome is certainly not trivial, but it is not the same as enhancing student achievement or other types of learning outcomes.

The Nature of Differences in Discourse and Interaction Characterisitics between Children's Homes and Classrooms.   Descriptive studies (Au, 1980; Gregory, 1998; Schmidt, 1995; Xu, 1999) provide good evidence that expectations for social interaction differ between the home and school environments of some language-minority students. These discontinuities included use of only the second language at school, classroom teacher–student discourse patterns that decreased meaningful adult–child interactions, less opportunity for student rehearsal of appropriate responses, and teaching in some classrooms that stressed isolated skill practices, rather than more meaningful literacy experiences (prevalent in some of the children's homes, but not all). There were fewer discrepancies between home and school discourse when an explicit attempt was made by teachers to match classroom instruction to children's home discourse.

Other Sociocultural Characteristics of Students and Teachers

In this section, we move beyond specific issues of discourse and interaction to examine the role of other noninstructional sociocultural factors.

These include such factors as student and family beliefs, attitudes, learning styles, motivation, behaviors, specific or general knowledge, and interests that are rooted in cultural or social group membership; the teacher–student cultural, ethnic, and linguistic match; teacher beliefs; classroom organization; and the degree of teacher versus student control of learning activities and content. A particular emphasis here is on the impact of culturally familiar instructional materials, meaning their content is rooted in culturally specific experiences or events.

The basic hypotheses of these studies is that (a) the attributes a child brings to school (knowledge, beliefs, attitudes, motivations, behaviors, experiences with specific contexts and situations) influence how he or she deals with school; (b) schools embody a specific variant of these factors; and (c) the greater the differences in these attributes and the school experiences, the greater the hindrance to learning. Therefore, effective educational practice requires narrowing this distance between home experiences and school demands. This hypothesis allows for two distinct explanations of how the effects of sociocultural factors on literacy may operate. One, an affect-based explanation, is that sociocultural compatibility creates increased motivation and interest, better mood and attitude, greater participation, and ultimately higher achievement. The second, a cognitively based explanation, is that sociocultural compatibility produces its effects mainly by increasing familiarity with new information and activating and promoting connections to existing cultural knowledge. The current research base does not allow us to determine the validity of these competing explanations, but this is an area that strongly warrants systematic investigation and theoretical explication.

We first examine studies that address the role of culturally relevant materials in literacy outcomes. We then consider studies examining the impact of cultural relevance in comparison with that of text language. As we see, there is some evidence for an impact of culturally familiar materials on learning outcomes such as reading comprehension; however, there is stronger evidence for the effects of text language (i.e., more familiar text language produces better comprehension). We then review studies that address a variety of other sociocultural factors, such as attitudes and family practices.

The Influence of Other Sociocultural Characteristics of Students and Teachers. Overall, the studies that address the role of culturally relevant materials in literacy outcomes provide some, although weak, support for the proposition that culturally relevant reading or curriculum materials promote literacy development, and, conversely, that culturally unfamiliar materials can interfere with comprehension and literacy growth (Davies, 1991; Lasisi, Falodun, & Onyehalu, 1988; Abu-Rabia,

1995). Various design issues limit what we can conclude from the studies. The familiarity of text content certainly influences comprehension, but it is not clear what role is played by cultural familiarity per se.

Studies that examine the effects of culturally meaningful materials in comparison with those of text language provide some support for the impact of culturally relevant materials on reading performance, but they indicate that text language exerts a stronger influence (Abu-Rabia, 1998a, 1998b). Students perform better when they read materials in the language they know better and when the text language is clearly written and accessible.

Studies examining other socioculturally related factors generally, including sociocultural variables in home-based and school-based instructional settings, knowledge and attitudes about the host country, and teachers' language, have methodological problems that limit the conclusions that can be drawn (Abu-Rabia, 1996; Chilora & Harris, 2001; Hannon & McNally, 1986; Hernández, 1991; Ima & Rumbaut, 1989; Jiménez, 1997; Kenner, 1999; Lasisi *et al.*, 1988; McCarty, 1993; Schon, Hopkins, & Vojir, 1984; Trueba *et al.*, 1984). Other studies find no effects of sociocultural factors (García-Vázquez, 1995; Schon *et al.*, 1984) or very weak or limited effects (Aarts and Verhoeven, 1999) once factors such as socio-economic status and language spoken in the home are taken into account. Most of these studies fall under the general rubric of *culturally compatible, culturally responsive,* or *culturally accommodating* instruction, but conceptually this is a murky literature. Despite useful attempts to provide an organizing conceptual framework (e.g., Tharp, 1989), there appears to be no common ground for collecting and interpreting data on sociocultural factors in literacy learning. For example, some authors (e.g., Lasisi *et al.*, 1988) consider use of the home language in classroom instruction to be a cultural accommodation. Others (e.g., Kenner, 1999) implicitly include children's experiences with mainstream mass media as part of their cultural experience. Although defining *cultural experience* in this way may be accurate, it complicates what we mean when we say that culture influences learning or that student culture must be taken into consideration when designing instruction for students from diverse cultural or linguistic backgrounds. Do we mean culture as in children's or families' traditional culture—ways of life, customs, beliefs, behavioral norms, values, and so on, associated with a particular ethnic or national-origin group? Or do we mean culture as in the characteristics and features of children's and families' lived experiences, a different construct? In point of fact, cultures are dynamic and always evolving. The boundaries between traditional culture and children's lived culture, which may have little to do with a researcher's conception of the children's culture, become increasingly blurred (see Goldenberg & Gallimore, 1995).

The general thesis that such factors influence literacy outcomes remains highly plausible, but the lack of (a) consistent definitions and research methods, (b) a focus on measured literacy outcomes, and (c) a larger theoretically driven organizing framework inhibits the design, systematic investigation, and, most important, interpretation of the existing research. Moreover, students' cultural affiliations are frequently confounded with SES—for which there is strong evidence of an impact on literacy outcomes—rendering interpretations even more problematic.

The Nature of Other Sociocultural Characteristics of Students and Teachers. Ten studies examined the role of sociocultural factors. Although these factors are not explicitly instructional, they tend to be relevant to instruction. For example, process approaches advocated by this group of authors create opportunities for students and teachers to bring sociocultural (and personal) elements into the classroom curriculum and instruction. The authors of some of these studies provide examples of the alienation experienced by some culturally diverse children if no effort is made to integrate them into the classroom (Schmidt, 1995). Numerous studies provide examples of teachers' giving legitimacy to children's personal, communal, or cultural backgrounds in the classroom by allowing them to write about topics that interest them (Blake, 2001; Moll & Díaz, 1987; Moll, Sáez, & Dworin, 2001; Townsend & Fu, 1998), to use their first language if it enables them to express themselves better (Hornberger, 1990; Jiménez & Gersten, 1999; Moll *et al.*, 2001), to take the time they need to develop their second-language competency (Townsend & Fu, 1998), to validate cultural experiences related to literacy (Jiménez & Gersten, 1999; Masny & Ghahremani-Ghajar, 1999), and to build home–community relationships (Masny & Ghahremani-Ghajar, 1999; Moll, 1986). One study (Hornberger, 1990) suggests it is possible to improve motivation, purpose, and interaction in classrooms even if the native language is not used. In this study, although a teacher did not share a common cultural/linguistic background with her students, she made up for this by creating classroom-based shared experiences, such as class trips and an annual camping trip, and classroom games that focused on literacy.

Taken as a whole, the studies provide useful descriptions of the methods and manner in which teachers have been able to use children's personal, communal, or cultural backgrounds in the classroom. The studies are overwhelmingly based on case study approaches and ethnographic or other qualitative methods. As a body, they document the nature of sociocultural differences in the classroom and continue to raise questions regarding the effects of those differences on students' learning opportunities and achievement outcomes. Unfortunately, these studies do not provide a clear answer to the question of whether classroom accommodations are specific examples of universal effective teaching practices or whether they represent a unique form of teaching particularly beneficial to specific sociocultural populations of students.

Moreover, although many of the authors offer suggestions to address these issues, it seems premature, based on the available research, to specify how classroom practices and contexts influence students or how to address these issues effectively from an instructional perspective. Clearly, research that connects careful documentation of these strategies with student literacy outcomes would begin to provide evidence that classroom sociocultural accommodations actually help children develop literacy skills.

Parents and Families

The role of parents and families in children's academic achievement has been a topic of inquiry for more than 40 years.

The Influence of Parents and Families.   Consistent with a great deal of other research, studies in this area reveal that language-minority families influence their children's literacy development. Three findings emerged from our review of this literature.

First, language-minority parents express willingness and often have the ability to help their children succeed academically (Goldenberg, 1987; Brooker, 2002). For various reasons, however, schools underestimate and do not take full advantage of parents' interest, motivation, and potential contributions. Although views about literacy and literacy practices may differ between home and school, literacy activities are not absent in home settings.

Second, more home literacy experiences and opportunities are generally associated with superior literacy outcomes, but findings in this regard are not consistent. Measures of parent and family literacy often predict literacy attainment (Arzubiaga *et al.*, 2002; Brunell and Saretsalo, 1999; Goldenberg and Gallimore, 1991; Reese, Garnier, Gallimore, and Goldenberg, 2000), but two studies found that parents' reading behavior was unrelated to children's literacy outcomes (Aarts & Verhoeven, 1999; Pucci & Ulanoff, 1998). Features of family life (e.g., domestic workload, religious activities) appear to influence the value children place on reading and their self-concepts as readers. SES—particularly parent education—is clearly associated with literacy outcomes.

Third, but with some important exceptions, the relationship between home language use and children's literacy outcomes tends to be language-specific. In other words, home experiences in the first and second languages are positively correlated with child literacy achievement in the first and second languages, respectively (Aarts & Verhoeven, 1999; Brunell & Linnakylä, 1994; Brunell & Saretsalo, 1999; Buriel & Cardoza,

1988; Cahill, 1987; Connor, 1983; Dolson, 1985; Hansen, 1989; Kennedy & Park, 1994; Monzó & Rueda, 2001). However, home experiences in the first or second language tend to be negatively correlated, although weakly, with child literacy achievement in the other language: Greater use of the first language predicts lower achievement in second-language literacy, whereas greater use of the second language predicts lower achievement in first-language literacy (see Table 5.1). Six studies report finding negative associations between first-language use in the home and second-language achievement (Aarts & Verhoeven, 1999; Buriel & Cardoza, 1988; Connor, 1983; Hansen, 1989; Kennedy & Park, 1994; Monzó & Rueda, 2001), but three studies (Cahill, 1987; Dolson, 1985; Hancock, 2002) report contrary findings—namely, that greater use of the first language in the home was associated with higher literacy achievement in the second language. The Hancock study is particularly important because it involved an experimental manipulation of the language of literacy materials sent home. Because of conflicting and inconclusive findings, no strong practice or policy recommendations are possible with respect to language use in the home. The need for additional research is obvious.

One conclusion that can be drawn from the studies reviewed here is that schools should look for ways to engage parents in children's literacy development (although, again, what language parents should be encouraged to promote at home is far from clear). There is ample evidence that language-minority parents are motivated and, in many cases, capable of actions that would lead to improved student outcomes. Moreover, studies of apparently successful school contexts suggest that parent–home–community involvement helps explain school success. Advocates of parent involvement argue that schools should actively seek ways to collaborate with parents for children's academic benefit (e.g., Epstein, 1992, 1996; Goldenberg, 1993).

Yet even aside from the language issue, the research base presents a dilemma. On the one hand, we have evidence of low-income and minority parents' willingness and ability to help their children succeed academically, but, on the other hand, the evidence for the impact of parent involvement efforts on children's achievement is surprisingly thin. Indeed, two research reviews that have appeared since 1990 challenge the notion that parent involvement programs have demonstrable effects on student outcomes (Mattingly et al., 2002; White, Taylor, & Moss, 1992). Mattingly et al. show that the strongest claims for effectiveness come from studies with the weakest designs (i.e., those lacking suitable control groups). These conclusions, however, have been strongly challenged in meta-analyses by Jeynes (2003, 2005).

Although we have considerable evidence that parents are positively disposed to helping their children—perhaps especially in the area of

TABLE 5.1
First- and Second-Language Use in the Home and First- and Second-Language Literacy Achievement*

	First-Language Literacy Achievement			Second-Language Literacy Achievement		
	Positive	*Negative*	*None*	*Positive*	*Negative*	*None*
First-language use in the home	• Brunell & Linnakylä (1994) • Brunell & Saretsalo (1999) • Cahill (1987) • Dolson (1985)		• Aarts & Verhoeven (1999)	• Cahill (1987) • Dolson (1985?) (nonsig. but moderate effect size) • Hancock (2002)	• Aarts & Verhoeven (1999?) (unclear variable construction) • Buriel & Cardoza, 1988 (language spoken as child & for third generation) • Connor (1983) • Hansen (1989) • Kennedy & Park (1994) (Asian students only) • Monzó & Rueda (2001?) (possible negative association)	• Buriel & Cardoza (1988) • Kennedy & Park (1994) (Mexican students only)

110

Second-language use in the home	• Brunell & Linnakylä (1994) • Brunell & Saretsalo (1999) • Dolson (1985)	• Aarts & Verhoeven (1999) • Cahill (1987)	• Aarts & Verhoeven (1999) • Buriel & Cardoza (1988)? (language spoken as child & for third generation only) • Connor (1983) • Hansen (1989) • Kennedy & Park (1994) (Asian students) • Koskinen et al. (2000)? (teacher rating and student self-report effects) • Monzó & Rueda (2001)?	• Dolson (1985)? (non sig., but moderate effect size)	• Buriel & Cardoza (1988) • Cahill (1987) • Kennedy & Park, (1994) (Mexican students) • Koskinen et al. (2000)

* A question mark (?) following an entry indicates there is some ambiguity or uncertainty about the data but that the study probably goes in the indicated cell. The note in parenthesis briefly identifies the ambiguity or uncertainty, with more extensive explanation provided in the text.

early literacy, where parents possess the attitudes and many have at least rudimentary literacy skills and knowledge to help their children—we know less about the likely effects on children's literacy development. A potential problem that should be acknowledged is that parents who do not speak the societal language are unable to assist their children in that language and cannot initiate or sustain communication with the school unless special personnel or programs are in place. The academic expectations of educators for students and their parents may place an undue burden on these families.

The Nature of Parent and Family Literacy Beliefs and Practices. Several studies have described differences between home–community and school literacy beliefs and practices. Some of this work has focused on home motivation, attitudes, values, and beliefs, and some has focused on oral language and literacy experiences. Three of these studies looked at home values, beliefs, and attitudes, as well as language and literacy experiences at home and at school (Huss, 1995; Huss-Keeler, 1997; Volk & De Acosta, 2001); one study examined home values, beliefs, and attitudes (Gregory, 1994); and one examined language and literacy experiences at home and at school (Mulhern, 1997).

Some of these studies highlight differences between students' home, community, and school in the uses of literacy. In several of the studies, for example, literacy was found to be associated with belonging to a religious community (Gregory, 1994; Huss, 1995; Volk & De Acosta, 2001). With respect to pedagogical differences, some of the literacy practices in homes tended to be more "rigid and formal" (Huss-Keeler, 1997), such that the meaning of texts was seen as inherent and not open to negotiation. Other studies document similarities between home–community and school. In one study, for example, literacy events were social interactions involving at least one other person (Volk & De Acosta, 2001) at home and, in some instances, in school.

A picture based on static and clear-cut differences between home and school is not accurate, however. For example, Volk and De Acosta (2001) suggest that a view of home–school relationships as either match or mismatch is too simplistic, in that "there are many literacies that are similar in some ways and different in others" (p. 220). Moreover, the relationships shift over time as the literacy practices in the two domains interact. For example, although it was found that the purposes of reading in both home and school were to acquire information, communicate, and maintain relationships with others, there were purposes unique to each setting. In the community, literacy was viewed as a means to gain access to God's word, whereas in school it was viewed as a way to gain pleasure. Children's experiences with literacy at home involving collaboration with others may have transformed their literacy experiences at school, in which they altered their individual classroom reading and writing times into social activities.

The studies also document the considerable misunderstanding that exists among teachers about the home and community literacy experiences of their students, as well as about parental and community expectations for achievement (Huss, 1995; Huss-Keeler, 1997). It appears from the studies that many of these misunderstandings are a result of cultural differences (e.g., parents believe they should trust teachers to do the teaching, and thus it is not the parental role to go to school, whereas teachers see parents as uninterested; Huss-Keeler, 1997). When such gaps have been bridged, teacher attitudes are less negative about language-minority parents and children. Huss-Keeler documents how even one home visit altered teachers' perceptions of parents' interest in their children's learning despite the parents' lack of English proficiency. Thus, it is important to help teachers understand their students' culture and home experiences. Several authors propose that professional development aimed at clarifying these cultural differences and providing a forum for discussion about them should be an important component of a school's program to ameliorate such misunderstandings between home, school, and community.

One study (Mulhern, 1997) also documents the importance of helping parents understand the kind of instruction children are receiving in school so that misunderstandings do not arise when children work at home. For example, emergent writing (in which children spell words the way they think they are spelled, without stopping to look them up) may be promoted in school, but may not be part of parents' repertoire because they were not taught this way. One way of creating more consonance between home and school may be by teachers modeling an activity and involving both parents and students (Quintero & Huerta-Macías, 1990).

A final note is that the collection of studies reviewed here portrays family experiences as diverse and shaped not only by culture, but also by personal attributes (Gutiérrez & Rogoff, 2003). As an example, Volk and De Acosta (2001) point to discrepancies among families of similar cultural backgrounds in the way they define the literacy events relevant to teaching reading and writing. Some families emphasized more explicit instruction in letter–sound relationships as key, whereas others drew on a broader range of resources to create literacy experiences for their children. This finding once again cautions against overgeneralizing individuals' attributes on the basis of cultural group membership or ethnicity.

Policies at the District, State, and Federal Levels

Many authors have speculated about the impact on literacy outcomes of various public educational policies, but there have been surprisingly few empirical investigations.

The Influence of Public Policies. The research base in this area is inadequate to permit firm conclusions, but the few existing studies are suggestive. Shannon (1995) describes the impact on students of the implicit (unofficial) U.S. language policy that privileges English and how a classroom teacher countered this impact with practices that appeared to have positive effects on students' literacy development. Findings of Brunell and Linnakylä's (1994) study of Swedish speakers in Finland could be interpreted as consistent with the hypothesis that language policies and practices recognizing the value of more than one language can minimize the negative effects of language-minority status on student literacy outcomes. Both studies, however, are open to alternative interpretations.

The Nature of Public Policies. It is notable that we could locate only one study on state and federal policies related to second-language learners. The one study we found indicates that specific federal or state policies play out differently in classrooms than they were envisioned to do. As documented by Stritikus (2001), a host of other factors, including other federal and state policies, as well as "the local school context, the teachers' political and ideological views, and their educational histories, is likely to play a large role in determining the nature of instruction" (p. 305).

Language Status or Prestige

As with the research on policy, one can hypothesize that the status of a language would influence the achievement of speakers of that language. Being a member of a low-status language group may have negative effects on self-concept, motivation, and learning opportunities, all of which can depress literacy attainment. Spanish, for example, is thought to be a low-status language in the United States (Carreira, 2000), and disproportionate numbers of Spanish speakers achieve at low levels in U.S. schools.

The Influence of Language Status or Prestige. Three studies provide suggestive evidence in support of the hypothesis that language status or prestige may influence student literacy outcomes (Brunell & Linnakylä, 1994; Lam, 2000; Shannon, 1995). Differences in achievement between language-minority (Swedish-speaking) and language-majority children in Finland—where both languages are of equal status—are modest compared with differences between some language-minority (e.g., Spanish-speaking) and language-majority children in the United States, where English is considered the high-status language. Yet other explanations are possible. For example, Scandinavian countries have particularly high literacy levels. Highly literate contexts, rather than equal language status, could explain the fact that there are relatively minor differences in the achievement of majority and minority speakers in Scandinavian countries. Moreover, SES differences in general are less extreme in Scandinavian countries than in the United States, where there are enormous economic differences among families and ethnic groups (Smeeding, 2002). The relative parity among different ethnic groups in Scandinavian societies may explain more equitable achievement outcomes across these groups.

The Nature of Language Status or Prestige.   When teachers show that they value students' first language, that language tends to be accepted by students in the class (Clark, 1995; Manyak, 2001; Reyes, Laliberty, & Orbanosky, 1993), but when teachers fail to value it (McCollum, 1999) other students may take on a more negative attitude about that language. However, value placed on the first language (Lotherington, Ebert, Watanabe, Norng, & Ho-Dac, 1998) may not be sufficient to promote first-language and literacy development. For example, even if there is institutional support, students are influenced by the status of peers; in schools where peers with the most status speak the second language, students tend to value that language (McCollum, 1999). As noted in Shannon (1995), it is difficult for teachers to support first-language use when it is not accepted in the larger community. Moreover, the studies suggest that any potential effects of language prestige cannot be evaluated without consideration of related sociocultural variables such as SES, ethnicity, and cultural differences. Nevertheless, the studies do suggest the relatively strong press to acquire English. The impact of this factor on second language and literacy outcomes cannot be stated unequivocally given the state of the research. It remains a promising area of investigation.

METHODOLOGICAL ISSUES

The studies reviewed in this chapter are extremely diverse methodologically and draw heavily from a qualitative research tradition. There are few experiments among the studies reviewed here.

The scarcity of experimental designs is understandable because sociocultural processes are difficult to manipulate. The field has been influenced more by anthropology and linguistics—disciplines that traditionally have not employed experimental designs—than by educational psychology and related fields. More often than not, the emphasis in this body of research has been on describing sociocultural factors, rather than on empirically demonstrating a link between sociocultural factors and student learning or other outcomes. Although experimental designs offer the strongest basis for causal inferences about the efficacy of specific interventions, carefully documented non-experimental studies can be used to enhance our understanding of relationships among variables. Moreover, qualitative studies can also support causal claims or hypotheses when they are carefully documented and consider specific "mechanisms"—linkages and processes. As is true of quantitative research, findings from qualitative studies are especially compelling when the results are replicated in a variety of settings and conditions. Quantitative studies (experimental or non-experimental), however, are better for establishing generalizability since they typically involve more subjects than qualitative studies. Of course, there can be validity threats and alternative explanations even with strong experimental designs.

Another issue of concern is unsubstantiated claims. For example, some authors argue that culturally sensitive or culturally accommodated instruction helps promote student literacy achievement, but they fail to provide evidence that the approach had any culturally sensitive or accommodating features. Moreover, there is often some question as to whether the approach under study had any true effects. Authors might claim effects, but the validity of these claims is difficult to determine because insufficient data are reported.

It is important to note that space constraints of journal publications make it difficult for ethnographic research and narrative reporting to be shown at their best. These methods require more space than is typically allowed by journals to document methods and analysis techniques appropriately. The absence of comprehensive methodological detail in many of the studies included here might have been a consequence of these constraints, rather than the quality of the study. Indeed, we had difficulty distinguishing between high-quality studies that had been squeezed into too little space and poor studies. Rather than risk eliminating potentially high-quality work with some conclusions worth thinking about, we erred on the side of inclusiveness. At the same time, although some of the included studies have shortcomings, others managed in a small amount of space to report findings with adequate empirical grounding.

In summary, the following are among the methodological issues we noted in our review of studies. Many, but not all, refer to the qualitative studies:

- Insufficient specification about investigator time spent in the research setting.
- Insufficient specification of data collection techniques, data analysis techniques, number of subjects, and number of observations.
- Data not presented to confirm/disconfirm author's point of view explicitly.
- No information about how representative examples were selected.
- No information about the frequency or typicality of reported key occurrences.
- No information about whether competing interpretations were considered and evaluated.
- Insufficient triangulation across several data sources.
- Making inferences and drawing conclusions not warranted by the data reported.

As already discussed, many of the studies reviewed are descriptive and do not address directly whether the sociocultural dimensions they target have an impact on student outcomes. Within the summary for each question, we discuss these studies separately because (a) many of these studies provide a rich source of descriptive material, as well as theory, hypotheses, and questions to be explored in future research; and (b) we use this opportunity to point out that many of the studies in this area are silent on the question of how sociocultural factors influence student outcomes. In this context, we call attention to a recent commentary by Sleeter (2004, p. 135):

> Ethnographic work may be ignored in policy debates when ethnographers do not speak to the language of power. Currently that language is achievement test scores. In order to insert our work more directly into discussions of school reform, we need to link findings, where relevant, to achievement data.... I am concerned that those who subscribe to decontextualized ways of understanding school reform will simply ignore insights of ethnography when achievement data are not included.

We agree with Sleeter that we must connect sociocultural factors with student learning as assessed by valid measures.

RECOMMENDATIONS FOR FUTURE RESEARCH

Specific Features of the Immigrant Experience

Given the numbers of language-minority students who are immigrants, research should systematically examine specific features of the immigrant experience that may have an impact on language-minority students' literacy development and try to disentangle these features from other, related factors, such as SES or home literacy experiences. Although some studies exist, many confounds limit the knowledge base in this area. The following questions require further study: What are the independent and combined effects of immigration status, SES, and home literacy experiences on literacy outcomes? How specifically does immigration status influence opportunity to learn apart from SES? What specific behaviors, beliefs, and attitudes of immigrant parents mediate the acquisition of literacy for language-minority students? Are these different for different immigrant groups? How do these factors change with more time in the host country?

Accommodations to Home and School Discourse

Research should investigate more carefully and systematically the relationship between home and school discourse, focusing in particular on potential mismatches and the effects on student outcomes when mismatches are reduced or eliminated. Many studies have identified significant differences between home and school environments. But the current state of the literature does not allow us to draw strong conclusions regarding the effects of these differences on literacy outcomes, or the effects when these differences are eliminated or minimized by altering the instructional environment. Such differences may indeed be important in literacy development, so there is a need for detailed and well-designed studies that address this issue straightforwardly.

Particularly useful would be well-designed experiments comparing instruction designed to eliminate or minimize discourse mismatches for a particular language-minority group (e.g., students of Mexican descent) with effective generic instruction that does not include such a component. An additional useful control would be to include in the study another sociocultural group (e.g., English-speaking, of European descent) that would receive the identical set of contrasting instructional treatments. This design would allow a test of whether instruction designed to minimize home–school discourse differences would be more effective than typical instruction, or whether such instruction facilitates literacy development for both sociocultural groups. In such a study, it would be important to design the control condition carefully so that the discourse-accommodating instruction would be compared with effective instruction. It would be useless and misleading to compare it with instruction already known to be poor. Ideally, the two instructional conditions would be as similar as possible, differentiated only by key discourse features employed by the teacher and designed to be accommodating to students' home discourse style.

Qualitative or ethnographic studies could also shed useful light on this hypothesis by using this type of methodology to collect detailed, fine-grained data on the nature of the classroom interactions and students' and teachers' responses to instruction.

Questions for further exploration also include: What specific home- and community-based discourse features need to be accommodated in classroom instruction to improve student outcomes? For example, if children come from cultures where turn-taking and wait-time rules are significantly different from those of the classroom, what is the effect on student outcomes if teachers alter these rules? Do the effects of these accommodations vary depending on specific types of classroom settings and activities, for example, during interactive reading instruction? In addition, do these accommodations affect different literacy outcomes (e.g., achievement, motivation, interest, reading behaviors)?

Other Sociocultural Accommodations to Instruction

Research needs to systematically examine sociocultural accommodations and their effects on language-minority students' literacy outcomes. Although a significant amount of work has been done on sociocultural factors involved in teaching and learning, much of it is plagued by methodological and theoretical problems. Often this research is descriptive only, such that outcomes are implied or assumed, but not directly examined. Relevant variables often are not well specified; there are frequently confounds among independent variables; and a lack of differentiation among culture, SES, race/ethnicity, prior experience, and language is common. Hypotheses about sociocultural accommodations need to be investigated more explicitly, more systematically, and in relation to student literacy outcomes. Many of these hypotheses overlap substantially with the discourse-based hypotheses discussed earlier.

The overarching question in this domain is: To what extent does accommodating instructional features (e.g., social organization of the classroom) or curriculum (e.g., academic content) to language-minority students' sociocultural characteristics result in improved student cognitive, affective, and ultimately academic outcomes? If such a result can be demonstrated, is it attributable to operationalizing existing learning principles, or are different principles involved? For example, does more relevant material increase motivation and thus achievement, or does it focus attention so that instructional time is more productive? Are there universal effective teaching strategies or some that are differentially effective? Are there interactions between generic instructional strategies (e.g., direct teaching, cooperative learning) and language-minority students' sociocultural characteristics? Do particular instructional approaches result in better or worse cognitive, affective, and/or academic outcomes for certain sociocultural groups, or are effective strategies equally effective for all groups?

The recommended research designs are analogous to those proposed earlier. The prior questions can be pursued effectively with experimental design procedures or more qualitative/ethnographic methods. What is critical are (a) a comparative design, whereby students in a culturally accommodated condition are compared with similar students in an effective, but not culturally accommodated condition; and (b) a measure or gauge of student literacy (or literacy-related) outcomes. Again, inclusion of another ethnolinguistic group would add to the study's informative value.

Characteristics of Effective Parental Involvement Strategies

Are parental involvement strategies or programs effective in improving academic achievement for language-minority students? If so, what are the characteristics of effective programs that involve parents? The existing research suggests that parent or family factors have an impact on the literacy development of language-minority students, and parents are often willing to help their children succeed academically. More information is needed on how specific parental behaviors and attitudes are related to enhanced literacy development. Do the salient parental factors influencing children's literacy outcomes change over time? In what ways can schools foster and take better advantage of parent/home resources at different ages and grades? What developmental differences may suggest that different parental factors are at work in the early stages of literacy acquisition as opposed to later? Are some parents more or less responsive to being involved in their children's educational attainment? What differentiates these parents? What means can be used to engage less responsive parents? There is a great need to develop, implement, and evaluate (in terms of student outcomes) techniques and programs that can promote parent involvement to enhance student literacy development.

Observational, naturalistic, interview, and possibly survey studies could help find answers to these questions. As discussed before, experimental designs offer fundamental advantages, in that they permit systematic comparison of parents' and students' responses/outcomes under different and documented conditions. Adding a qualitative component would increase the probability of producing detailed and valid understanding about how such interventions and programs influence— or fail to influence—participants.

The effect of language use in the home is an important additional area for study. All of the correlational studies reviewed found positive within-language correlations, such that home experiences in one language positively correlate with at least some literacy outcomes in that language. Moreover, with two exceptions, there are negative across-language correlations, such that home experience in one language is negatively correlated with literacy outcomes in the other language for at least some measures. Because causality cannot be inferred from correlations, we need to understand what explains these correlations. One possibility is simply that more time spent in one language promotes greater competence in that language and detracts from competence in another language.

However, this explanation runs counter to the two experimental studies reviewed here. One study found that promoting Spanish home literacy activities produced a positive effect on English preliteracy achievement in kindergarten, whereas the other study found that promoting English home literacy activities had no effect on English literacy achievement in first grade. The time-on-task explanation also runs counter to findings reported in Chapter 4 suggesting positive transfer in literacy domains across languages.

Other explanations must be explored—for example, the quality and content of parent–child interactions. It might be the case that home language that is more academically oriented has a different relationship with student outcomes than home language that is more conversational or informal. The experiment demonstrating the effects of promoting Spanish literacy in the home on English preliteracy development suggests just this possibility. Two other aspects of parents' home language use need to be studied: the relationship between parents' language use and their language competence, and parents' explanations for why they use one language or the other or a combination of the two. Different answers would have different implications for policy and practice recommendations.

Beyond such studies, it would be extremely useful to conduct additional experimental interventions in which families would be randomly assigned to conditions that varied the balance of first- and second-language use in the home. Such a study, admittedly, would be controversial and difficult to carry out. If done successfully, however, it would yield extremely useful data about (a) how alterable home language patterns are among language-minority families, and (b) what effects can be expected from attempts to alter home language use.

The Effects of School and Other Policies on Language-Minority Students' Literacy Development

There is a great need for policy studies linking school, district, state, and federal policies to language-minority students' literacy development. One highly visible policy initiative, which began in California and is now drawing attention throughout the country, is designed to end primary-language instruction in schools. What is the effect of this policy shift on student literacy outcomes? Beyond such dramatic and highly publicized shifts, various states have different policy frameworks for educating language-minority students. Can we discern their effects on language-minority students' achievement?

A shift in federal policy has occurred with regard to language of instruction. Title VII of the Improving America's Schools Act (P.L. 103–382, 1994) promoted "multilingual skills" and provided funding for many two-way bilingual programs throughout the United States, but Title III of the No Child Left Behind Act of 2001 (P.L. 107–110, 2002) makes no mention of the benefits of maintaining and promoting multiple language skills. Moreover, NCLB has created a high-stakes accountability environment that is unprecedented at the federal level yet limits how many years ELLs can be tested in their native language (three in most cases with up to two more on a case-by-case basis) for language arts accountability purposes (see Chapter 7) How, if at all, have these changes in federal policy affected learning opportunities and literacy development among English-language learners?

At the district and school levels, myriad policies are in place for identifying, placing, instructing, and exiting from special services English-language learners. What are the effects of those policies on learning opportunities and literacy attainment?

Finally, policies with respect to the education of language-minority children vary internationally. Can we gauge the effects of these policies on language-minority populations in different countries and assess how they compare with policies in the United States?

The Role of Language Status/Prestige in Students' Literacy Development

There is a need to investigate more systematically, and in different language-use, community, and national contexts, the hypothesis that language status or prestige influences student literacy development. While the research suggests that there are differences in the status and prestige of different languages, is language status related to or does it influence language-minority students' cognitive, affective, and/or academic outcomes? Does this vary by language status or across different language groups? Will enhancing the status of the home language help improve language-minority students' cognitive, affective, and academic outcomes? If enhancing the status of students' home language is effective in promoting literacy development, what are the most promising ways to accomplish this?

There is some suggestion that technology could play a role in mediating language status issues (e.g., Lam, 2000). Given the rapidly increasing importance of technology in educational practice, a related question is whether technology (such as the Internet) as a medium of communication or instruction can attenuate the deleterious effects of a low-status language or, alternatively, help promote a higher status for a language. If technology can promote higher language status, what is the effect on student literacy development? Some of these questions would be amenable to experimental manipulations and evaluation.

Recommendations for Study Design and Methodology

Greater Attention to Assessing and Reporting Student Literacy Outcomes. Many studies in this area describe particular contexts and then draw inferences about their effects on student literacy development. But there is a surprising absence of outcome data. The inferences are often reasonable, but they do not substitute for data. The lack of achievement data is particularly characteristic of studies that address the issue of culturally compatible or culturally accommodating instruction. Despite a belief among many in the field that instruction tailored to different cultural groups is superior to instruction based on general principles of teaching and learning, there is a paucity of data to support this claim. The best studies suggest that student engagement and participation, which are not the same as achievement, can be enhanced through the use of culturally compatible instruction, but even these studies are open to numerous alternative explanations.

The Application of Quality Criteria to Ethnographic Research. Because a large portion of the research in this area is qualitative or ethnographic, certain criteria should apply if the findings from this type of research are to contribute to our understanding of the field. First, researchers should document having collected observations from multiple sources and having employed multiple techniques for uncovering or cross-checking varying perspectives on complex issues and events. Second, they should provide information about the relative frequency of certain events or occurrences. Third, they should examine competing or alternative explanations. Fourth, they should make an effort to explain the range of variation in the data. Finally, their generalizations should be based on the data collected.

The Use of Mixed Research Designs. There is a need for mixed research designs that combine the best of quantitative and qualitative research methods. Quantitative methods allow for large numbers of subjects and data that are relatively easy to process. They also permit a degree of generalization, depending on how subjects are selected, as well as the calculation of effect sizes. Qualitative data permit more in-depth study of behavior and its links to other aspects of settings and contexts, and also may provide insight into the mechanisms and processes through which various factors produce specific outcomes. When combined, these two approaches to social research have a much greater probability of shedding light on complex topics than has either one individually (Green, Camilli, & Elmore, in press; Weisner, 2005).

REFERENCES

Aarts, R., & Verhoeven, L. (1999). Literacy attainment in a second language submersion context. *Applied Psycholinguistics*, 20(3), 377–393.

Abu-Rabia, S. (1995). Attitudes and cultural background and their relationship to English in a multicultural social context: The case of male and female Arab immigrants in Canada. *Educational Psychology*, 15(3), 323–336.

Abu-Rabia, S. (1996). Druze minority students learning Hebrew in Israel: The relationship of attitudes, cultural background, and interest of material to reading comprehension in a second language. *Journal of Multilingual and Multicultural Development*, 17(6), 415–426.

Abu-Rabia, S. (1998a). Attitudes and culture in second language learning among Israeli–Arab students. *Curriculum and Teaching*, 13(1), 13–30.

Abu-Rabia, S. (1998b). Social and cognitive factors influencing the reading comprehension of Arab students learning Hebrew as a second language in Israel. *Journal of Research in Reading*, 21(3), 201–212.

Arzubiaga, A., Rueda, R., & Monzó, L. (2002). Reading engagement of Latino children. *Journal of Latinos and Education*, 1(4), 231–43.

ASCD Advisory Panel on Improving Student Achievement (1995). In R. Cole (Ed.), *Educating everybody's children: Diverse teaching strategies for diverse learners* (pp. 9–20). Alexandria, VA: Association for Supervision and Curriculum Development.

Au, K. H.-P. (1980). Participation structures in a reading lesson with Hawaiian children: Analysis of a culturally appropriate instructional event. *Anthropology and Education Quarterly*, 11(2), 91–115.

Au, K. H.-P., & Mason, J. M. (1981). Social organizational factors in learning to read: The balance of rights hypothesis. *Reading Research Quarterly*, 17(1), 15–52.

Blake, B. E. (2001). Fruit of the devil: Writing and English language learners. *Language Arts*, 78(5), 435–441.

Brooker, L. (2002). "Five on the first of December!" What can we learn from case studies of early childhood literacy? *Journal of Early Childhood Literacy*, 2(3), 292–313.

Brunell, V., & Linnakylä, P. (1994). Swedish speakers' literacy in the Finnish society. *Journal of Reading*, 37(5), 368–375.

Brunell, V., & Saretsalo, L. (1999). Sociocultural diversity and reading literacy in a Finland–Swedish environment. *Scandinavian Journal of Educational Research*, 43(2), 173–190.

Buriel, R., & Cardoza, D. (1988). Sociocultural correlates of achievement among three generations of Mexican American high school seniors. *American Educational Research Journal*, 25(2), 177–192.

Cahill, D. P. (1987). Bilingual development of Italo–Australian children. *Australian Review of Applied Linguistics*, 4, 101–127.

California State Department of Education. (1986). *Beyond language: Social and cultural factors in schooling language minority students*. Los Angeles: Evaluation, Dissemination and Assessment Center, California State University. 341

Carreira, M. (2000). Validating and promoting Spanish in the United States: Lessons from linguistic science. *Bilingual Research Journal*, 24, 333–352.

Chilora, H., & Harris, A. (2001). *Investigating the role of teacher's home language in mother tongue policy implementation: Evidence from IEQ research findings in Malawi*. Washington, DC: American Institutes for Research/USAID, Improving Educational Quality (IEQ) Project.

Clark, E. R. (1995). "How did you learn to write in English when you haven't been taught in English?": The language experience approach in a dual language program. *Bilingual Research Journal*, 19(3/4), 611–627.

Cole, R. (Ed.). (1995). *Educating everybody's children: Diverse teaching strategies for diverse learners*. Alexandria, VA: Association for Supervision and Curriculum Development.

Connor, U. (1983). Predictors of second-language reading performance. *Journal of Multilingual and Multicultural Development*, 4(4), 271–288.

Davies, A. (1991). Performance of children from non-English speaking background on the New South Wales Basic Skills Tests of Numeracy: Issues of test bias and language proficiency. *Language Culture and Curriculum*, 4(2), 149–161.

Dolson, D. P. (1985). The effects of Spanish home language use on the scholastic performance of Hispanic pupils. *Journal of Multilingual and Multicultural Development*, 6(2), 135–155.

Durán, R. (1983). *Hispanics' education and background*. New York: College Entrance Examination Board.

Epstein, J. (1992). School and family partnerships. In M. Alkin (Ed.), *Encyclopedia of educational research* (6th ed., pp. 1139–1152). New York: Macmillan.

Epstein, J. (1996). Perspectives and previews on research and policy for school, family, and community partnerships. In A. Booth & J. Dunn (Eds.), *Family and school links: How do they affect educational outcomes?* (pp. 209–246). Mahwah, NJ: Lawrence Erlbaum Associates.

Forman, E., Minick, N., & Stone, C. (1993). *Contexts for learning: Sociocultural dynamics in children's development*. Oxford: Oxford University Press.

García-Vázquez, E. (1995). Acculturation and academics: Effects of acculturation on reading achievement among Mexican-American students. *Bilingual Research Journal*, 19(2), 304–315.

Goldenberg, C. (1987). Low-income Hispanic parents' contributions to their first-grade children's word-recognition skills. *Anthropology and Education Quarterly*, 18(3), 149–179.

Goldenberg, C. (1993). The home–school connection in bilingual education. In B. Arias & U. Casanova (Eds.), *Ninety-second yearbook of the National Society for the Study of Education. Bilingual education: Politics, research, and practice* (pp. 225–250). Chicago, IL: University of Chicago Press.

Goldenberg, C., & Gallimore, R. (1991). Local knowledge, research knowledge, and educational change: A case study of early Spanish reading improvement. *Educational Researcher*, 20(8), 2–14.

Goldenberg, C., & Gallimore, R. (1995). Immigrant Latino parents' values and beliefs about their children's education: Continuities and discontinuities across cultures and generations. In P. R. Pintrich & M. Maehr (Eds.), *Advances in motivation and achievement: Culture, ethnicity, and motivation* (Vol. 9, pp. 183–228). Greenwich, CT: JAI.

Green, J., Camilli, G., & Elmore, P. (Eds.) (in press). *Complementary methods for research in education*. Washington, DC: American Educational Research Association.

Gregory, E. (1994). Cultural assumptions and early years' pedagogy: The effect of the home culture on minority children's interpretation of reading in school. *Language Culture and Curriculum*, 7(2), 111–124.

Gregory, E. (1998). Siblings as mediators of literacy in linguistic minority communities. *Language and Education*, 12(1), 33–54.

Gutiérrez, K. D., & Rogoff, B. (2003). Cultural ways of learning: Individual styles or repertoires of practice. *Educational Researcher, 32*(5), 19–25.

Hancock, D. R. (2002). The effects of native language books on the pre-literacy skill development of language minority kindergartners. *Journal of Research in Childhood Education, 17*(1), 62–68.

Hannon, P., & McNally, J. (1986). Children's understanding and cultural factors in reading test performance. *Educational Review, 38*(3), 237–246.

Hansen, D. A. (1989). Locating learning: Second language gains and language use in family, peer and classroom contexts. *NABE: The Journal of the National Association for Bilingual Education, 13*(2), 161–180.

Hernández, J. S. (1991). Assisted performance in reading comprehension strategies with non-English proficient students. *Journal of Educational Issues of Language Minority Students, 8*, 91–112.

Hornberger, N. H. (1990). Creating successful learning contexts for bilingual literacy. *Teachers College Record, 92*(2), 212–229.

Huerta-Macías, A., & Quintero, E. (1992). Code-switching, bilingualism, and biliteracy: A case study. *Bilingual Research Journal, 16*(3/4), 69–90.

Huss, R. L. (1995). Young children becoming literate in English as a second language. *TESOL Quarterly, 29*(4), 767–774.

Huss-Keeler, R. L. (1997). Teacher perception of ethnic and linguistic minority parental involvement and its relationships to children's language and literacy learning: A case study. *Teaching and Teacher Education, 13*(2), 171–182.

Ima, K., & Rumbaut, R. G. (1989). Southeast Asian refugees in American schools: A comparison of fluent-English-proficient and limited-English-proficient students. *Topics in Language Disorders, 9*(3), 54–75.

Jacob, E., & Jordan, C. (Eds.). (1987). Explaining the school performance of minority students [Special Issue]. *Anthropology and Education Quarterly, 18*(4).

Jeynes, W. (2003). A meta-analysis: The effects of parental involvement on minority children's academic achievement. *Education and Urban Society, 35*, 202–218.

Jeynes, W. (2005). A meta-analysis of the relation of parental involvement to urban elementary school student academic achievement.? *Urban Education, 40*, 237–269.

Jiménez, R. T. (1997). The strategic reading abilities and potential of five low-literacy Latina/o readers in middle school. *Reading Research Quarterly, 32*(3), 224–243.

Jiménez, R. T., & Gersten, R. (1999). Lessons and dilemmas derived from the literacy instruction of two Latina/o teachers. *American Educational Research Journal, 36*(2), 265–301.

Kauffman, P., Chávez, L., & Lauen, D. (1988). *Generational status and educational outcomes among Asian and Hispanic 1988 eighth graders.* (NCES 1999–020). Washington, DC: National Center for Education Statistics.

Kennedy, E., & Park, H.- S. (1994). Home language as a predictor of academic achievement: A comparative study of Mexican- and Asian-American youth. *Journal of Research and Development in Education, 27*(3), 188–194.

Kenner, C. (1999). Children's understandings of text in a multilingual nursery. *Language and Education, 13*(1), 1–16.

Koskinen, P. S., Blum, I. H., Bisson, S. A., Phillips, S. M., Creamer, T. S., & Baker, T. K. (2000). Book access, shared reading, and audio models: The effects of supporting the literacy learning of linguistically diverse students in school and at home. *Journal of Educational Psychology, 92*, 23–36.

Kucer, S. B., & Silva, C. (1999). The English literacy development of bilingual students within a transitional whole language curriculum. *Bilingual Research Journal, 23*(4), 347–371.

Lam, W. S. E. (2000). L2 literacy and the design of the self: A case study of a teenager writing on the internet. *TESOL Quarterly, 34*(3), 457–482.

Lara-Cinisomo, S., Pebley, A. R., Vaiana, M. E., Maggio, E., Berends, M., & Lucas, S. R. (2004). A matter of class. *RAND Review*, 28(3). Retrieved March 3, 2005, from http://www.rand.org/publications/randreview/issues/fall2004/index.html

Lasisi, M. J., Falodun, S., & Onyehalu, A. S. (1988). The comprehension of first- and second language prose. *Journal of Research in Reading*, 11(1), 26–35.

Leseman, P. & de Jong, P. (1998). Home literacy: Opportunity, instruction, cooperation and socialemotional quality predicting early reading achievement. *Reading Research Quarterly*, 33, 294–318.

Lotherington, H., Ebert, S., Watanabe, T., Norng, S., & Ho-Dac, T. (1998). Biliteracy practices in suburban Melbourne. *Australian Language Matters*, 6(3), 3–4.

Love, K. (1996). Talk around text: Acquiescence or empowerment in secondary English. *Australian Review of Applied Linguistics*, 19(2), 1–25.

McCarty, T. L. (1993). Language, literacy, and the image of the child in American Indian classrooms. *Language Arts*, 70(3), 182–192.

McCarty, T. L., Wallace, S., Lynch, R. H., & Benally, A. (1991). Classroom inquiry and Navajo learning styles: A call for reassessment. *Anthropology and Education Quarterly*, 22(1), 42–59.

McCollum, P. (1999). Learning to value English: Cultural capital in a two-way bilingual program. *Bilingual Research Journal*, 23(2/3), 133–134.

Manyak, P. C. (2001). Participation, hybridity, and carnival: A situated analysis of a dynamic literacy practice in a primary-grade English immersion class. *Journal of Literacy Research*, 33(3), 423–465.

Masny, D., & Ghahremani-Ghajar, S.-S. (1999). Weaving multiple literacies: Somali children and their teachers in the context of school culture. *Culture and Curriculum*, 12(1), 72–93.

Mattingly, D., Prislin, R., McKenzie, T., Rodríguez, J., & Kayzar, B. (2002). Evaluating evaluations: The case of parent involvement programs. *Review of Educational Research*, 72, 549–576.

Moll, L. C. (1986). Writing as communication: Creating strategic learning environments for students. *Theory Into Practice*, 25(2), 102–108.

Moll, L. C., & Díaz, S. (1987). Change as the goal of educational research. *Anthropology and Education Quarterly*, 18(4), 300–311.

Moll, L. C., Sáez, R., & Dworin, J. (2001). Exploring biliteracy: Two student case examples of writing as a social practice. *Elementary School Journal*, 101(4), 435–449.

Monzó, L., & Rueda, R. (2001). *Constructing achievement orientations toward literacy: An analysis of sociocultural activity in Latino home and community contexts* (CIERA Report No. 1–011). Ann Arbor, MI: Center for the Improvement of Early Reading Achievement.

Mulhern, M. M. (1997). Doing his own thing: A Mexican-American kindergartner becomes literate at home and school. *Language Arts*, 74(6), 468–476.

Ogbu, J., & Matute-Bianchi, M. (1986). Understanding sociocultural factors: Knowledge, identity, and school adjustment. In California State Department of Education, *Beyond language: Social and cultural factors in schooling language minority students* (pp. 73–142). Los Angeles: Evaluation, Dissemination and Assessment Center, California State University.

Pucci, S. L., & Ulanoff, S. H. (1998). What predicts second language reading success? A study of home and school variables. *International Review of Applied Linguistics*, 121–122, 1–18.

Quintero, E., & Huerta-Macías, A. (1990). All in the family: Bilingualism and biliteracy. *Reading Teacher*, 44(4), 306–312.

Reese, L., Garnier, H., Gallimore, R., & Goldenberg, C. (2000). Longitudinal analysis of the antecedents of emergent Spanish literacy and middle-school English reading achievement of Spanish-speaking students. *American Educational Research Journal*, 37(3), 633–662.

Reyes, M. D. L. L., Laliberty, E. A., & Orbanosky, J. M. (1993). Emerging biliteracy and cross-cultural sensitivity in a language arts classroom. *Language Arts*, 70(8), 659–668.

Rogers-Zegarra, N., & Singer, H. (1980). Anglo and Chicano comprehension of ethnic stories. *Yearbook of the National Reading Conference*, 29, 203–208.

Rumbaut, R. (1995). The new Californians: Comparative research findings on the educational progress of immigrant children. In R. Rumbaut & W. Cornelius (Eds.), *California's immigrant children*. San Diego: Center for U.S.–Mexican Studies.

Saravia-Shore, M., & García, E. (1995). Diverse teaching strategies for diverse learners. In R. Cole (Ed.), *Educating everybody's children: Diverse teaching strategies for diverse learners* (pp. 47–74). Alexandria, VA: Association for Supervision and Curriculum Development.

Schmidt, P. R. (1995). Working and playing with others: Cultural conflict in a kindergarten literacy program. *The Reading Teacher*, 48(5), 404–412.

Schon, I., Hopkins, K. D., & Vojir, C. (1984). The effects of Spanish reading emphasis on the English and Spanish reading abilities of Hispanic high school students. *The Bilingual Review*, 11(1), 33–39.

Shadish, W. (1994). Critical multiplism: A research strategy and its attendant tactics. In L. Sechrest & A. Figueredo (Eds.), *New directions for program evaluation* (pp. 13–57). San Francisco, CA: Jossey-Bass.

Shannon, S. M. (1995). The hegemony of English: A case study of one bilingual classroom as a site of resistance. *Linguistics and Education*, 7(3), 175–200.

Sirin, S. (2005). Socioeconomic status and academic achievement: A meta-analytic review of research. *Review of Educational Research*, 75, 417–453.

Sleeter, C. (2004). Context-conscious portraits and context-blind policy. *Anthropology and Education Quarterly*, 35(1), 132–136.

Smeeding, T. (2002). Globalisation, inequality, and the rich countries of the G–20: Evidence from the Luxembourg Income Study. In D. Gruen, T. O'Brien, & J. Lawson (Eds.), *Globalisation, living standards, and inequality: Recent progress and continuing challenges* (pp. 179–206). Canberra, Australia: J. S. McMillan.

Stritikus, T. T. (2001). From personal to political: Proposition 227, literacy instruction, and the individual qualities of teachers. *International Journal of Bilingual Education and Bilingualism*, 4(5), 291–309.

Suárez-Orozco, C. M., & Suárez-Orozco, M. (1996). *Transformations: Immigration, family life, and achievement motivation among Latino adolescents*. Stanford, CA: Stanford University Press.

Tharp, R. (1989). Psychocultural variables and constants: Effects on teaching and learning in schools. *American Psychologist*, 44, 349–359.

Townsend, J. S., & Fu, D. (1998). A Chinese boy's joyful initiation into American literacy. *Language Arts*, 75(3), 193–201.

Trueba, H., Moll, L. C., & Díaz, S. (1984). *Improving the functional writing of bilingual secondary school students* (Report No. 400–81–0023). Washington, DC: National Institute of Education.

Volk, D., & De Acosta, M. (2001). "Many differing ladders, many ways to climb . . .": Literacy events in the bilingual classroom, homes, and community of three Puerto Rican kindergartners. *Journal of Early Childhood Literacy*, 1(2), 193–224.

Weisner, T. S. (Ed.). (2005). *Discovering successful pathways in children's development: Mixed methods in the study of childhood and family life*. Chicago, IL: University of Chicago Press.

White, K. R. (1982). The relation between socioeconomic status and academic achievement. *Psychological Bulletin*, 91(3), 461–481.

White, K., Taylor, M., & Moss, V. (1992). Does research support claims about the benefits of involving parents in early intervention programs? *Review of Educational Research*, 62, 91–125.

Wilkinson, L. C., Milosky, L. M., & Genishi, C. (1986). Second language learners' use of requests and responses in elementary classrooms. *Topics in Language Disorders, 6*(2), 57–70.

Xu, H. (1999). Reexamining continuities and discontinuities: Language-minority children's home and school literacy experiences. *Yearbook of the National Reading Conference, 48,* 224–237.

6

Instruction and Professional Development

Diane August, Isabel L. Beck, Margarita Calderón, David J. Francis, Nonie K. Lesaux, and Timothy Shanahan, with Frederick Erickson and Linda S. Siegel

This chapter reviews research on instruction and professional development related to literacy in language-minority children. The five sections focus on the following research questions:

- What impact does language of instruction have on the literacy learning of language-minority children? Is it better to immerse students in English-language instruction only, or are there benefits to bilingual instruction?
- What can be done to improve achievement in reading, writing, and spelling for language-minority children?
- What do we know about classroom and school practice designed to build literacy in language-minority children?
- What do we know about literacy instruction for language-minority children in special education settings?
- What does the research tell us about the role of teachers' beliefs and attitudes in the literacy development of language-minority children, and what do we know about professional development for these teachers?

BACKGROUND

These research questions are contextualized within a broad conceptual framework describing the development of literacy in language-minority children and youth. According to this framework, many individual student factors such as age of arrival in a new country, educational history, and cognitive capacity influence literacy development. In addition, literacy development is influenced by language and literacy profiency in the native language, as well second-language oral proficiency skills (all are influences on literacy development unique to the second-language learning situation). Moreover, the sociocultural context in which children are acquiring their second language influences learning. Finally, particular educational settings and interventions influence the course of development (this framework is described more fully in Chapter 1).

METHODOLOGY

The criteria used for selecting the studies reviewed in this chapter are consistent with the criteria used in the other chapters. However, the criteria for the review of language of instruction differ in some important ways from the previously described criteria. For example, there have been past reviews of the influence of language of instruction so it was essential that our review be consistent with those previous reviews to allow for comparisons of results; this meant that we had to include studies in this section that had been conducted prior to 1980. Additionally, to provide an adequate evaluation of such instruction, the instructional efforts studied here had to provide at least 6 months of teaching to the students, and in most cases, the programs were studied for at least 1 year.

Different research methods are useful for addressing different types of questions. The diversity of research questions posed in this chapter necessitates the examination of studies that use a variety of research methods. Experiments, quasi-experiments, and single-subject designs are useful for determining what works because these research methods allow us to causally link instructional efforts with student learning. Studies on language of instruction, effective literacy teaching, and special education attempt to answer these kinds of "what works" questions, and, consequently, these reviews rely wholly (language of instruction, effective literacy teaching) or partly (special education) on experimental studies. Although logically the experimental paradigm allows for a determination of causal relationships, interpretive caution is still needed as such studies may vary in quality—how well a study controls for alternative explanations of effects, how well its conditions match those in actual classrooms, and how thoroughly it describes the intervention and context in which the intervention occurs. Furthermore, the results of even the best studies are probabilistic; we have greater confidence in results that have been successfully replicated many times in independent studies. With regard to studies of effective literacy teaching and special education with language-minority children, there rarely were multiple studies on the same approaches and learning outcomes, and for this reason no meta-analysis was attempted (though we did calculate effect sizes for each study to facilitate subjective comparisons of particular approaches). For language of instruction, where replication studies were available, a full meta-analysis of results is provided.

This chapter also includes ethnographic studies and case studies. Ethnographic studies—narrative descriptions of schools and classrooms—are useful for documenting the contexts in which language-minority students are educated. Ethnographic studies are cited in the sections on classroom and school practices, special education, and teachers and professional development. These studies provide descriptions of changes in students' or teachers' cognitive or linguistic behaviors, the instructional approaches used to achieve these changes, and the context in which the approach was implemented. Ethnographies and case studies, like experiments, vary in quality. The best of these studies are based on theory and use rigorous measures aligned with the goals of the study. Ultimately, these studies can generate only hypotheses about the influence instruction may have on learning (because they make no systematic manipulation of the instruction, they have no control group), but they can help identify subtle factors that may affect learning, they can be a useful basis for establishing hypotheses for future inquiry, or, when joined with experimental studies, they can help explain why certain experimental results are obtained. When qualitative methods such as ethnographies were the sources of data, we used the systematic interpretive procedures already described in Chapter 1.

FINDINGS

Language of Instruction

For many years, discussion of effective reading programs for English-language learners has revolved around the question of whether and how children's first language should be used in an instructional program. The focus of this section is on studies that compare bilingual programs with programs that use only English. In addition to the studies focused on the acquisition of literacy by language-minority students ($n = 16$), this section incorporates findings from one heritage language study and three

Canadian French immersion studies. Appendix 6.A (Table 6.A.1) includes evaluation studies in the present review and other reviews that compare one approach to the other (Rossell & Baker, 1996; Greene, 1997; Slavin & Cheung, 2004; Willig, 1985).

French Immersion Studies. Although studies of French immersion programs are not directly relevant to the question of the effectiveness of bilingual programs for language-minority students acquiring the national language, they are important in providing a broader under-standing of the role of the sociocultural context in literacy development. Several Canadian studies of French immersion programs, in which native-English-speaking children are taught entirely or primarily in French in the early elementary years (e.g., Barik & Swain, 1978; Genesee, Sheiner, Tucker, & Lambert, 1976), have played an important role in debates about bilingual education.

The findings from these French immersion studies paint a consistent picture: At least for the overwhelmingly middle-class English-speaking students involved, French immersion had no negative effect on English reading achievement, and it gave students an opportunity to acquire facility in a second language, French. The relevance of these findings to the U.S. situation is in suggesting that similar second-language immer-sion programs, as well as two-way bilingual programs, for English-proficient children are not likely to hinder students' English reading development.

Studies Conducted With Language-Minority Students. Fourteen studies included in our review compared language-minority students in the elementary grades who were taught to read using either bilingual or English-only instruction (Alvarez, 1975; Campeau et al., 1975; Cohen, Fathman, & Merino, 1976; Danoff, Coles, McLaughlin, & Reynolds, 1978; De la Garza & Medina, 1985; Doebler & Mardis, 1980–1981; Huzar, 1973; Lampman, 1973; J. A. Maldonado, 1994; J. R. Maldonado, 1977; Plante, 1976; Ramírez et al., 1991; Saldate, Mishra, & Medina, 1985; Valladolid, 1991). Three of these elementary studies used random assignment to the instructional conditions while 11 used a procedure which matched students on pretest variables, such as reading and oral proficiency, or on pre-reading skills. Two studies (Covey, 1973; Kaufman, 1968) compared these instructional approaches with students in the secondary grades, and both employed random assignment.

Heritage Language Studies. One study we reviewed (Morgan, 1971) examined the effectiveness of a program in which language-minority children received instruction in their heritage language. In this case, the heritage language was French.

Findings   To evaluate the impact of bilingual education as compared with English-only instruction, we analyzed the estimated effect sizes from the 15 studies by using the *Comprehensive Meta-Analysis (CMA) Version 2* software (Borenstein, 2005). Appendix 6.B (Table 6.B.1) provides a table with results for each study, sample, outcome, and grade that went into the meta-analysis. For all studies, positive effect sizes indicate a difference favoring bilingual education, and negative effects indicate a difference favoring English-only instruction. Effect sizes were corrected to prevent small-sample bias (Hedges, 1981). In averaging across effect sizes, we treated each study sample as the unit of analysis. Thus, the 15 studies yielded 71 effect sizes across 26 samples. For the sake of computing average effect sizes, we averaged across different reading outcomes and grades within the same study sample to derive a weighted average for that study sample. These weighted average effect sizes appear in Table 6.1, along with their estimated standard errors and 95% confidence intervals. These weighted averages were then averaged to estimate the mean effect size and its standard error under each of two models: a fixed effects model and a random effects model. The weighted average across all study samples appears in Table 6.2, along with an estimate of the standard error, the lower and upper limits of a 95% confidence interval, and a test that the mean effect size equals zero. In addition to computing the average effect size across all studies, we also computed the mean separately for the studies that used randomization. This estimate appears in Table 6.2 as well. Finally, because Maldonado (1994) produced a somewhat larger effect size than the remaining randomized controlled trials, and because information reported in Maldonado (1994) was internally inconsistent indicating possible errors in our estimate of the effect size, we also computed the mean effect size separately for the randomized studies without Maldonado to assess the overall impact of this one large effect size on the mean estimate of the effects of the randomized studies. These estimates appear in the final two rows of Table 6.2.

Scanning Table 6.1 reveals a range of effect sizes from negative to positive, with at least some statistically significant positive and negative effect sizes (i.e., effect sizes that are statistically different from 0). Overall, 16 of the 26 estimated effect sizes are positive, 8 are negative, and 2 are 0. At the same time, only 7 of the 16 positive effect sizes have confidence intervals that exclude 0, and only 4 of the 8 negative effect sizes exclude 0. The effect sizes vary somewhat across the studies (Q =323.7, df =25, $p <$ .0001). Although the weighted average of the effect sizes is significant (mean =.18, SE =.033, $p <$ .0001 under the fixed effects model; mean =.33, SE =0.127, p =.011 under the random effects model; Table 6.2), there is variation in the results. For this reason, we separately examined the studies that used random assignment.

TABLE 6.1
Effect size statistics for individual studies

| | | | | Statistics for Each Study | | | | | |
RCT	Study Name	Subgroup Within Study	Hedges' g''	Standard Error	Variance	Lower Limit	Upper Limit	Z Value	p Value
Yes	Maldonado, 1994	Sample 1	2.1212	0.5440	0.2959	1.0550	3.1874	3.8992	.0001
	Saldate et al., 1985	Sample 1	-0.2829	0.2521	0.0636	-0.7770	0.2112	-1.1223	.2617
	de la Garza, 1985	Sample 1	0.1910	0.2194	0.0482	-0.2391	0.6211	0.8703	.3841
	Ramírez et al., 1991	Sample 1	0.1774	0.1484	0.0220	-0.1135	0.4684	1.1953	.2320
	Ramírez et al., 1991	Sample 2	0.0947	0.0954	0.0091	-0.0923	0.2817	0.9930	.3207
	Ramírez et al., 1991	Sample 3	0.0796	0.1049	0.0110	-0.1259	0.2852	0.7591	.4478
	Valladolid, 1991	Sample 1	-0.6052	0.1968	0.0387	-0.9909	-0.2196	-3.0758	.0021
	Alvarez, 1975	Sample 1	-0.1863	0.2390	0.0571	-0.6548	0.2822	-0.7795	.4357
	Alvarez, 1975	Sample 2	-0.2541	0.2389	0.0571	-0.7224	0.2142	-1.0634	.2876
	Campeau et al., 1975	Sample 2	1.8279	0.2426	0.0589	1.3523	2.3034	7.5340	.0000
	Campeau et al., 1975	Sample 3	1.3929	0.2628	0.0691	0.8778	1.9080	5.2999	.0000
	Campeau et al., 1975	Sample 5	2.6311	0.2230	0.0497	2.1941	3.0681	11.8001	.0000
	Campeau et al., 1975	Sample 6	0.2420	0.1357	0.0184	-0.0239	0.5080	1.7837	.0745
	Campeau et al., 1975	Sample 7	0.8540	0.1585	0.0251	0.5434	1.1646	5.3889	.0000
	Campeau et al., 1975	Sample 8	0.4553	0.1716	0.0294	0.1191	0.7916	2.6540	.0080
	Cohen et al., 1976	Sample 1	-0.1741	0.3904	0.1524	-0.9392	0.5911	-0.4459	.6557
	Cohen et al., 1976	Sample 2	-1.1518	0.4591	0.2108	-2.0516	-0.2519	-2.5087	.0121
	Cohen et al., 1976	Sample 3	-1.5981	0.5539	0.3068	-2.6838	-0.5125	-2.8851	.0039
	Danoff et al., 1978	Sample 1	-0.2621	0.0690	0.0048	-0.3974	-0.1269	-3.7992	.0001

(Continued)

TABLE 6.1
(Continued)

		Subgroup			Statistics for Each Study				
RCT	Study Name	Within Study Hedges' g^u	Standard Error	Variance	Lower Limit	Upper Limit	Z Value	p Value
Yes	Huzar, 1973	Sample 1	0.0136	0.2201	0.0485	−0.4178	0.4451	0.0619	.9506
Yes	Kaufman, 1968	Sample 1	0.0477	0.2355	0.0555	−0.4139	0.5092	0.2025	.8396
Yes	Kaufman, 1968	Sample 2	0.4696	0.2989	0.0893	−0.1161	1.0554	1.5714	.1161
	Maldonado, 1977	Sample 1	0.3580	0.1845	0.0340	−0.0036	0.7195	1.9404	.0523
Yes	Plante, 1976	Sample 1	0.7750	0.4097	0.1679	−0.0281	1.5780	1.8915	.0586
Yes	Covey, 1973	Sample 1	0.6583	0.1555	0.0242	0.3534	0.9631	4.2323	.0000
	Morgan, 1971	Sample 1	0.2541	0.1441	0.0208	−0.0283	0.5365	1.7635	.0778

Note: STANDARD errors do not take into account potential effects of clustering within studies. Confidence intervals, z-values, and p-values should be interpreted with caution.

TABLE 6.2
Statistics for Average Effect Sizes

Model	Studies Include	Statistics for Average Effect Size						
		Hedges' g''	Standard Error	Variance	Lower Limit	Upper Limit	Z Value	p Value
Fixed	All studies	0.1835	0.0329	0.0011	0.1191	0.2479	5.5838	.0000
Random	All studies	0.3251	0.1271	0.0162	0.0760	0.5743	2.5575	.0105
Fixed	RCTs	0.4515	0.0997	0.0099	0.2560	0.6470	4.5273	.0000
Random	RCTs	0.5380	0.2140	0.0458	0.1185	0.9574	2.5136	.0119
Fixed	RCTs except Maldonado, 1994	0.3934	0.1014	0.0103	0.1946	0.5923	3.8782	.0001
Random	RCTs except Maldonado, 1994	0.3650	0.1638	0.0268	0.0440	0.6859	2.2287	.0258

Separate examination of the randomized studies (6 samples and 12 individual effect sizes) produced a somewhat larger weighted average effect size that was also statistically different from 0 under both the fixed and random effects models (mean =0.45, SE =.11, p < .0001 under the fixed effects model; mean =.54, SE =0.21, p =.012 under the random effects model). In addition, the test for heterogeneity again showed that the effect sizes were not consistent across the studies (Q =18.7, df =5, p =.002), although in this case 4 of 6 effect sizes are positive and 2 fall between 0 and 0.05. That is, all effect sizes are in the same direction, but they vary in magnitude. These findings suggest a moderate advantage for bilingual education, but the analysis included one study with a very large effect size 2.12 (Maldonado, 1994) that might be exerting too much influence on this finding. There were several reporting problems in the Maldonado study (1994), and for that reason we reanalyzed the RCTs without this study. Again the weighted average of the treatment effects indicates a statistically significant, moderately sized, average treatment effect favoring bilingual approaches to literacy instruction (mean =.39, SE =.10, p < .0001 under the fixed effects model; mean =.365, SE =0.16, p =.026 under the random effects model). Eliminating Maldonado from the collection of all 26 effect sizes has a minimal effect on the estimates of average effect sizes, and does not alter the interpretation of findings.

In summary, it seems reasonably safe to conclude that bilingual education has a positive effect on English reading outcomes that is small to moderate in size. Unfortunately, many questions regarding how to make bilingual instruction maximally effective for students, and the factors that moderate this effectiveness, remain unanswered. We would have liked to conduct an exhaustive examination of potential moderator variables in the analyses conducted here, but, because of limited resources and time, could not do so. To the extent that the studies provided relevant information, such an analysis could yield some benefit to understanding the research literature and instructional effectiveness.

In addressing the inherent problem of selection bias, the studies of Huzar (1973) and Plante (1976) are particularly important, despite taking place a quarter of a century or more ago. Both were multiyear experiments for which, because of the use of random assignment, we can rule out selection bias as an explanation for the findings. Both started with children in the early elementary grades and followed them for 2 to 3 years. It is interesting that both used a model that would be unusual today—paired bilingual reading instruction provided by different teachers in Spanish and English, with transition to all-English instruction by second or third grade. The use of both Spanish and English reading instruction each day resembles the experience of Spanish-dominant students in two-way bilingual programs (see Calderón &

Minaya-Rowe, 2003) more than typical transitional bilingual models, which delay English reading instruction to second or third grade.

Only two studies of secondary programs met our inclusion criteria, but both were high-quality randomized experiments. Covey (1973) found substantial positive effects of Spanish instruction for low-achieving language-minority ninth graders, and Kaufman (1968) found mixed but slightly positive effects of a similar approach with low-achieving language-minority seventh graders.

Finally, with respect to language-minority students experiencing reading difficulties, Maldonado's (1994) study found dramatically higher achievement gains for learning-disabled children transitioned over a 3-year period from Spanish to English than for those taught only in English. Although the Maldonado (1994) study could not be appropriately combined statistically with the other studies, it is important to note that the results were nevertheless consistent with the overall analysis.

In summary, where differences between two instructional conditions were found, these differences typically favored the bilingual instruction condition both with elementary and secondary students, and across a range of abilities. Moreover, children in the bilingual programs not only developed facility with English literacy to the same extent as their peers taught in English, but also developed literacy skills in their native language. Thus, they achieved the advantage of being bilingual and biliterate.

The studies reviewed here evidenced many flaws. Future research into this question would do better if it randomly assigned a large number of children to be taught in English or their native language; these students would be pretested on outcomes of interest, as well as on language proficiency in their first and second languages; and the students' progress would be followed long enough for the latest-transitioning children in the bilingual condition to have completed their transition to English and have been taught long enough in English to permit a fair comparison. In addition, researchers would carefully document the nature and quality of the instruction. Unfortunately, only a few small studies of this kind have ever been conducted As a result, the findings of studies that have compared bilingual and English-only approaches must continue to be interpreted with great caution. (The Institute for Education Sciences is currently funding three quasi-experimental studies comparing outcomes for students taught in English only with those taught with some use of the native language.)

Effective Literacy Teaching

In this section, we focus on studies of two fundamental approaches to literacy improvement: (a) one that examines enhanced instruction in particular elements of literacy (phonemic awareness, phonics, sight vocabulary, meaning vocabulary, oral reading fluency, reading comprehension, writing, and spelling), and (b) one that examines all other interventions aimed at improving literacy among English-language learners. This section only includes intervention studies that employed experimental, quasi-experimental, or single-subject designs.[1] Appendix 6.C (Table 6.C.1) reports information about the instructional approach employed in each study.

Elements of Literacy. We found only 17 studies addressing effects of explicitly teaching phonemic awareness, phonics, oral reading fluency, meaning vocabulary, reading comprehension, and writing that met the inclusion criteria outlined earlier, and we found no such studies of instruction in spelling or sight vocabulary for language-minority students. By comparison, the National Reading Panel reviewed more than 400 studies on these topics for native English speakers, and that report did not deal with writing and did not review doctoral dissertations or technical reports as we did. With so few studies available, we could not perform a true meta-analysis for any of the literacy components (there were never three conceptually comparable studies on any of the elements). Table 6.3 includes effect sizes for instructional approaches aimed at enhanced teaching of specific literacy elements.

Phonemic awareness instruction helps young children to hear the separate sounds (the phonemes) within words, and phonics instruction teaches the relationships between letters and sounds and how to use these relationships to pronounce printed words. Research shows that explicit phonemic awareness and phonics instruction confers an early learning advantage for first-language students. For instance, the National Reading Panel examined 52 studies of phonological awareness instruction and another 38 studies of phonics instruction, and these studies consistently showed that this kind of instruction was effective with young children, as determined by a wide range of measures, including beginning reading comprehension. In contrast, we could only find five small studies that examined the teaching of phonological awareness and phonics to language-minority children (Gunn, Biglan, Smolkowski, &

---

[1]An experiment randomly assigns students to the experimental and control groups, whereas a quasi-experiment assigns preexisting groups to conditions and uses statistical controls to account for characteristics on which the groups may differ. Single-subject designs measure baseline performance and then intervene with some type of instruction; the learning is closely monitored for each subject, and various procedures are used to increase the possibility that this learning is due to the intervention (well-designed single-subject studies can strongly suggest causation, but not with the same degree of certainty as can a comparable-quality randomized control trial). We can increase our certainty about the effectiveness of a given approach further when a study is replicated; this simply means that the study has been carried out multiple times with the same results.

TABLE 6.3
Effect Sizes for Instructional Approaches Aimed at Enhanced Teaching of Specific Literacy Elements to English-Language Learners[a]

Study	N	Grade	Home Language	Type of Study[b]	Pretest Differences[c]	Treatment Duration[d]	Effect Size	Confidence Interval	Signif
Phonemic awareness & phonics									
Gunn et al., 2000	184	K–3	Spanish	RCT	No	21 weeks	.29	.07–.52	Yes
Gunn et al., 2002	117	K–3	Spanish	RCT	No	2 weeks	.38	.22–.55	Yes
Kramer et al., 1983	15	1–3	Spanish	RCT	No	4 weeks	*	—	Yes
Larson, 1996	33	1	Spanish	RCT	No	7 weeks	2.82	1.83–3.82	Yes
Stuart, 1999	112	Pre & K	Sylheti	Quasi-Exp.	Yes	12 weeks	.46	.38–.55	Yes
Oral reading fluency									
De La Colina et al., 2001	74	1–2	Spanish	Single Subject	No	12 weeks	*	—	
Denton, 2000	93	2–5	Spanish	RCT	No	8 weeks	.05	-.10–.49	No
Vocabulary									
Carlo et al., 2004	142	5	Spanish	Quasi-Exp.	*	15 weeks	*	—	Yes
Pérez, 1981	75	3	Spanish	RCT	No	13 weeks	1.12	.78–1.47	Yes
Vaughn-Shavuo, 1990	30	1	Spanish	RCT	No	3 weeks	1.40	.59–2.18	Yes
Reading comprehension									
Bean, 1982	45	4–5	Spanish	RCT	No	1 day	*	—	
Shames, 1998	58	9–11	Haitian Creole	Quasi-Exp.	Yes	36 weeks	.20	-.36–.75	No
Swicegood, 1990	95	3	Spanish	Quasi-Exp.	*	6 weeks	.05	-.35–.45	No

(Continued)

TABLE 6.3
(Continued)

Study	N	Grade	Home Language	Type of Study[b]	Pretest Differences[c]	Treatment Duration[d]	Effect Size	Confidence Interval	Signif
Writing									
Franken et al., 1999	20	9–12	Mixed	RCT	No	6 weeks	–.16	–46–13	No
Gómez et al., 1996	72	5	Spanish	RCT	No	6 weeks	.32	.18–45	Yes
Prater et al., 1993	46	4–6	Spanish	RCT	No	3 weeks	.60	.30–90	Yes
Sengupta, 2000	100	9–12	Chinese	Quasi-Exp.	Yes	36 weeks	.81	.36–1.24	Yes

[a] If the literary outcome measures were in the students' home language, the study is printed in italics. Only one of these studies used home-language measures.

[b] RCT = Randomized controlled trial; Quasi-Exp. = quasi-experiment; Single Subject = single-subject or multibaseline design.

[c] For quasi-experimental studies; this indicates whether some kind of statistical adjustment was necessary because of pretest differences in the sample.

[d] Treatment duration is an estimate of the number of weeks of treatment (often the original studies indicated a number of months or a starting and ending date).

* Insufficient information provided in the article to allow determination.

Ary, 2000; Gunn, Smolkowski, Biglan, & Black, 2002; Kramer, Schell, & Rubison, 1983; Larson, 1996; Stuart, 1999). Despite the paucity of studies, the findings of all five of these studies are consistent with the overall findings of the first-language research (only one of these studies measured reading comprehension).

Additional research is needed both to replicate these findings and to help determine whether special routines or emphases are needed in these areas in teaching English-language learners from various language backgrounds. The study of Kramer *et al.* (1983) aimed specifically at evaluating instruction designed to help students hear sounds that could be confusing for those of a particular language background. Other studies of this type might be useful in helping to design instructional approaches to phonological awareness and phonics that would be particularly effective with specific populations of English-language learners.

There is more to reading than just decoding, however. Students need to develop fluency with reading, meaning that they need to be able to accurately read words in text, to read these words with sufficient speed, and to read with proper expression so that the reading sounds meaningful (i.e., with the appropriate prosodic shape to permit language interpretation—including pausing, emphasis, etc.). The National Reading Panel reviewed the results of 51 studies on the teaching of oral reading fluency, and concluded that such teaching was beneficial to students. Oral reading fluency instruction had a positive impact on these students' word recognition skills, fluency, and reading comprehension. Despite the attention devoted to fluency teaching for native speakers, we found only two such studies with English-language learners (De la Colina, Parker, Hasbrouck, & Lara-Alecio, 2001; Denton, 2000). Both studies reported positive results, indicating that oral reading fluency instruction was beneficial to second-language learners.

Word meaning or vocabulary is another important component of literacy learning. Reading comprehension depends greatly upon the reader's accurate interpretation of the meanings of the words in a text. The National Reading Panel reviewed 45 studies on the teaching of vocabulary to first-language students, and found consistent improvements in reading comprehension due to such teaching. Given the fundamental importance of vocabulary to reading comprehension and the obvious limitations in the vocabulary knowledge of English-language learners (who have not had the same opportunity as native speakers for oral exposure to English words before learning to read), it is surprising that we found only three experimental studies of English vocabulary teaching, one of which was brief (Carlo *et al.* 2004; Perez, 1981; Vaughn-Shavuo, 1990). Nevertheless, all three of these studies revealed a positive benefit in learning to read due to the vocabulary teaching, consistent with the evidence for first-language students.

While decoding, fluency, and vocabulary instruction all have been shown to influence reading comprehension, it is possible to teach students comprehension strategies as well. Such teaching usually emphasizes the use of organized ways of thinking about the information in a text; for example, students might be taught to compare what they know with the text information, how to ask and answer one's own questions about a text, or how to summarize what is read. The National Reading Panel reviewed 205 studies of such instructional strategies, and concluded that strategy instruction conveyed a clear learning advantage for first-language students.

In contrast, we found only three studies that examined ways of teaching reading comprehension to English-language learners (Bean, 1982; Shames, 1998; Swicegood, 1990), and these had some inconsistent results. From this it is clear that such instruction *can* help language-minority students to read better, but much more research would be needed to determine the best ways to promote reading comprehension.

Another important dimension of literacy is writing, that is being able to communicate one's own ideas through written language. The importance of writing and its relationship to reading has been clearly demonstrated (Tierney & Shanahan, 1992), and a recent review of experimental/quasi-experimental studies included 116 studies that focused on writing instruction with first-language students (Graham & Perin, in press). These studies showed that there were many effective ways of helping students to write better.

In contrast, we found only four experimental studies of writing instruction with English-language learners (Franken & Haslett, 1999; Gomez, Parker, Lara-Alecio, & Gomez, 1996; Prater & Bermudez, 1993; Sengupta, 2000). Generally, these studies found that language-minority students benefit from structured writing procedures in which students are explicitly taught to write well, and from peer-editing approaches in which students revise their writing on the basis of feedback from others. Again, these findings are consistent with the findings drawn from research on first-language students.

With so few experimental studies on instruction in any of the individual components of literacy and with such great variability in study designs, it is difficult to generalize from the findings. It seems fair to say that these 17 studies yielded results that are largely consistent with the findings for native-speaking populations. Although these results are insufficient to prove that the same instructional routines found to benefit native speakers are equally effective with English-language learners, they in no way contradict this idea (Fitzgerald, 1995a, 1995b).

It is important to note that of the 17 studies synthesized here, only 6 employed comprehension measures. When comprehension was included, the studies were less likely to find benefits from the instruction (e.g., Denton, 2000). Also, when reading improvements were observed, they were less pronounced if reading comprehension was included in the battery of measures (e.g., Gunn, Biglan *et al.*, 2000; Gunn, Smolkowski *et al.*, 2002). Overall, the effects observed in these studies were somewhat smaller than those reported for the comparable National Reading Panel studies, and this was especially true for reading comprehension. (One exception to this was vocabulary; explicit vocabulary instruction with second-language students had bigger impacts on learning than was usually reported in the first-language studies.)

The limited English proficiency of the language-minority students may be implicated in these findings. In the area of phonics instruction, for example, the National Reading Panel found that for English-speaking students, phonics instruction had a consistently positive impact on all literacy measures for beginning readers, but only on decoding outcomes for students in the upper elementary grades. It may be wise to provide phonics support for older students who are struggling with reading, but only in the context of instruction in other literacy elements including vocabulary and comprehension. Phonics shows students how to decode, which helps them as long as the words they are trying to decode are in their oral language repetoire. English-language learners may lack oral counterparts for the words they decode; under such circumstances, the impact of phonics on text comprehension will be more variable and less certain. The same could be said of oral reading fluency instruction and comprehension instruction, both of which show substantial impacts on the reading comprehension of native English speakers, but a much smaller impact on English-language learners. Both of these may work better when students have greater facility with oral English.

The positive findings for these studies suggest that teaching specific reading and writing elements can be beneficial to second-language students. The smaller effect sizes, however, particularly for reading comprehension, suggest the potential importance of building greater knowledge of oral English simultaneously so the literacy tools provided by instruction can be used to maximum advantage. Chapter 3 showed the implications of oral language proficiency in reading comprehension, and those findings suggest the potential importance of greater oral language development in order to obtain maximum benefit from the types of instruction evaluated here.

Furthermore, that instruction in the literacy elements benefits English-language learners much in the way it does native-English learners, does not mean that there is no need to adjust these instructional approaches to make them effective with English-language learners (Gersten & Baker, 2000). Indeed, some of the studies reviewed here allude to such adjustments. For example, it may be useful to give greater attention to particular sounds (those not in the first language) when working to build auditory discrimination skills in English-language learners (Kramer *et al.*, 1983). Similarly, teaching English vocabulary is effective, but progress may be most rapid when this instruction is connected to the students' home language, such as by providing a home-language equivalent or synonym for new words or focusing on shared cognates when available. (The issue here is not whether the students' home language should be taught as part of literacy instruction, but whether it should be used as the basis for some aspects of this instruction.) Future research needs to be more explicit about the kinds of adjustments for English-language learners that are made in successful programs.

Complex Approaches. Not all attempts to improve literacy instruction focus on individual literacy elements. In many cases, the effort at improvement tries to address instruction in multiple aspects of literacy simultaneously or addresses the elements more indirectly or in a less targeted manner. Unfortunately, there were few experimental studies that examined the effectiveness of these more complex innovations aimed at improving the literacy performance of English-language learners. With so few studies of any given approach—even when the results were promising—it is not possible to conclude that any of these approaches consistently confers an advantage to learners. We would characterize the quality of research evidence in this area as weak to moderate in terms of rigor of design and certainty of conclusions the studies allow. Table 6.4 displays effect sizes for instructional approaches aimed at enhanced teaching approaches of multiple literacy elements.

One example of this kind of approach is Success for All (SFA). SFA is a complex instructional program that initially teaches language-minority students in their home language, that restructures classrooms, targets several of the elements of literacy, and provides monitoring of learning and tutoring for students who struggle. The effect of SFA on the reading development of English-language learners was examined in three separate studies that met our selection criteria (Dianda & Flaherty, 1995; and a technical report that includes two studies, Slavin & Madden, 1998), and a positive impact was demonstrated in each of these for at least some literacy measures.

Similarly, it is widely claimed that encouraging students to read will have a positive impact on reading achievement, due to the additional practice that would be stimulated. The results from studies on encouraging language-minority students to read more (Elley, 1991; Tsang, 1996; Tudor & Hafiz, 1989; Schon, Hopkins, & Davis, 1982; Schon, Hopkins, & Vojir, 1984, 1985) indicated that encouraging students to read English text, such as by providing reading materials and time for students to read, had a positive impact on English reading

TABLE 6.4
Effect Sizes for Instructional Approaches Aimed at Enhanced Teaching of Multiple Literacy Elements to English-Language Learners[a]

Study	Intervention	N	Grade	Home Language	Type of Study[b]	Pretest Diff.[c]	Treatment Duration[d]	Effect Size	Confidence Interval	Signif.
Encouraging reading & writing										
Elley, 1991		535	4-5	Fijian	Quasi	Yes	72 weeks	.60	.53-.66	Yes
		459	5-6							
Schon et al., 1982		114	2-4	Spanish	Quasi	Yes	32 weeks	*	–	No
Schon et al., 1984		272	9-12	Spanish	Quasi	Yes	17-30 weeks	-.08	-.38-.21	No
Schon et al., 1985		400	7-8	Spanish	Quasi	Yes	34 weeks	-.20	-.52 to .12	No
Tudor et al., 1989		45	4-5	Panjabi	Quasi	No	13 weeks	*	–	Yes
Tsang, 1996		144	8-12	Cantonese	RCT	No	20 weeks	.27	.11-.24	Yes
Reading to children										
Hancock, 2002		77	K	Spanish	RCT	No	57 weeks	.66	.10-1.22	Yes
Hastings-Góngora, 1993		11	K	Spanish	RCT	No	5 weeks	*	*	No
Ulanoff et al., 1999		60	3	Spanish	Quasi	Yes	1 day	*	*	Yes
Tutoring & remediation										
Escamilla, 1994		46	1	Spanish	Quasi	*	12-16 weeks	1.15	.87-1.43	Yes
Syvanen, 1997		16	4-5	?	Quasi	Yes	19 weeks	.12	-.41-.67	No
Other investigations										
Calderón et al., 1998	Cooperative group	222	2-3	Spanish	Quasi	Yes	72 weeks	.59	.14-1.03	Yes
Cohen et al., 1980	Mastery learning	150	1	Spanish	RCT	No	4 weeks	.51	.28-.74	Yes

(Continued)

TABLE 6.4
(Continued)

Study	Intervention	N	Grade	Home Language	Type of Study[b]	Pretest Diff.[c]	Treatment Duration[d]	Effect Size	Confidence Interval	Signif.
Goldenberg et al., 1992	Parents	10	K	Spanish	Quasi	No	36 weeks	.53	-.20–1.26	No
Neuman et al., 1992	Captioned TV	129	7–8	Mixed	Quasi	Yes	12 weeks	.55	.37–.71	Yes
Saunders, 1999	Multi-year bilingual transition program	125	2–5	Spanish	Quasi	No	144 weeks	.57	.04–1.10	Yes
Saunders et al., 1999	Instructional conversations and literature logs	116	4–5	Spanish	RCT	No	4 days	.55	.25–.85	Yes
Tharp, 1982	Kamehameha Early Educ Program	204	1	Hawaiian	RCT	No	36 weeks	.20	.13–.45	Yes
Waxman et al., 1994	Time use	88	1–5	Spanish	Quasi	Yes	26 weeks	.65	.36–.94	Yes
	Content ESL	52	1–5	Spanish	Quasi	No	26 weeks	.01	-.32–.34	No
Success for all										
Dianda et al., 1995		147	K–1	Spanish	Quasi	No	72 weeks	.76	—	Yes
Slavin et al., 1998: AZ		138	1	Spanish	Quasi	No	36 weeks	.45	.27–.63	Yes
Slavin et al., 1998: Fairhill		50	1–3	Spanish	Quasi	Yes	72 weeks	.20	-.12–.53	No

[a] If the literacy outcome measures were in the students' home language, the study is printed in italics. Only three of these studies used home-language measures.

[b] RCT = Randomized controlled trial; Quasi = quasi-experiment.

[c] For quasi-experimental studies; this indicates whether some kind of statistical adjustment was necessary because of pretest differences in the sample.

[d] Treatment duration is an estimate of the number of weeks of treatment (often the original studies indicated a number of months or a starting and ending date).

* Insufficient information provided in the article to allow determination.

outcomes. Similar efforts to increase the amount of reading in the home languages did not show any immediate impact on English reading, however.

Reading aloud to children is widely touted as a way to increase reading achievement, but the quality of evidence on such reading with language-minority children is so limited that the best we can say is that students may be able to develop English vocabulary through this approach (Hancock, 2002; Hastings-Gongora, 1993; Ulanoff & Pucci, 1999).

Two studies investigated tutoring and remediation efforts with second-language students (Escamilla, 1994; Syvanen, 1997) and these showed positive effects. Likewise, studies of enhanced literature discussions and extended language arts routines showed promise, but two of the three studies of these approaches considered the impact of this kind of instruction only upon student performance on single lessons, rather than on more general literacy achievement (Saunders, 1999; Saunders & Goldenberg, 1999; Tharp, 1982). Cooperative grouping conferred a benefit (Calderón, Hertz-Larawitz, & Slavin, 1998), as did captioned TV (Neuman & Koskinen, 1992), but these results were drawn from single studies, so further investigation is needed to confirm these findings.

There are obviously too few studies of any of these interventions to allow the conclusion that any of these approaches will consistently lead to literacy improvement for language minority children. However, taking the entire set of studies together, some important insights into effective instruction for English-language learners can be drawn. For example, it is evident, given the consistency of the positive findings here, that efforts to improve the literacy instruction of language-minority children have a good chance of success. There is no reason to believe, on the basis of these studies, that the improvement of instruction for these students is too difficult to undertake.

Also, when improvement in reading comprehension was used as an outcome measure, as was done in 18 of the 22 studies, it is evident that the results are less positive than when reading comprehension is omitted. Even more telling than this is the fact that, for any comparison made in these 22 studies, all failures to accomplish significant differences were for reading comprehension. Two of the three studies with positive results that included reading comprehension as an outcome measure (Dianda & Flaherty, 1995; Elley, 1991; Tharp, 1982) reported less improvement on comprehension than on the other measures used. It is fair to say that sizable positive reading comprehension outcomes were relatively rare, and that future efforts to improve reading achievement for English-learners need to put much greater emphasis on building the background knowledge, language development, and cognitive tools needed to comprehend well.

Finally, efforts to provide students with substantial experience with English (such as by encouraging them to read English-language materials beyond the instructional day or reading to them to build their vocabulary) have shown some value. This pattern of results is evident in studies that encouraged students to read as well as in those aimed at developing more thorough discussion routines around literature.

Qualitative Studies of Classroom and School Practices

This section examines schooling practices and contexts related to literacy development in language-minority students. It addresses, respectively, (a) instructional techniques designed to improve specific components of literacy, (b) comprehensive instructional programs designed to build literacy, (c) effective classrooms and schools, and (d) school change. Although some studies in this chapter examine factors addressed in the previous two sections, the treatment of these studies in this section is different in that it reviews case studies and ethnographic research rather than experimental and quasi-experimental studies.

Instructional Techniques Designed to Improve Specific Components of Literacy. We describe approaches designed to teach basic, word-level skills (word recognition, decoding, and spelling), text- or discourse-level skills (vocabulary, reading comprehension, reading fluency, and writing), or to target both kinds of skills concurrently, and to increase students' participation in classroom discourse and literacy-related behavior.

The teaching methods examined in this collection of studies vary widely. They included a Spanish version of Reading Recovery called *Descubriendo la Lectura* (Escamilla & Andrade, 1992); a phonological awareness and phonics program (Hus, 2001); instruction in reading strategies, in some cases using reciprocal teaching as a method of developing students' strategy use (Hernández, 1991; Wright, 1997); collaborative strategic reading, intended to promote content learning, language acquisition, and comprehension (Klingner & Vaughn, 2000); sustained silent reading (Pilgreen & Krashen, 1983); reading clubs (Kreuger & Townshend, 1997); paired reading (Li & Nes, 2001); and efforts to increase student discourse (Martínez-Roldan & López-Robertson, 2000) or literacy-related outcomes (Genishi, Stires, & Yung-Chan, 2001; Kenner, 1999; Ramos & Krashen, 1998). Some studies investigated whether methods of instruction used with native speakers of English helped Spanish-speaking language-minority students if the instructional materials or techniques were translated and used in the students' first language—in these cases, Spanish (Escamilla & Andrade, 1992; Hernández, 1991). The remaining studies investigated instructional methods derived from research and theory on language acquisition for native English speakers; this instruction was delivered in English.

Studies focused on a spectrum of grade levels, from kindergarten through high school. Those examining word-level skills targeted children in kindergarten through third grade, whereas those emphasizing text-level skills targeted children in the upper elementary grades and high school. There was also variation in the student samples. Studies included struggling learners (Escamilla & Andrade, 1992; Kreuger & Townshend, 1977; Wright, 1997), those solely limited in English proficiency (Hernández, 1991; Li & Nes, 2001), and those with a mix of proficiency levels (Genishi et al., 2001; Hus, 2001; Kenner, 1999; Martínez-Roldan & López-Robertson, 2000; Pilgreen & Krashen, 1983; Ramos & Krashen, 1998; Wolf, 1993).

In general, the findings of these studies are consistent with those reported in the previous section. Because many of these are case studies or evaluation studies, their designs do not allow us to preclude alternative explanations of the results they report. Other factors may have led to the positive student outcomes, including regular classroom instruction (many of the instructional approaches were delivered outside of regular instruction) or students' maturation. As in the previous section, these studies suggest that instructional emphasis on key reading components improved students' literacy learning. Students who were taught phonics explicitly improved their phonological awareness and decoding skills (Escamilla & Andrade, 1992; Hus, 2001). Instruction aimed at building comprehension skills more directly suggest that language-minority students may benefit from instructional approaches that are effective with monolingual students (Palincsar & Brown, 1984, 1985; Paris, Cross, & Lipson, 1984). Students improved in comprehension in Spanish, English vocabulary, the abilty to identify factual, interpretive, and evaluative statements, and to respond effectively to literature in English through various instructional approaches including reciprocal teaching (Hernández, 1991), collaborative group work (Klingner & Vaughn, 2000), or metacognitive strategies instruction (Wright, 1997). The students in the other studies that also borrowed from the first-language literacy research—SSR (Pilgreen & Krashen, 1983), an approach modeled on Reading Recovery (Kreuger & Townshend, 1997), and the use of paired reading (Li & Nes, 2001)—also improved in the targeted skills (reading ability, interest in reading and reading habits, oral English reading, English reading accuracy and fluency).

As with the findings of quasi-experimental research reported in the previous section, however, some of the approaches found to be successful have attributes that would make them especially suitable for English-language learners. Two studies (Escamilla & Andrade, 1992; Hernández, 1991) provided instruction in students' native language—in this case,

Spanish. In addition, several studies focused on making English word meanings clear through such techniques as picture cues (Hus, 2001) and other techniques (Kreuger & Townshend, 1997); extracting the meaning of text by identifying and clarifying difficult words and passages (Klingner & Vaughn, 2000); consolidating text knowledge through summarization (Klingner & Vaughn, 2000); and providing extra practice reading words, sentences, and stories (Pilgreen & Krashen, 1983; Wright, 1997).

These studies raise some important issues about the nature of effective literacy instruction. One issue that emerges from these studies has to do with strategy use versus teacher's scaffolding of text as a mechanism for improving students' comprehension. For example, Hernández (1991) presumably focused on teaching students strategy use. However, the teacher did many things that scaffolded instruction: The researcher/teacher started the lesson by discussing students' experiences related to the story content and introducing new vocabulary, and concluded the lesson by framing questions for group response, summarizing part of the text for group response, prompting predictions, and clarifying ambiguities. Student leaders gradually took over this role. Future studies on strategy use would benefit from clearly distinguishing the two methods of building comprehension, as well as pairing assessments of strategy use with measures of actual literacy skills (e.g., comprehension or writing) to look at outcomes more broadly.

Another issue relates to differential effects of the approaches studied on students with varying degrees of English proficiency (Klingner & Vaughn, 2000) and capability, with some students needing more intensive or qualitatively different types of instruction (Kreuger & Townshend, 1997; Wright, 1997). In the Kreuger and Townshend study, for example, four students did not benefit from an intervention, possibly because they had multiple learning problems. In the Wright study, the low scores of some students are attributed to students' intellectual and social difficulties. The English-language learners in Klingner and Vaughn's study made the smallest gains in vocabulary. Language-minority students are a highly heterogeneous group, and the various approaches studied must be interpreted in this light and designed to take these differences into account.

The studies reviewed in the preceding section can help inform the design of instructional methods and strategies. However, because the studies were prospective case studies, and as such did not employ control groups, the findings are only suggestive. Approaches that appear to effect positive change should be submitted to more rigorous evaluations using experimental or quasi-experimental designs. Other methodological issues that weaken these studies include the brief duration of the instructional approach used in many of the studies and the use of researcher-developed outcome measures with no reported information about validity or reliability or the relationship to standardized assessments commonly used to measure the same literacy constructs in children.

This section has also reviewed studies that looked at students' participation in literacy learning. One study reviewed here explored students' participation in classroom discourse related to literacy events (Martínez-Roldan & López-Robertson, 2000) and two studies involved unique classroom situations associated with literacy development (Kenner, 1999; Ramos & Krashen, 1998). The rich detail provided by the authors of the subset of these ethnographic studies provide a window into how students engage in classroom literacy events. However, there is scant information about how the representative examples were selected or about their frequency or typicality. Such studies can be valuable, but it would further our understanding of literacy development greatly if such studies linked their observations to student learning outcomes. One cannot assume that increased discourse in English will translate into improved literacy outcomes. In examining child–child interactions, Saville-Troike (1984) found that "three of the five highest achieving students (in English) used their native languages with peers to the virtual exclusion of English, while the other two top achievers rarely spoke to other children during ESL or regular classroom sessions" (p. 209).

Comprehensive Instructional Programs. The studies reviewed in this section provide insights into more complex or complete approaches to literacy instruction, including approaches that do not target a specific literacy element or that target multiple elements simultaneously. While all the studies reviewed here examined comprehensive programs or components of such programs, the nature of the programs and their goals varied considerably. Three of the studies examined students' overall literacy development in balanced-literacy programs (Fitzgerald & Noblit, 1999, 2000; Kucer & Silva, 1999). A fourth study (Araujo, 2002) explored kindergarten English-language learners' development in a curriculum consisting of circle reading, phonics/handwriting, and journal writing. A fifth study (Kucer, 1999) compared the responses of two students to whole-language instruction they received in one classroom. A sixth study (Kuball & Peck, 1997) considered students' writing development in whole-language instruction. A seventh study (Pérez, 1994) examined what Spanish-dominant students learned during whole-language Spanish instruction. The remaining studies focused on the development of specific aspects of students' reading and writing performance when exposed to specific instructional techniques delivered within the context of the designated instructional model. These instructional techniques include strategy wall charts aimed at overcoming blocks when reading, writing, or spelling (Kucer, 1995); dialogue journals and literature logs (Reyes, 1991); a writer's workshop (Au & Carroll, 1997); and cloze lessons (Kucer, 1992).

Although the participants in these studies represent a range of language backgrounds (Portuguese, Spanish, Native Hawaiian) and ages (kindergarten through sixth grade), most of the studies focused on children whose home language was Spanish, and no studies addressed middle or high school students. The approaches to studying these programs were varied, but in most cases, both qualitative and quantitative data were gathered in the same classrooms so that researchers could construct hypotheses about classroom practices and measure students' literacy growth and ultimate attainment. These studies' careful examination of the details of these practices contributes to our understanding of the complexity involved in implementing effective literacy instruction with language-minority students.

The studies described (a) document activities intended to promote extended oral and written discourse; (b) create venues where speaking, reading, and writing are interrelated; and (c) provide opportunities for students to actively construct knowledge using authentic literature, rich discussions around text, and process approaches to writing. They are grounded in the theory that language mediates learning (Vygotsky, 1978), and that children construct knowledge through their engagement in peer interactions and through scaffolded interactions with adults (Spivey, 1997). Many of the programs document improvement in selected facets of children's language and literacy development: spelling and word recognition (Aruajo, 2002), phonological awareness, word-recognition strategies, word meaning, global knowledge of reading, sentiments of wanting to read, and more mature communicative competence (Fitzgerald & Noblit, 2000); composition skills for Spanish-speaking students and graphophonemic literacy for some students (Kuball & Peck, 1997); meaning construction and knowledge of grammatical relations, as well as retelling ability (Pérez, 1994); language sense (production of more syntactically and semantically acceptable sentences) and improvements in story retelling, writing, and spelling (Kucer & Silva, 1999); and writing (Au & Carroll, 1997).

However, although the studies document the progress that some students make in developing literacy, they also highlight that this progress is not uniform, with the same instructional program producing differential student outcomes. Some students develop language and literacy skills, whereas others do not progress at the same pace. For example, Araujo (2002) indicates that, "while most children made some progress, the range between modest and dramatic improvement was widespread" (p. 244). Fitzgerald and Noblit (2000) document the differential growth in reading in which "at the end of the year, lowest readers performed as their better-reading counterparts did at midyear" (p. 17). Kuball and Peck (1997) indicate that, although 25% of the students achieved advanced-level graphophonemic literacy skills for kindergarten children, 75% of the English-language learners remained at the prephonemic level. Pérez (1994) notes that, although 16 students improved in their use of meaning construction and grammatical relations, 6 students did not.

A conclusion that might be drawn from these findings is that, even within theory-based instructional programs, some children will need additional support to keep pace with their classmates. Also, although some authors claim that the reason some children do not make progress is that "they were not developmentally ready" (Kuball & Peck, 1997, p. 227), others (Kucer & Silva, 1999; Pérez, 1994) suggest the need for more balanced approaches that includes explicit instruction in phonics and writing (a claim that is consistent with the findings reported in the previous section on Effective Literacy Teaching).

One important theme in these studies is the value of attending to the individual needs of students, since English-language learners are not a homogeneous group. For example, Fitzgerald and Noblit (2000) used varied approaches to meet the needs of various students. The teacher provided a variety of daily reading activities in varied settings. The teacher also held reading meetings with students grouped according to their achievement level. She provided a classroom library organized by reading level from which children could choose books to read. During writing, each child was given individual attention by either the teacher or her instructional aide. Finally, for the English-language learners in the class, the teacher altered her instruction by incorporating such tactics as speaking more slowly and using simpler vocabulary, but she did not alter her expectations and did not change the language of instruction for these students. When teachers do not accommodate individual differences, students may have more difficulty acquiring literacy. Kucer (1999) found that two English-language learners responded differently to whole-language curriculum because of different interests and concerns. One child responded well to the teacher's whole-language approach, but the other was unable to respond successfully to the curriculum as presented.

Teachers' expectations for students with differing levels of English proficiency, and instructional approaches aligned with the expectations, may influence students' literacy development. In a study conducted by Neufeld and Fitzgerald (2001), the teacher's expectations for the English-language learners in her low reading group (she believed that they could not learn to read before they had requisite levels of oral proficiency) and the consequent instructional emphasis (e.g, focusing on the alphabet, spelling, neat writing, and oral English with little systematic and sustained practice in word reading) resulted in students' failure on an end-of-year reading measure.

In these studies, teaching is shown to play an important role in students' success. For example, Kucer (1999) attributes one child's failure with the curriculum in part to its delivery, described as routinized and unchanging throughout the school year. Although the instructional mediations offered by the teacher appeared to be sufficient for one child, the researcher suggests that the other student might have benefited from "instructional detours," events that focus on a particular difficulty a child is having (Cazden, 1992). The data show that, rather than taking these detours, the teacher simply repeated the same instructions when the child's performance was lacking. The results of these studies also indicate that the level of teacher scaffolding may be important during whole-language instruction. For example, in Kucer's (1995) study, although the focus of instruction was ostensibly on student strategy use, the teacher spent a lot of class time working with students to ensure they understood the text; in response groups, the teacher read the book chorally with the students a second time and then discussed the text from a variety of perspectives, clarifying things students did not understand.

The studies indicate that the nature of the language in which children are learning to read matters. Spanish-speaking children instructed in Spanish mastered decoding skills more easily than did English-speaking children instructed in English (Kuball & Peck, 1997). This is likely related to the differences between English and Spanish in the depth of the orthography of the respective languages.

An important finding from two studies (Fitzgerald & Noblit, 2000; Neufeld & Fitzgerald, 2001) is that, with the exception of vocabulary, although students may progress at different rates, their growth follows similar paths. The implication is that, over time, with good instruction, lower-level readers will ultimately attain the same goals as higher-level readers. As noted previously, this may be the case, but some children may need more intensive and qualitatively different kinds of interventions (National Institute for Child Health and Human Development, 2000) if they are going to catch up more quickly to their monolingual peers. Moreover, although they may eventually catch up in other literacy skills, it was not the case for vocabulary. At the end of first grade, all but one of the English-language learners scored in the bottom half of the class on one test of knowledge of English word meanings.

Professional development can play an important role in improving instruction. Several of the studies document teachers using classroom routines and strategies that appeared ineffective with English-language learners (Kucer, 1999; Reyes 1991). The authors suggest that mentoring and professional development may have made a difference in these circumstances. For example, in the study by Reyes, "although the literature journals and logs indicated that the students either did not comprehend or could not produce in English what they did comprehend" (p. 309), the teacher did not modify her teaching to accommodate students' needs. More specifically, she did not help students select books that were at an appropriate reading level or monitor and scaffold their reading. The KEEP experience (Au & Carroll, 1997) highlights the importance of supporting teacher change and the need for systems that are intensive, elaborate, and enduring to accomplish this change. In the KEEP program, there was intensive mentoring by the KEEP consultants; as noted in the study description, each consultant worked with only one to three project teachers and observed and mentored in classrooms twice a week. This level of support is considerably more than occurs in most schools. The authors advocate providing teachers with sustained coaching so they can develop the practices necessary to succeed, including organizing the classroom to support a constructivist approach, creating opportunities for student-centered learning, employing appropriate instructional practices, and developing an assessment system tied to instruction. Two critical tools in supporting teacher change were the classroom implementation checklist and grade-appropriate benchmarks used to assess student progress.

The studies also demonstrate that teachers may have received professional development in implementing popular programs like Writer's Workshop. However, because the workshops did not focus on how to modify the approaches to suit the linguistic needs of English-language learners, the instructional strategies that teachers learned and were implementing may not have been appropriate (Reyes, 1991).

Effective Classrooms and Schools.   Largely in response to findings by researchers (Coleman *et al.*, 1966; Jencks *et al.*, 1972) who suggested that differences in student achievement were due to factors outside the control of schools (e.g., home environment), studies appeared (e.g., Edmonds, 1979, Purkey & Smith, 1983) that challenged this conclusion by identifying effective schools and the characteristics that made them effective. In this section, we review eight studies that follow this tradition. However, unlike the original effective schools research that designated schools as effective based on measures of school achievement, the authors of these studies employed a theoretical framework and previous research findings to define *effective literacy instruction* and then used this framework to observe instruction. In some cases, while observing, the researchers also refined their framework. One study (Padrón, 1994) used a previously designed observation instrument to gather data on classrooms with language-minority students.

In their series of studies, Gersten and Jiménez (1994), Jiménez and Gersten (1999), Short (1994), and Padrón (1994) examine the quality of instruction by using a framework they have developed. A theme that runs through these studies is that teaching within these frameworks and implementing these techniques are not easy.

To a great extent, these attributes overlap with those of effective instruction for monolingual students. For example, attributes identified by the researchers include implicit and explicit challenging of students, active involvement of all students, providing activities that students can complete successfully, and scaffolding instruction for students through such techniques as building and clarifying student input and using visual organizers, teacher mediation/feedback to students, and classroom use of collaborative/cooperative learning. In many cases, however, there are techniques related to second-language acquisition such as sheltered English and respect for cultural diversity.

The value of these studies is that they identify potential explanatory factors. These factors need to be either bundled and tested experimentally as an intervention package or examined as separate components to determine whether they actually lead to improved student performance—a point made by the authors (Gersten & Jiménez, 1994).

School Change.   We found two studies that examined how school staff members work together to implement changes designed to improve literacy outcomes for language-minority students. One of these studies (Weaver & Sawyer, 1984) documented the change process at a small rural elementary school with a predominantly Anglo student population when teachers sought outside assistance from a local university to support the language growth of two Vietnamese students who arrived at the school not yet speaking English. The other study (Goldenberg & Gallimore, 1991) examined changes that occurred at an elementary school, located in a district with a 90% Hispanic student enrollment, where 80% of the Hispanic students had limited English proficiency.

These studies demonstrate the progress schools can achieve when staff work together to address specific issues, and highlight the importance of mobilizing staff to focus on the needs of language-minority students, even when such students are few in number. They provide heartening evidence that a concerted school effort involving teachers and administrators, together with outside agents (university researchers and specialists), can make a difference. These studies also point to the importance of sustained and comprehensive efforts because change is slow and circuitous, and language-minority students, especially those who live in poverty, face many challenges in achieving grade-level standards of literacy.

Literacy Instruction for Language Minority Children in Special Education Settings

In this section, we review studies examining the context in which language-minority students with special needs are educated and studies of instructional approaches designed for students with special needs.

The studies described in this section employed diverse research methods, including ethnography (Hughes, Vaughn, & Schumm, 1999; Jiménez, 1997; Ruiz, 1995; Wolf, 1993) and case studies (Fawcett & Lynch, 2000; Graves, Valles, & Rueda, 2000), as well as methods typical of the literature on children educated in special settings, such as multiple-baseline designs (Rousseau, Tam, & Ramnarain, 1993; VanWagenen, Williams, & McLaughlin, 1994), parallel-treatment designs (Rohena, Jitendra, & Browder, 2002),[2] and alternating-treatment designs (Echevarría, 1996; Perozzi, 1985). Two studies were quasi-experiments (Bos, Allen, & Scanlon, 1989; Klingner & Vaughn, 1996).

The samples in a majority of the studies are small; of the 10 studies examining instructional approaches, 8 included 5 or fewer children. As Rohena and colleagues (2002) suggest, "the small number of participants in a study limits the findings, and additional research is needed to extend the findings to a larger sample and diverse groups of individuals (other language minority background students)" (p. 182).

Instructional efforts that were grounded in different theoretical models were found to be promising. For example, behavioral approaches to developing sight word reading (Rohena et al., 2002) and vocabulary (Perrozi, 1985) were successful, but so were approaches that were more cognitive or learning strategy oriented (Klingner & Vaughn, 1996) or that took a more holistic, interactive approach (Echevarría, 1996). Given the small sample sizes and lack of controls in some of the studies, more research is needed to explore the effectiveness of these approaches. Table 6.5 indicates the effect sizes for these studies.

Although all the studies reviewed here involved language-minority students in special education settings, a wide range of students is represented across the studies. In some cases, the children may not have been learning disabled, but were poor readers as a consequence of their limited English proficiency or lack of exposure to reading instruction in

---

[2] A multiple probe across participants with a parallel-treatment design (PTD) was used to evaluate and compare the effectiveness and efficiency of two instructional conditions with respect to reading sight words. According to the authors, the PTD is "well suited for comparing the effectiveness and efficiency of instructional procedures" and "combines elements of the multiple probe (multiple baseline) design and uses random assignment and counterbalancing to control for extraneous variables for the purpose of comparing two antecedent manipulations with independent responses of equal difficulty" (Rohena et al., 2002, p. 174; cited in Sindelar et al., 1985).

TABLE 6.5
Effect Sizes for Instructional Approaches Designed for Language-Minority Students in Special Education Settings

Study	N	Grade	Home Language	Type of Study	Pretest Differences	Treatment Duration	Effect Size	Confidence Interval	Signif.
Alternating treatment									
Echevarría, 1996	5	2–3	Spanish	ATD	Not appropriate for effect size calculation				
Perozzi, 1985	6	Pre-K	Spanish/English	ATD	Not appropriate for effect size calculation				
Multiple baseline									
Rousseau et al., 1993	5	6	Spanish	MB	Not appropriate for effect size calculation				
VanWagenen et al., 1994	3	7	Spanish	MB	Not appropriate for effect size calculation				
Parallel treatment									
Rohena et al., 2002	4	7–8	Spanish	PT	Not appropriate for effect size calculation				
Quasi-experiments									
Klingner & Vaughn, 1996	26	9–11	Spanish	Quasi-Exp.	Yes				
• Gates-MacGinitie							–.03	–.8–.74	No
• Comprehension							–.39	–1.17–.38	No
• Strategy							–.58	–1.36–.21	No
Randomized control trial									
Bos et al., 1989	42	4–6	Spanish	RCT		3 days	.81	.47–1.16	Yes

161

their second language (see Appendix 6.D for a description of identification procedures). In the study of VanWagenen et al. (1994), for example, children were assigned to the special education teacher because of the need for intensive instruction in word-recognition meaning, pronunciation, and application of grammatical structures. The designation was based solely on scores on the Woodcock Reading Mastery Test. Although the two students studied by Fawcett and Lynch (2000) scored very low on the reading and spelling subtests of the Dyslexia Screening Test, they demonstrated strengths on the nonverbal subtests (postural stability and bead threading), compared with norms for their age. They also achieved high scores on the semantic fluency test, which measures speed of access to information within a specified category (in this case, animals) and is considered indicative of verbal intelligence (Frith, Landerl, & Frith, 1995). In addition to cross-study differences, there appears to have been a range of levels of disability within studies because students differed greatly in the progress they achieved in response to the same instructional approach. Thus, in interpreting the study findings, it is essential to consider students' individual profiles and how these profiles interact with particular instructional approaches.

Of note is that approaches that have been found effective in English may also work for children learning in their native language. For example, Echevarría (1996) found that instructional conversations implemented in Spanish with Spanish-speaking children were effective; these approaches have been found to be effective with students learning in English as a second language as well (Saunders & Goldenberg, 1999). These studies also suggest that modifications designed to make English instruction more comprehensible for language-minority students can be helpful. For example, VanWagenen et al. (1994) used an assisted-reading approach that introduced vocabulary and comprehension first; Rousseau et al. (1993) found that teaching key vocabulary was more effective than listening previewing in enhancing literal recall, and that the combination of the two strategies was more effective than either alone; and Klingner and Vaughn (1996) allowed students to use their first language to clarify meaning. Clearly, more research is needed to determine whether these findings will hold up in studies explicitly designed to investigate them, comparing tailored and untailored interventions, rather than tailored interventions and instruction as usual.

Students' native language appeared to help them in learning a second language. Perrozi (1985) found that three children, each with a different pattern of language development—normal, mild delay, and disordered—learned English receptive vocabulary more rapidly when the vocabulary was initially taught in the child's native language. Although Rohena et al. (2002) did not find that language of instruction had a differential effect on sight word learning, they remind readers that the verbal prompts in English were simple and within participants' level of English proficiency. They also note that language of instruction may be less important in developing sight word reading than in developing text-based components of literacy, such as comprehension. Maldonado (1994) found that second- and third-grade Spanish speakers with learning disabilities taught initially in Spanish and transitioned into English outperformed a control group that received traditional special education in English. The students in the two groups had similar characteristics, including age, education, experience, learning disability, language proficiency, and socioeconomic status (SES). See also findings reported in Chapter 4 that indicate transfer from first- to second-language literacy.

The level of students' English-language proficiency appears to interact with the instructional approach employed. Several studies found that instructional approaches were successful only if students had requisite levels of English. For example, Klingner and Vaughn (1996) found that children with the potential to benefit most from the intervention had some initial reading ability and fairly high levels of second-language oral proficiency.

These studies also indicate that the context in which children learn influences their discourse and development. As noted earlier, Ruiz (1995) documents differences in students' performance in less formal contexts. Echevarría (1996) demonstrates that, during instructional conversation lessons, significantly higher levels of academic discourse occurred, and students attained a higher level of conceptual development. The broader school context can also influence children's literacy development. Graves *et al.* (2000) report that teachers believed school-level initiatives (reduction in time allocated to writing, uniform switch to English) had a detrimental effect on students' writing progress. Wolf (1993) found that, through Reader's Theater, students labeled at risk were able to interpret text and perform a scene from a story they were reading.

One important issue raised by these studies is the manner in which students are identified as learning disabled and the assessments used to track their progress. In some cases, limited information about the selection process is provided (although the measures are reported, the criteria for inclusion are not; individual student scores are not provided). With regard to identification and tracking student progress, in many cases the information is difficult to interpret because it is based solely on researcher-developed assessments, and no information is given about what the scores mean—more specifically, how these students compare with other children with similar needs or with children without learning issues. Many of the authors fail to provide information about the reliability or validity of the assessments used or about interrater reliability when more open-ended assessments were used. Some studies (Rohena *et al.*, 2002; Rousseau *et al.*, 1993) caution that, although the data may suggest that the instructional approaches employed had powerful effects on students' reading ability, it is important to examine whether those effects were long-lasting, as well as whether they generalize to other reading materials, tasks, or situations. Finally, studies should be designed to differentiate between a language delay and a reading disability.

In several studies (Bos *et al.*, 1989; Hughes, Vaughn, & Schumm, 1999; Klingner & Vaughn, 1996), intelligence tests were used to determine which students were placed in special education settings. It is common to use intelligence (IQ) tests in the diagnosis of learning disabilities and other educational difficulties; in many cases, the so-called discrepancy definition is used. According to this definition, to be learning disabled, an individual must have a discrepancy between a score on an IQ test and an achievement test. Serious questions have been raised about this practice in the case of individuals who are being assessed in their first language (e.g., Siegel, 1989, 1992), and this approach may be even more inappropriate with language-minority children and youth. It is often assumed that IQ tests measure reasoning and problem-solving ability independently of specific knowledge and cultural norms. However, most IQ tests have a language component that requires the vocabulary and knowledge of complex syntax in English, and culturally specific background knowledge. More recent definitions of learning disabilities do not rely on this discrepancy model, but instead focus on students' ability to learn given appropriate schooling.

Teacher Beliefs and Professional Development

This section reviews seven studies that examine teachers' beliefs and attitudes, which are thought to influence how teachers perceive, process, and act on information in the classroom (Clark & Peterson, 1986; Mangano & Allen, 1986). It then turns to five studies of professional development for teachers who work with language-minority children to develop their literacy skills. Three studies (Calderón & Marsh, 1988; Hoffman, Roser & Farest, 1988; Saunders & Goldenberg, 1996) focused on professional development for English-as-a-second-language (ESL) and bilingual education teachers, and two examine training programs for teachers of language-minority students with learning disabilities (Haager & Windmueller, 2001; Ruiz, Rueda, Figueroa, & Boothroyd, 1995). To be included in this section, studies had to meet the inclusion criteria established for the Panel as a whole (see Chapter 1). However, the reporting of student outcomes was not a requirement.

Two studies examined teacher beliefs in effective classrooms and found that the teachers had high expectations for language-minority learners and valued cultural differences. Studies (Johnson, 1992; Orellana, 1995) suggest that teachers' beliefs and theoretical orientation may influence their classroom practices, and it has been claimed (Johnson, 1992) that teacher training "create[s] opportunities for teachers to . . . become aware of how their own beliefs relate to the way they perceive, process, and act upon information in literacy instruction" (p. 101). Teacher training may influence teacher beliefs (Rueda & García, 1996), and this may help teachers become more aware of how their attitudes and beliefs influence their instruction. The studies also found that teachers teaching in similar contexts may hold different beliefs about the students they teach (Browne & Bordeaux, 1991)—a difference that may be related to the match between teachers' and students' cultural backgrounds

The attributes of professional development deemed important for all teachers (American Educational Research Association, 2005) were affirmed as important in the five professional development studies conducted in second-language learning contexts. These studies all examined professional development lasting for at least a year. The professional development consisted of ongoing meetings between teachers and those providing the professional development, opportunities for classroom practice coupled with mentoring and coaching, and teacher learning communities. The teacher education was always focused on specific strategies for improving instruction for language-minority students, the theory that informs the strategies, and how to apply the strategies in classrooms: improving how teachers read aloud to young children (Hoffman *et al.*, 1988); combining direct and constructivist methods (Saunders & Goldenberg, 1996); teaching oral language, reading, and writing in different instructional contexts (Calderon & Marsh, 1988); improving early reading interventions (Haager & Windmueller, 2001); and introducing a literacy curriculum for learning disabled students (Ruiz *et al.*, 1995).

These studies also suggest what might be unique to professional development focused on teachers who work with language-minority students. Calderón and Marsh (1988) highlight the importance of staff development that builds on theory, effective teacher craft, and close collaboration between researchers and teachers given the paucity of experimental research on literacy instruction for this group of students (see the previous section on effective literacy teaching for a discussion of the research on effective practice). Professional development for mainstream teachers has a much more robust research base from which to draw (National Institute of Child Health and Human Development, 2000). In addition, the studies suggest that, to develop a coherent program of instruction for language-minority students, it is important to involve all staff involved in their education (i.e., bilingual and

English-language specialists, learning disabilities specialists if called for, and classroom teachers) in the same professional development efforts (Haager & Windmueller, 2001; Ruiz *et al.*, 1995). Although this may be important for all students, it is especially important for language-minority students who tend to be served by multiple school personnel.

The findings also demonstrate that creating change in teachers can be a time-consuming process that requires considerable investment on the part of all involved. Four of the professional development efforts studied took place over extended periods of time (1–3 years); all involved many meetings and workshops or an intensive summer program (32 hours of contact time) and, in some cases, follow-up in classrooms. In addition, all the efforts involved an outside collaborator with expertise—in the case of these studies, there was close collaboration with university researchers.

The studies suggest that, "regardless of the specific research questions posed, it is best to think of professional development as including three outcomes: change in teachers' classroom practices, change in their beliefs and attitudes, and change in students' learning outcomes" (Guskey, 1986; cited in Ruiz *et al.*, 1995, p. 622). However, they also suggest that change is not unidirectional. For example, although some researchers found that changing teachers' perceptions may be the first step in this process (Richardson, 1991; cited in Haager & Windmueller, 2001, pp. 247–248), changing instructional practices in ways that produce positive student outcomes can change teacher beliefs (Calderón & Marsh, 1988). Ruiz *et al.* (1995) described two dimensions of change—practices and beliefs; both involved transitional processes, and during the transition there was no particular order in which they occurred. The authors indicate further that such factors as teachers' ethnic background and students' background may influence the directionality of the relationship between these factors.

In many cases, the data collected were suitable for answering the research questions posed. For example, the goal of two studies (Saunders & Goldenberg, 1996; Ruiz *et al.*, 1995) was to examine changes in teachers' instructional paradigms. In both cases, researchers used transcriptions of professional development sessions and teacher interviews to document this change. In addition, Ruiz *et al.* (1995) documented teachers' classroom practices before and after the professional development to examine the congruence between the professional development and practice. However, in cases where the focus of the professional development was on providing teachers with strategies for changing student performance, it is important to examine both changes in teachers' instructional methods and changes in student performance as a means of validating that both the content and delivery of the professional development were appropriate.

In using student outcomes to assess effective professional development, it is critical to ensure that teacher effectiveness is not confounded with student capacity. Value-added assessment systems have been developed to examine the relationships among school systems, schools, teachers, and students' academic growth over time (Sanders & Horn, 1998), taking into account student capacity. In examining links between professional development and student performance, other factors should be considered, including school and district policies that influence learning (e.g., class size, allocation of teachers to classrooms, and required curricular materials). To gauge effectiveness, most studies reviewed here examined teachers' reports of change or actual changes in their teaching behavior. Larger-scale studies employing more complex designs are needed to examine the relationship between professional development for teachers and the progress of their language-minority students.

CROSS-CUTTING THEMES

Influence of Educational Settings and Instructional Approaches on Learning

How children are taught obviously affects learning. The studies reviewed in this chapter took varying approaches to understanding how teaching influences the literacy learning of language-minority children and youth.

Methods and Approaches for Teaching Literacy to Language-Minority Students. It is evident that there are simply not enough quasi-experimental and experimental studies to allow for a thorough specification of how best to teach literacy to language-minority students. The number of studies that evaluated the effectiveness of various approaches to teaching literacy more effectively were tiny in comparison to the number of such studies that provide information on first-language literacy learning. Given the substantial emphasis on the use of research-based instruction within No Child Left Behind, it is essential that there be a greater effort to conduct research that will define such instruction.

One positive pattern of results from this collection of studies was the idea that the types of literacy teaching found to be effective with native English speakers appears largely to be effective with English-language learners, too. However, caution is needed so as to not overstate this finding. Even in the studies here, there were essential adjustments to these instructional routines. Although the nature of such adjustments needs to be explored more directly in future research, studies suggest the advisability of altering curriculum coverage depending on the similarity between English and the native language and the students' levels of attainment of their native language and of fine-tuning instructional routines, including relying on the students' home language in some ways.

Qualitative studies of classroom and school practices suggest several possible ways to accomplish this fine-tuning, including identifying and clarifying difficult words and passages within texts to facilitate the development of comprehension; consolidating text knowledge through summarization; giving students extra practice in reading words, sentences, and stories. Some studies also revealed the value of instructional routines that include giving attention to vocabulary, checking comprehension, presenting ideas clearly both verbally and in writing, paraphrasing students' remarks and encouraging them to expand on those remarks, and using physical gestures and visual cues to clarify meaning.

Developing Students' English Proficiency. Several studies indicate that students are less able to take advantage of interventions geared to promote incidental learning in English if they do not have requisite levels of English proficiency. For example, one study examined the impact of using captioned TV as a way to build word knowledge for middle-grades second-language learners. Generally, captioned TV outperformed a condition in which students only read the textbook. However, the authors also found that higher levels of English proficiency were associated with more learning of vocabulary. In discussing the findings, the authors note that the more linguistic competence the students had, the more they acquired, supporting the need for substantial direct teacher intervention in building oral English proficiency for students who are below a threshold of linguistic competence in their new language.

Moreover, teaching English-language learners strategies (for decoding or comprehension) can be effective, but it should be combined with concerted efforts to build students' facility in English. The reason is that strategies of various types are unlikely to help students who do not have the requisite language proficiency to comprehend the text. Substantial instruction and support in developing English proficiency were evident in some studies, but not in others, and this difference may help explain the inconsistency in success with comprehension strategies or the smaller effect sizes for these procedures with second-language students.

Quality of Teaching. Despite the importance of teaching, we only found five studies that focused on professional development. The results demonstrate that creating change in teachers is a time-consuming process that requires considerable investment on the part of the change agents, as well as the teachers. The five professional development efforts studied took place over extended periods; all involved extensive and intensive engagement, and, in some cases, follow-up in classrooms. In addition, outside university-based collaborators with expertise assisted. The studies indicate that teachers found professional development to be most helpful when it provided opportunities for hands-on practice, with teaching techniques readily applicable to their classroom, in-class demonstrations with their own or a colleague's students or more personalized coaching.

Systemic Efforts and Overall School Success.   Findings from studies of effective classrooms and schools identify attributes related to positive student outcomes. To a great extent, the attributes overlap with those of effective schools for native English speakers, such as implicit and explicit challenging of students, active involvement of all students, providing activities that students can complete successfully, and scaffolding instruction for students through such techniques as building and clarifying student input and using visual organizers, teacher mediation/ feedback to students, and classroom use of collaborative/cooperative learning. In some cases, however, there are techniques related to second-language acquisition such as sheltered English and respect for cultural diversity. There is a need for experimental investigation into the ultimate effectiveness of these approaches.

Difficulty of Creating School Change.   Several studies we reviewed show the progress schools can achieve by having staff work together to address specific school issues. Such studies highlight the importance of mobilizing staff to focus on the needs of language-minority students, even when the students are few in number, and provide evidence that a concerted school effort involving outside agents (researchers and specialists) and school personnel (principals, specialists, and classroom teachers) can make a difference in student outcomes. In these studies, the schools sought assistance from local universities, which assisted with staff development and school change efforts. The studies also highlight the importance of supporting teacher change and the need for support systems that are intensive, elaborate, and enduring to accomplish this goal. Two critical tools in supporting teacher change were a classroom implementation checklist and grade-appropriate benchmarks used to assess student progress.

Importance of Individual Differences

Students' development of literacy is influenced by a range of individual factors, including age of arrival in a new country, educational history, socioeconomic status (SES), and cognitive capacity. This point is highlighted by the differential effects of instruction on students of different ages, with differing degrees of English proficiency and varied cognitive capacity. Children's interests and concerns can also play a role. It is critical to keep in mind that language-minority students are a highly heterogeneous group, and that instruction must be designed to take such differences into account.

The studies reviewed also demonstrate the benefits of attending to the individual needs of students. For example, one study referred to earlier documents how a teacher successfully addressed the individual needs of her students. Most pertinent for second-language learners, the teacher did not lower expectations for these students but did make modifications to her instruction to help ensure they understood what she was saying (Fitzgerald & Noblit 2000).

Developmental Nature of Literacy Acquisition

Literacy development requires the acquisition of word-level (those involved in word reading and spelling) and text-level skills (those involved in the interpretation and communication of meaning). Young English-language learners follow a developmental trajectory—similar to that of native speakers—in the acquisition of literacy, and this trajectory appears to be similar for children regardless of their language background (see Chapter 3, this volume). However, in some cases, the rate is slower for English-language learners. For example, when native speakers and English-language learners are taught together, both make gains in vocabulary learning, but the vocabulary knowledge of the English-language learners tends to remain below that of their native-speaking peers. These differences result, in part, from lower levels of initial oral English proficiency.

It should be noted that, in the development of second-language literacy, the nature of the native and second languages matters as well as the experience students have had in developing first-language literacy. For example, Spanish-speaking children instructed in Spanish mastered decoding skills more easily than did English-speaking children instructed in English. Moreover, instruction for students who are literate in their first language could be more targeted, emphasizing those skills not yet obtained through the first language while paying less attention to easily transferable skills already mastered.

In successful instructional programs, children learn precursor skills and use them as building blocks for acquiring later, more complex skills. However, some language-minority students may begin acquiring literacy for the first time in the upper grades, while others may have already learned literacy in their first language. Unfortunately, because of the dearth of longitudinal studies examining the instruction of language-minority students, there is little information about how best to provide instruction in early precursor skills that develop concurrently with the skills or subsequent to them.

Influence of Native-Language Literacy and Second-Language Oral Proficiency on Second-Language Literacy Development

Language-minority students who are literate in their first language are likely to be advantaged in the acquisition of English literacy. Studies demonstrate that language-minority students instructed in their native language (usually Spanish) and English perform, on average, better on English reading measures than language-minority students instructed only in English. This is the case at both the elementary and secondary levels. The strongest evidence supporting this claim comes from randomized studies, which indicate a moderate effect in favor of bilingual instruction. However, recent evaluations of scientifically based beginning reading programs used to teach non-English-speaking children to read in English are showing promising results, suggesting that if children receive good instruction with appropriate scaffolding, they are able to master early reading skills in English. This is an important finding in that first-language instruction is not an option in many schools where children speak multiple languages or where staff are not capable of providing first-language instruction.

Less evident, but no less important, is the benefit of instructional routines that, although focused on the teaching of English, exploit students' native language—for example, by using Spanish words as synonyms in vocabulary instruction or conducting instructional conversations that permit some interpretation to take place in the home language. Conversely, no immediate benefit was found to English comprehension in having students engage solely in extensive amounts of Spanish reading, indicating the importance of providing instruction in students' second as well as first language.

As noted earlier, the results of several studies indicate that children with lower levels of English oral proficiency gain less advantage from instruction relative to more English-proficient students. In addition, we found lower effect sizes for many instructional approaches when used with English-language learners—especially when reading comprehension was the outcome measure; oral proficiency in English appeared to be necessary for students to obtain maximum benefit.

The Role of Sociocultural Context in Literacy Development

As noted previously, use of language-minority students' native language is one important element of the sociocultural context in which these students are educated. Two studies found that programs incorporating culturally appropriate curricula resulted in positive literacy and literacy-related gains for Native American children in these programs. The culturally appropriate curricula used instructional strategies such as "informal participation structures containing overlapping speech, mutual participation of students and teacher, co-narration, volunteered speech, instant feedback and lack of penalty for wrong answers" (Tharp, 1982, p. 519). However, these programs combine many elements, and it is difficult to determine exactly what it is about the programs that made them effective. It may be that improved methods of teaching reading and writing, as well as culturally appropriate curricula, enhanced students' literacy. Future resrach is clearly needed. Other studies found that it was possible to set up classroom instructional activities that gave language-minority students greater opportunity to share their ideas and perspectives (social) or use their native language, and noted increased participation in classroom discourse. However, additional research is necessary to determine whether increased interaction in the second language leads to higher levels of proficiency and literacy in that language.

METHODOLOGICAL ISSUES

Strengths of the Studies

There was considerable variation in the quality of research across all study types. We found excellent studies in each category. Some of the experimental and quasi-experimental studies were well designed, with reliable pre- and post-test measurements, checks on fidelity, and equivalency of control and experimental groups. The qualitative research employed a wide variety of methods to collect data about the classroom context, student behavior, and instructional approaches for literacy development. Additional information about students' performance was obtained from reading, writing, and oral language assessments; samples of student work; and school documents. The detailed descriptions of an approach or context, of students' work or behavior, and of the criteria used to assess them enhance our understanding of the dynamic and complex nature of schooling.

Shortcomings of the Studies

Although the studies met the inclusion criteria for this chapter, they had shortcomings. Of most concern, the quasi-experimental studies rarely provided a clear description of the adjustments that were made to various instructional routines used with English-only students to meet the needs of English-language learners. As useful as it is to know that a particular program or language approach results in a benefit to students, it is important to understand exactly how this approach was used. Too few studies used randomized control experiments and too few looked at instruction for as long as a school year; our confidence in the results would be greater if such approaches were used. Given that the effect sizes tended to be smaller with English-language learners than with native speakers, it would have been helpful to have English-language proficiency measures to help understand whether outcomes were mediated by language proficiency, and which students within the group succeeded most as a result of the approach. There is also a need for more descriptive data on the students and their context within these experimental efforts to discern the circumstances under which instruction works best.

With regard to the qualitative studies, a first set of issues revolves around the quantity and quality of the data collected to document an approach, the context in which the approach was implemented, or the impact it had on students. Often insufficient detail about an instructional approach or its implementation is given. Researchers often measured the impact of instruction using their own unvalidated measures, and failed to provide evidence of the psychometric adequacy of their procedures or instruments. Without standardized measures or sufficient information about the measures, it is impossible to determine if an instructional approach really conferred a benefit to the language-minority students. Another assessment issue arises when authors only measure selected outcomes (e.g., coherence and organization in writing, but not in spelling or grammar), which results in an incomplete picture of student competence in a multifaceted ability, such as writing or oral language proficiency. Finally, some authors do not describe how they synthesize or analyze their data.

A second set of issues for qualitative studies revolves around how well the findings are supported by the information collected. First, in some cases researchers do not collect observations from multiple sources or employ multiple techniques for identifying or cross-checking what they found. Second, many studies do not situate narrative vignettes and quotes from participants within a framework of evidence about the range and frequency of variation in these events, making it impossible to determine how well the reported findings match the actual events. Third, some authors do not consider alternative or competing explanations. They may, for example, attribute outcomes to an instructional technique, but fail to consider the impact of other educational experiences the students are having throughout their school days. Often, findings could easily be related to other variables (e.g., levels of first- or second-language proficiency, SES of the students or group of students, grade level, sociocultural context). Fourth, some authors fail to explain the range of variation in the data presented. For example, findings from several studies suggest that, for language-minority students as a group, level of language proficiency may have influenced study findings, but this influence is not documented or explained in a discussion of the findings. A final issue is whether the generalizations presented are supported by the data collected. In some cases, there is a tendency to overgeneralize and go beyond the scope of the study with conclusions.

It is important to note that high-quality studies of literacy development in language-minority students can be difficult to accomplish in school settings, given the paucity of funds allocated for such research. Conducting research capable of identifying a best course of action is expensive. In the past, federal funds have been devoted largely to evaluations of federally supported programs, comparison studies aimed at evaluating the efficacy of English immersion versus some native-language use, and survey research that provides descriptions of the language-minority populations and the settings in which they are educated. That agenda needs to be expanded.

FUTURE RESEARCH

This chapter reveals the great need for more and better research into what schools should do to improve literacy among language-minority students. Beyond the obvious need for more studies and more replications further evaluating promising instructional innovations, there is a need for a more sophisticated approach to research than has usually been apparent. Educational outcomes may be influenced by individual, sociocultural, cross-linguistic, and developmental factors. What is needed is an ambitious research agenda that pursues a systematic analysis of the effectiveness of instructional routines and the adjustments teachers make in these routines to foster success *within the context* of these individual and contextual factors that moderate and mediate literacy learning outcomes for language-minority students.

Moreover, we need to use research findings to craft new theories and inform various paradigms that in turn can be used to inform both future research and practice. Theory plays an important role in practice because findings from one study, or even a collection of studies, will never be sufficient to address the unique circumstances of any new educational situation. Educators need to understand relevant theories if they are to respond effectively to the unique circumstances they confront in meeting the diverse needs of students in their classrooms.

Methodological Recommendations for Improving the Research Base

As noted, a fundamental problem with much of the experimental research reviewed here was that the authors provided too little information about the English-language learners, their context, and the nature of the instruction being provided.

Future research should report children's level of literacy or language attainment in the native language and second language so it is possible to make sense of variations in effectiveness. Moreover, studies on the teaching of language-minority students should routinely document the similarities and differences between the approaches used with the language-minority students and these same approaches used with native speakers. With such descriptions, it would be possible to determine whether different adjustments are needed for students with different first languages or at varied levels of English proficiency. Finally, the studies need to use valid, reliable literacy measures and consider the long-term (not just the immediate) impact of the instruction.

Although case studies and ethnographic reports cannot determine the efficacy of instruction, they can be valuable in providing insight into the kinds of instructional adjustment that need to be tested in the experimental evaluations. Qualitative research is potentially useful (on its own and when combined with experimental designs), but quality standards are needed to ensure the trustworthiness of the observational procedures employed and to circumscribe the interpretations and generalizations drawn from such work. These standards should be employed in the training of researchers, and journal editors and grant reviewers should apply them in determining which studies to publish and which to fund.

In documenting an approach or context in which an approach was implemented, criteria should include the number of observations per unit of analysis,[3] duration of these observations, detail (specificity and concreteness) provided in reporting these observations, and appropriateness of the methods used for documentation. With regard to whether and how findings and themes are supported by data, criteria should include the sufficiency of diverse sources of information (triangulation), provision of information about the relative frequency of certain events or occurrences (typicality or atypicality), examination of

---

[3]For example, if the unit of analysis is the classroom, how many times was it visited? If it was a particular kind of lesson within the classroom, how many such lessons were observed? If it was a particular kind of instructional move (including moves using the mother tongue in instruction), how many instances of that move were observed?

competing or alternative explanations, explanation of the range of variation in the data presented, and presentation of generalizations presented based on the data collected.

Given the complexity of educating language-minority students, there is a need for more sophisticated research designs making use of multiple methods of inquiry. The NRP (National Institute of Child Health and Human Development, 2000) came to a similar conclusion after reviewing research on reading instruction with native English speakers. The circumstances are even more complex and the need for mixed-method designs is even more crucial with English-language learners. Within the context of experimental and quasi-experimental studies evaluating the efficacy of particular instructional approaches with this population, there is a need for close and careful observation of the implementation of these approaches and the milieu in which they are implemented. Mixed-method designs employing multiple research methods are the most likely avenue for achieving this level of understanding. Research of this type requires collaboration among experts from diverse areas of interest and the availability of the funding and infrastructure necessary to collaborate in this manner.

Substantive Recommendations for Improving the Research Base

Research is needed to replicate the findings described in this volume in order to build greater confidence in the findings. Especially needed are longitudinal studies that examine the long-term benefits of the various procedures that have been tried so far.

Research should go beyond identifying specific instructional approaches that are effective to examine how these approaches can be scaled up in such a way that they remain effective across contexts and populations. It has often been noted that results of research studies can be difficult to implement on a larger scale. Thus, research that goes from hypothesis to proven effectiveness in a classroom or school to effectiveness on the school- or district-wide level is needed to identify the conditions and mechanisms that would allow a research-proven approach to be applied with broader benefit.

Research needs to address not only the development of basic language proficiency and early literacy, but also the acquisition of higher level literacy skills. Chapter 3 of this volume shows that English-language learners often match native English speakers in word recognition, phonemic awareness, and spelling without necessarily attaining comparable levels of comprehension and writing in English. Public hearings held by the Panel as well as the research reviewed revealed a strong need for information on how to facilitate the literacy learning of adolescent students. Research is needed to identify effective ways to support learning of content knowledge attained through literacy in history, science, mathematics, and other school subjects.

Finally, research on literacy instruction for language-minority students should address the learning needs of students with special needs and learners at different levels of English proficiency (including older newcomers), with different levels of content knowledge, at different ages, at different levels of language and literacy attainment in the native language, and with different native-language backgrounds. Earlier we noted the need for better reporting of these characteristics so that we can glean the maximum amount of information from these studies. Here we go beyond that point to call for explicit studies of what works with different types of learners. Because teachers work with classrooms of children with diverse strengths and needs, research additionally needs to explore how to differentiate instruction so teachers can maximally accommodate the needs of all children within a classroom. Direct studies of this type will help validate the correlational evidence and enhance our understanding of how to teach all language-minority students to read and write most effectively

APPENDIX 6.A

TABLE 6.A.1
Evaluation Studies Included in the Present Review and Other Reviews

Study	Characteristics	Willig, 1985	Rossell & Baker, 1996	Greene, 1997	Slavin & Cheung, 2004
Alvarez, 1975	Elementary school; matched design		X		X
Campeau et al., 1975	Elementary school; matched design		X		X
Cohen et al., 1976	Elementary school; matched design		X		
Covey, 1973	Secondary school; random assignment	X	X	X	X
Danoff et al., 1978	Elementary school; matched design	X	X	X	
de La Garza & Medina, 1985	Elementary school; matched design		X		
Doebler & Mardis, 1980–81*	Elementary school; matched design				X
Huzar, 1973	Elementary school; random assignment	X	X	X	X
Kaufman, 1968	Secondary school; random assignment	X	X	X	X
Lampman, 1973*	Elementary School; Matched Design		X		
Maldonado, 1977	Elementary school; matched design		X		X

(Continued)

TABLE 6.A.1
(Continued)

Study	Characteristics	Willig, 1985	Rossell & Baker, 1996	Greene, 1997	Slavin & Cheung, 2004
Maldonado, 1994	Elementary school; random assignment				X
Plante, 1976	Elementary school; random assignment				X
Ramírez, 1991	Elementary school; matched design		X	X	X
Saldate et al., 1985	Elementary school; matched design				
Valladolid, 1991	Elementary school; matched design		X		
Heritage Language Studies					
Morgan, 1971	Elementary school; matched design		X		X
French Immersion Studies					
Barik & Swain, 1975*	Elementary school; matched design		X		X
Barik & Swain, 1978*	Elementary school; matched design		X		
Barik et al., 1977*	Elementary school; matched design	X			X

* Not included in the meta-analysis.

APPENDIX 6.B

TABLE 6.B.1
Effect Sizes of Studies Included in the Meta-Analysis

Study Name	Subgroup Within Study	Outcome	Time Point	Biling-ED N	English-Only N	Std Diff in Means	Std Err	Hedges' g^u	Standard Error
Maldonado, 1994	Sample 1	Reading total	2	10	10	2.215	0.568	2.121	0.544
Saldate et al., 1985	Sample 1	Unknown	2	31	31	-0.287	0.255	-0.283	0.252
Saldate et al., 1985	Sample 1	Word reading	3	19	19	0.908	0.341	0.889	0.334
de la Garza, 1985	Sample 1	Reading comprehension	2	25	117	0.192	0.221	0.191	0.219
de la Garza, 1985	Sample 1	Reading comprehension	3	25	117	0.207	0.221	0.206	0.219
de la Garza, 1985	Sample 1	Reading vocabulary	2	24	118	0.496	0.226	0.494	0.225
de la Garza, 1985	Sample 1	Reading vocabulary	3	24	118	0.249	0.224	0.248	0.223
Ramirez et al., 1991	Sample 1	Reading total	1	67	139	0.178	0.149	0.177	0.148
Ramirez et al., 1991	Sample 1	Reading total	2	67	139	-0.258	0.149	-0.257	0.149
Ramirez et al., 1991	Sample 1	Reading total	3	67	139	0.154	0.149	0.154	0.148
Ramirez et al., 1991	Sample 2	Reading total	1	252	194	0.095	0.096	0.095	0.095
Ramirez et al., 1991	Sample 2	Reading total	2	252	194	-0.100	0.096	-0.099	0.095
Ramirez et al., 1991	Sample 2	Reading total	3	252	194	0.017	0.096	0.017	0.095
Ramirez et al., 1991	Sample 3	Reading total	1	170	194	0.080	0.105	0.080	0.105
Ramirez et al., 1991	Sample 3	Reading total	2	170	194	-0.276	0.106	-0.275	0.105
Ramirez et al., 1991	Sample 3	Reading total	3	170	194	-0.067	0.105	-0.067	0.105

(Continued)

TABLE 6.B.1
(Continued)

Study Name	Subgroup Within Study	Outcome	Time Point	Biling-ED N	English-Only N	Std Diff in Means	Std Err	Hedges' g''	Standard Error
Valladolid, 1991	Sample 1	Reading total	4	50	57	-0.610	0.198	-0.605	0.197
Valladolid, 1991	Sample 1	Reading total	5	50	57	-0.541	0.197	-0.538	0.196
Alvarez, 1975	Sample 1	Reading comprehension	2	51	26	-0.188	0.241	-0.186	0.239
Alvarez, 1975	Sample 1	Reading vocabulary	2	51	26	0.163	0.241	0.162	0.239
Alvarez, 1975	Sample 2	Reading comprehension	2	39	31	-0.257	0.242	-0.254	0.239
Alvarez, 1975	Sample 2	Reading vocabulary	2	39	31	0.072	0.241	0.071	0.238
Campeau et al., 1975	Sample 2	Reading total	1	104	27	1.839	0.244	1.828	0.243
Campeau et al., 1975	Sample 2	Reading total	2	94	21	0.924	0.249	0.918	0.247
Campeau et al., 1975	Sample 2	Reading total	3	75	22	-0.241	0.243	-0.239	0.241
Campeau et al., 1975	Sample 3	Reading total	1	106	19	1.401	0.264	1.393	0.263
Campeau et al., 1975	Sample 3	Reading total	2	95	35	1.434	0.217	1.426	0.216
Campeau et al., 1975	Sample 3	Reading total	3	101	29	0.761	0.216	0.757	0.215
Campeau et al., 1975	Sample 3	Reading total	4	75	20	0.271	0.252	0.269	0.250
Campeau et al., 1975	Sample 5	Reading total	1	125	46	2.643	0.224	2.631	0.223
Campeau et al., 1975	Sample 5	Reading total	2	97	57	0.406	0.168	0.404	0.168
Campeau et al., 1975	Sample 5	Reading total	3	85	63	0.882	0.174	0.877	0.173
Campeau et al., 1975	Sample 6	Reading total	1	119	100	0.243	0.136	0.242	0.136

(Continued)

TABLE 6.B.1
(Continued)

Study Name	Subgroup Within Study	Outcome	Time Point	Biling-ED N	English-Only N	Std Diff in Means	Std Err	Hedges' g^u	Standard Error
Campeau et al., 1975	Sample 6	Reading total	2	205	93	0.355	0.126	0.354	0.126
Campeau et al., 1975	Sample 6	Reading total	3	79	80	0.389	0.160	0.387	0.159
Campeau et al., 1975	Sample 7	Reading total	1	146	60	0.857	0.159	0.854	0.158
Campeau et al., 1975	Sample 7	Reading total	2	161	53	0.668	0.162	0.665	0.161
Campeau et al., 1975	Sample 7	Reading total	3	218	83	0.123	0.129	0.123	0.129
Campeau et al., 1975	Sample 7	Reading total	4	98	88	0.760	0.152	0.757	0.151
Campeau et al., 1975	Sample 8	Reading total	1	145	45	0.457	0.172	0.455	0.172
Campeau et al., 1975	Sample 8	Reading total	2	155	53	0.541	0.161	0.539	0.161
Campeau et al., 1975	Sample 8	Reading total	3	146	62	0.272	0.152	0.271	0.152
Campeau et al., 1975	Sample 8	Reading total	4	151	58	0.390	0.156	0.389	0.155
Cohen et al., 1976	Sample 1	Reading total	4	14	11	-0.180	0.404	-0.174	0.390
Cohen et al., 1976	Sample 1	Reading Total	5	7	7	-0.220	0.536	-0.206	0.502
Cohen et al., 1976	Sample 2	Reading total	3	12	9	-1.200	0.478	-1.152	0.459
Cohen et al., 1976	Sample 2	Reading total	4	7	7	-1.145	0.577	-1.072	0.540
Cohen et al., 1976	Sample 3	Reading total	2	7	9	-1.690	0.586	-1.598	0.554
Cohen et al., 1976	Sample 3	Reading total	3	7	7	-1.809	0.635	-1.694	0.594
Danoff et al., 1977	Sample 1	Reading total	2	722	297	-0.262	0.069	-0.262	0.069
Danoff et al., 1977	Sample 1	Reading total	3	905	469	-0.265	0.057	-0.265	0.057
Danoff et al., 1977	Sample 1	Reading total	4	941	515	0.097	0.055	0.097	0.055
Danoff et al., 1977	Sample 1	Reading total	5	731	144	-0.287	0.091	-0.287	0.091
Danoff et al., 1977	Sample 1	Reading total	6	341	68	-0.424	0.133	-0.423	0.133

(Continued)

TABLE 6.B.1
(Continued)

Study Name	Subgroup Within Study	Outcome	Time Point	Biling-ED N	English-Only N	Std Diff in Means	Std Err	Hedges' g''	Standard Error
Huzar, 1973	Sample 1	Reading total	2	41	40	0.014	0.222	0.014	0.220
Huzar, 1973	Sample 1	Reading total	3	43	36	0.313	0.227	0.310	0.225
Kaufman, 1968	Sample 1	Paragraph meaning	7	41	31	0.048	0.238	0.048	0.235
Kaufman, 1968	Sample 1	Paragraph meaning	8	31	19	0.115	0.292	0.113	0.287
Kaufman, 1968	Sample 1	Word meaning	7	41	31	0.220	0.239	0.217	0.236
Kaufman, 1968	Sample 1	Word meaning	8	31	19	0.311	0.293	0.306	0.288
Kaufman, 1968	Sample 2	Paragraph meaning	7	20	25	0.478	0.304	0.470	0.299
Kaufman, 1968	Sample 2	Word meaning	7	20	25	0.039	0.300	0.038	0.295
Maldonado, 1977	Sample 1	Reading total	2	47	79	0.360	0.186	0.358	0.184
Maldonado, 1977	Sample 1	Reading total	3	47	79	0.506	0.187	0.503	0.186
Maldonado, 1977	Sample 1	Reading total	4	47	79	0.475	0.187	0.473	0.186
Maldonado, 1977	Sample 1	Reading total	5	47	79	0.378	0.186	0.376	0.185
Plante, 1976	Sample 1	Reading total	2	15	10	0.801	0.424	0.775	0.410
Plante, 1976	Sample 1	Reading total	3	16	12	0.272	0.384	0.264	0.372
Covey, 1973	Sample 1	Reading total	9	89	84	0.661	0.156	0.658	0.156
Morgan, 1971	Sample 1	Paragraph reading	1	93	100	0.255	0.145	0.254	0.144
Morgan, 1971	Sample 1	Word reading	1	93	100	0.374	0.145	0.372	0.145

APPENDIX 6.C

TABLE 6.C.1

Distinguishing Two Types of Studies—Explicit Instruction in Literacy Components and Complex Approaches—With Studies Listed by Skill or Approach, as in Chapter 6[4]

	Sample			Intervention				
Study	N	Grade	Language Status Definition	Duration & Routine	Instructional Practices	Materials	Professional Development	Delivery

Explicit Instruction in Literacy Components

Phonemic Awareness & Phonics

Gunn et al., 2000	184	K–3	Determined by ethnicity: Hispanic and non-Hispanic 84% of Hispanic students spoke only or mainly Spanish	4–5 months and 15–16 months (up to 2 years) 25–30 minutes daily Pull-out Small group and one-on-one	2 instructional groups Reading Mastery (RM; Engelmann & Bruner, 1988) group, used in 1st and 2nd grades: Emphasizes phonemic awareness, sound-letter correspondence, sounding out and blending words Corrective Reading (CR; Engelmann,	Typical Reading Mastery materials Typical Corrective Reading materials Decodable texts	10 hours of pre-service training in testing, grouping, presenting lessons, signaling for student responses, correcting errors, motivating students with clear	Instructors: Assistants hired for project Fidelity: Weekly observations

(Continued)

[4] If the literacy outcome measures were in the students' home language, the study is printed in italics.

* No information provided in the study

| | Sample | | | Intervention | | | | |
Study	N	Grade	Language Status Definition	Duration & Routine	Instructional Practices	Materials	Professional Development	Delivery
Gunn 117 et al., 2002	117	K–3	(see Gunn et al., 2000 above)	(see Gunn et al., 2000 above)	Carmine, & Johnson, 1988) group, used in 3rd and 4th grades: Emphasizes phonics, decoding, fluency, and comprehension. Both methods used direct, explicit instruction, with modeling, practice, and feedback and skills taught until demonstrated mastery	(see Gunn et al., 2000 above)	expectations and feedback, and theoretical framework of effective reading instruction Twice monthly meetings Observed trainer teaching lessons as needed	(see Gunn et al., 2000 above)

(Continued)

185

Study	Sample			Intervention				
	N	Grade	Language Status Definition	Duration & Routine	Instructional Practices	Materials	Professional Development	Delivery
Kramer et al., 1983	15	1–3	Mexican-American students who could speak both Spanish and English	4 weeks 30 minutes per session, 4 days a week Pull-out Unspecified grouping	Phonemic awareness 1 new minimal contrast pair per week First 2 days of week, new sounds taught (one per day), and second 2 days of week previously taught pairs reviewed Sounds taught using names (e.g., Chile Choo for /ch/) and reviewed in oral and written exercises and games Individual, self-directed practice as free time allowed	Picture cards Other materials not specified	Not applicable	Instructor: Researcher Fidelity: Not applicable

(Continued)

| Study | Sample | | | Intervention | | | | | |
| | N | Grade | Language Status Definition | Duration & Routine | Instructional Practices | Materials | Professional Development | Delivery | |

Study	N	Grade	Language Status Definition	Duration & Routine	Instructional Practices	Materials	Professional Development	Delivery
Larson, 1996	33	1	Bilingual and second year ESOL Puerto Rican students	5–7 weeks 15 minutes per session, 2–3 times weekly Pull-out One-on-one	Phonemic awareness Letter-sound correspondences Modeling and practice in pointing to Elkonin boxes while pronouncing CVC words until 80% correct criterion met Then modeling and practice in moving letter tiles into Elkonin boxes while pronouncing CVC words until 80% correct criterion met Training occurred either in English only, or in Spanish until 80% criterion met and then in English	Elkonin boxes Plastic letter tiles	Not applicable	Instructor: Researcher Fidelity: Not applicable

(Continued)

| | Sample | | | Intervention | | | | |
Study	N	Grade	Language Status Definition	Duration & Routine	Instructional Practices	Materials	Professional Development	Delivery
Stuart, 1999	112	Pre & K	English as a Second Language learners	12 weeks 1 hour daily In-class Whole class	Phonological awareness Letter-sound correspondences Whole class instruction with small group follow-up activities	Phonics Handbook (Lloyd, 1992), photocopied worksheets, phonics workbooks, "finger" phonics books (small decodable texts), phonics books wall chart, phonics jigsaw puzzles, stencils, videos	Researcher met with teachers Teachers given Phonics Handbook, training video, and option to attend training seminar by program author (2 out of 3 attended)	Instructors: Classroom teachers Fidelity:*

Oral Reading Fluency

De La Colina et al., 2001	74	1–2	Spanish-English bilingual students enrolled in ESL	8,10, and 12 weeks 45 minutes per	Read Naturally (RN: Ihnot, 1997): Instruction focuses on building fluency and	Translated RN passages (60–350 word passages at	*	Instructors: Classroom teachers

(Continued)

Study	N	Grade	Language Status Definition	Duration & Routine	Instructional Practices	Materials	Professional Development	Delivery
			program who scored at lowest ESL category (beginning or non-English speaker)	In-class One-on-one	comprehension; Repeated readings, modeling, and self-monitoring (students graphed their fluency before and after repeated reading practice) with a few comprehension questions following each passage	mid-1st grade through 6th grade reading levels, 24 per level)	*	Fidelity: Weekly observations by researchers; Self-monitoring with implementation checklist
Denton, 2000	93	2–5	Spanish–English bilingual students in bilingual classrooms, adequately fluent in both languages, average reading skills in Spanish,	8 weeks 40 minutes per session, 3 days per week Unclear if pull-out or in-class Small group (2–	2 instructional groups Read Well (RW: Sprick Howard, & Fidanque, 1998): Emphasizes phonics, vocabulary, and comprehension; Explicit, systematic phonics instruction, practice in fully	RW: Small books with decodable text, some of which are "duet" texts with more sophisticated language that teacher read aloud for	Each tutor trained in both methods (RN for 2 hours; RW for 4 hours), which included viewing videos of methods and hands-on practice	Instructors: Undergraduate students with a special education major Fidelity: Supervised by graduate

(Continued)

	Sample			Intervention				
Study	N	Grade	Language Status Definition	Duration & Routine	Instructional Practices	Materials	Professional Development	Delivery
			poor reading skills in English	4 students) and one-on-one	decodable texts, during-reading discussion and questioning designed to build vocabulary and comprehension, and post-reading comprehension worksheets Read Naturally (RN; Ihnot, 1992): Emphasizes fluency, vocabulary, and comprehension; Student selects passage, pre-reading vocabulary and comprehension activities, student reads passage aloud,	students RN: Short, interesting texts, presumably leveled	Tutors taking school-based practicum in reading instruction and received ongoing instruction in principles of reading instruction including Direct Instruction for students at-risk and with learning disabilities	students including researcher with 1–6 observations of tutoring sessions; Self-monitoring with implementation checklists

(Continued)

| | Sample | | | | Intervention | | | | |
Study	N	Grade	Language Status Definition	Duration & Routine	Instructional Practices	Materials	Professional Development	Delivery
					graphs fluency, rereads with and without audio-tape modeling until fluency goal met, answers multiple choice questions on passage, tutor times and quizzes student, and final fluency rate graphed			
Vocabulary								
Carlo et al., 2004	142	5	Spanish-speaking students in bilingual or mainstream programs and monolingual English-only students	15 weeks 30–45 minutes, four days per week In-class	Text-centered vocabulary instruction Day 1: Spanish-speaking students given Spanish-language text (in written and	Detailed lesson plans Newspaper articles, diaries, first hand documents, and historical	Curriculum materials provided, which included detailed lesson plans and quasi-scripted lesson guides	Instructor: Classroom teachers Fidelity: Three lessons filmed and coded for fidelity with

(Continued)

Study	Sample		Language Status Definition	Intervention			Professional Development	Delivery
	N	Grade		Duration & Routine	Instructional Practices	Materials		
				Whole group, small group, individual	audio-taped format) Day 2: English-language text introduced to whole group, target words identified and vocabulary activity Days 3 & 4: Small groups complete vocabulary activity with words from text Day 5: Direct instruction and activities in high utility vocabulary learning topics, such as awareness of cognates and polysemy or derivational word analysis	accounts on immigration	Biweekly learning community meetings in which coming weeks' materials were previewed and previous weeks' experiences were reflected on	reliability estimates

(Continued)

Study	Sample		Language Status Definition	Intervention				
	N	Grade		Duration & Routine	Instructional Practices	Materials	Professional Development	Delivery
Pérez, 1981	75	3	Mexican-American students with low reading achievement scores	3 months 20 minutes daily In-class Unspecified grouping	Oral Language Activities: Reading is presented as a step in a process of communication with its foundation in oral language	Teacher packets with oral language activity guides and materials, covering idiomatic expressions, riddles, analogies, compound words, polysemous words, etc.	Training included packets with instructional materials and suggestions, demonstration of using materials, and workshops on teaching ELLs	Instructor: Classroom teachers Fidelity: *
Vaughn-Shavuo, 1990	30	1	Spanish dominant bilingual students, as determined by district criteria	3 weeks 30 minutes daily Pull-out Small group	2 instructional groups Intervention group: Vocabulary taught using sentences that formed narratives	Steps to English Vocabulary Cue Card #1–7 (Kernan, 1983) Steps to English, Teacher's	Not applicable	Instructor: Researcher Fidelity: Not applicable

(Continued)

	Sample			Intervention				
Study	N	Grade	Language Status Definition	Duration & Routine	Instructional Practices	Materials	Professional Development	Delivery
					Control group: Vocabulary taught using unconnected sentences	Manual, Level One (Kernan, 1983)		
					Both groups engaged in the same follow-up writing activities involving the target vocabulary words	Story grammar cards		
Reading Comprehension								
Bean, 1982	45	4–5	Orally fluent Spanish-English bilingual students according to scores on bilingual language proficiency test	1 day Session length uncertain Pull-out One-on-one	3 groups Each group read one version of experimental text, gave free recall retelling and then prompted retelling targeting ten key ideas in story	583 words from the opening of the story entitled "The Chase Twins" from <u>Miami Linguistic Readers</u> (D.C. Heath, 1966) reading series	Not applicable	Instructor: Not applicable Fidelity: Not applicable

(Continued)

| Study | Sample | | Language Status Definition | Intervention | | | | |
	N	Grade		Duration & Routine	Instructional Practices	Materials	Professional Development	Delivery
						(third grade readability level)		
						Version of story edited to make anaphoric pronoun references more explicit (624 words; fourth grade readability level)		
						Version of story edited to omit trivial events to make problem-solving macropropositional structure		

(Continued)

| | Sample | | | Intervention | | | | |
Study	N	Grade	Language Status Definition	Duration & Routine	Instructional Practices	Materials	Professional Development	Delivery
						more apparent and anaphoric pronoun references also made more explicit (427 words; fifth grade readability level)		
Shames, 1998	58	9–11	ESOL students in their first or second year of ESOL	1 year 51 minutes daily In-class Whole group	3 instructional groups Community Language Learning (CLL; Curran, 1972): Cooperative learning of second language using student-generated stories and dialogs; Students	CLL; CLL+CPS: Student-generated stories and dialogs CPS; CLL+CPS: American history textbook written	Research assistant and facilitators attended training in CLL for 4 hours Research assistant also attended CPS	Instructors: Research assistant delivered primary instruction 3 days a week and set up follow-up activities;

(Continued)

Study	Sample			Intervention				
	N	Grade	Language Status Definition	Duration & Routine	Instructional Practices	Materials	Professional Development	Delivery
					discuss a topic of interest to them, conversation is audio-taped, listened to, written down, and read; students then reflect on learning process

Comprehension Processing Strategies (CPS): Comprehension strategies (K-W-L charts and Question-Answer-Relation-ships) introduced and modeled in three languages, and practiced each week with new texts; Vocabulary and sight | especially LEP students, also some student-generated texts from CLL group | training for 4 hours | Classroom teacher delivered follow-up activities; Two bilingual community language facilitators present at all times

Fidelity: * |

(Continued)

Study	Sample		Language Status Definition	Intervention		Instructional Practices	Materials	Professional Development	Delivery
	N	Grade		Duration & Routine					
						words reviewed prior to reading, with letter-sound correspondences reviewed as needed			
						CLL + CPS: Methods alternated every two weeks beginning with CLL			
Swice-good, 1990	95	3	Bilingual Spanish-dominant Hispanic students enrolled in bilingual Spanish-English classes	6 weeks 90 minutes daily In-class Whole group		Self-generated questioning strategies Definition, modeling, and practice of strategy Practice occurred independently and in pairs and small groups	Third grade basal reader: Lima, Naranja, Limon (Flores, Guzman, Long, Macias, Somoza, & Tinajero, 1987)	Orientation, question-and-answer, and training sessions (unclear length)	Instructors: Classroom teachers Fidelity: Unscheduled classroom observations and visits; Teachers kept anecdotal logs

(Continued)

	Sample		Intervention					
	N	Grade	Language Status Definition	Duration & Routine	Instructional Practices	Materials	Professional Development	Delivery
Study								
Writing								
Franken et al., 1999	20	9–12*	Diverse students from a variety of countries (Taiwan, Hong Kong, Malaysia, Korea, India, Mexico, Macedonia, Fiji, etc.) learning English as a Second Language (ESL)	6 weeks 2 sessions amounting to a total of 2.5 hours per week In-class Whole group and student pairs	Instruction and practice in writing argumentative essays 2 groups of students: on alternate weeks one group of students worked with a self-selected peer and the other group worked independently First session was a double period in which students completed prewriting tasks, including study of a sample argumentative text, brainstorming, and mapping	Sample texts and writing prompts written on cue cards	*	Instructors: Classroom teacher and researcher Fidelity: *

(Continued)

| | Sample | | | | Intervention | | | | |
Study	N	Grade	Language Status Definition		Duration & Routine	Instructional Practices	Materials	Professional Development	Delivery
						Second session was a single period in which students wrote their own argumentative essays using a cue card with a writing prompt			
						First two weeks spent writing on general topics without outside textual support; second two weeks used more specific science topics and lists of facts; and third week used most specific topics and written texts as resources			

(Continued)

	Sample				Intervention			Professional Development	Delivery
Study	N	Grade	Language Status Definition		Duration & Routine	Instructional Practices	Materials		
Gómez et al., 1996	72	5	Students classified as Level I, II, and III in English language proficiency based on cumulative files, standardized achievement tests, informal assessments, and an interview		6 weeks 4.5 hours daily, 2–4 days per week In-class Whole group	2 instructional groups Free Writing (FW): Students selected their own topics and wrote for as long as they wanted; Teachers wrote responses to content of writing rather than correcting errors, engaging students in written dialogs; Students encouraged to plan and share their writing in small groups Structured Writing (SW): Topics assigned by teachers; Students wrote for 9 minutes;	*	FW and SW teachers and assistants trained separately in 2 3-hour sessions Received ongoing direction and support from researcher	Instructor: Classroom teachers and instructional assistants Fidelity: Supervision by researchers with daily monitoring using checklists Minor corrective consultations as needed

(Continued)

| Study | Sample | | | Intervention | | | | |
	N	Grade	Language Status Definition	Duration & Routine	Instructional Practices	Materials	Professional Development	Delivery
					Students worked alone and quietly; Teachers corrected errors, focusing on those deemed most important			
					All students permitted to write in English and Spanish			
Prater et al., 1993	46	4–6	Students in general education classrooms who had previously been in ESL or bilingual classrooms, who were judged limited English	3 weeks Daily (session length uncertain) In-class small group and individual	Students wrote one composition per week by selecting a writing20topic, writing a first draft, revising, editing, and completing a final rewrite	*	*	Instructor: Classroom teachers Fidelity:*
					Students in the small			

(Continued)

| Study | Sample | | Language Status Definition | Intervention | | | | |
	N	Grade		Duration & Routine	Instructional Practices	Materials	Professional Development	Delivery
			Proficient by their teacher		group condition discussed their potential topics and shared their first and revised drafts; also received instruction and modeling in group processes and responding to others' writing			
					Students in the individual condition completed all steps individually with only traditional written corrective feedback from the teacher			

(Continued)

Study	Sample			Intervention			Professional Development	Delivery
	N	Grade	Language Status Definition	Duration & Routine	Instructional Practices	Materials		
Sengupta, 2000	100	9–12	Bilingual students in English programs in Hong Kong	1 year 80-minute lesson, weekly In-class Whole group	Revision Instruction: Focus on making texts more "reader-friendly" in both organization and content through addition, deletion, re-ordering, and substitution during the production of multiple drafts Teachers gradually released responsibility by first offering extensive guidance, and then moving to peer-evaluation and finally self-evaluation with little scaffolding	Researcher provided lesson plans, pre-writing input for topics for all classes, and related teaching materials and guidelines	*	Instructors: Classroom teachers Fidelity: *

(Continued)

Study	Sample			Intervention					
	N	Grade	Language Status Definition	Duration & Routine	Instructional Practices	Materials	Professional Development	Delivery

Complex Approaches

Encouraging Reading & Writing

Study	N	Grade	Language Status Definition	Duration & Routine	Instructional Practices	Materials	Professional Development	Delivery
Elley, 1991	535 459	4–5 5–6	Fiji students learning to read in English after several years of Fijian or Hindi reading instruction	2 years SBE: Daily (session length uncertain) SSR: 20–30 minutes, daily In-class Whole group	2 instructional groups Shared Book Experience (SBE; Holdaway, 1979): Teacher reads book over several days with students increasingly joining in and lots of free-ranging discussion; Follow-up extension activities involving artistic interpretation, paired rereading, and acting Sustained Silent Reading (SSR):	250 new books, mainly illustrated storybooks	SBE: 3 day in-service SSR: Notes outlining approach and its principles distributed	Instructor: Classroom teachers Fidelity: Researchers visited schools every two months

(Continued)

Study	Sample			Intervention				Delivery
	N	Grade	Language Status Definition	Duration & Routine	Instructional Practices	Materials	Professional Development	
					Students encouraged to read silently for pleasure; Teachers motivated reading by displaying, talking about, and reading from books			
Schon et al., 1982	114	2–4	Hispanic students in bilingual classrooms	8 months At least 60 minutes weekly In-class Whole group	Provided free reading time Developed positive attitudes toward reading through fun and social activities, such as read alouds and book sharing	Extensive collection of Spanish-language books, selected for attractive illustrations, simple texts, and high interest	*	Instructors: Classroom teachers Fidelity:*

(Continued)

Sample				Intervention				
Study	N	Grade	Language Status Definition	Duration & Routine	Instructional Practices	Materials	Professional Development	Delivery
Schon et al., 1984	272	9–12	Hispanic students in remedial reading classes	4–7 months At least 12 minutes daily, or 55 minutes weekly In-class Whole group	Provided free reading time	Extensive collection of Spanish-language newspapers, magazines, and books, selected for range of readability and high interest	*	Instructors: Remedial reading teachers Fidelity: Bilingual resource person visited classes biweekly to guide and monitor teachers
Schon et al., 1985	400	7–8	Hispanic students in homogeneously grouped reading classes	8.5 months At least 45 minutes weekly In-class	Provide free reading time Encourage interested students to read Spanish materials	Extensive collection of Spanish-language newspapers, magazines, and	*	Instructors: Reading teachers Fidelity: Bilingual

(Continued)

| | Sample | | | Intervention | | | | |
Study	N	Grade	Language Status Definition	Duration & Routine	Instructional Practices	Materials	Professional Development	Delivery
				Whole group		books, selected for range of readability and high interest		resource person visited classes biweekly to guide and monitor teachers and update materials
Tudor *et al.*, 1989	45	4–5	Panjabi-speaking ESL students	3 months 1 hour daily After-school Individual	Sustained silent reading Students chose their own books and could take books home Students gave oral reports on their reading selection about once a week	Leveled books (104 titles, many with multiple copies) Dictionaries	Not applicable	Instructor: Researcher Fidelity: Not applicable

(Continued)

| | Sample | | | Intervention | | | | |
Study	N	Grade	Language Status Definition	Duration & Routine	Instructional Practices	Materials	Professional Development	Delivery
Tsang, 1996	144	8–12	Cantonese students in English programs in Hong Kong	20 weeks 40 minute sessions, 7–9 times every six days In class Individual	3 instructional groups Traditional Writing Instruction plus Unrelated Enrichment: Students required to complete 8 math assignments with minimal English required; Assignments marked and returned to students by researcher Traditional Writing Instruction plus Extensive Reading: Students required to read 8 books from a list a leveled books available in the school	In extensive reading group: Leveled books, including simplified classics, original books, and information-based books representing a variety of interests	*	Instructors: Classroom teachers Fidelity: Researcher verified teacher fidelity every 2 weeks for first 2 months and weekly thereafter

(Continued)

Study	Sample			Intervention				
	N	Grade	Language Status Definition	Duration & Routine	Instructional Practices	Materials	Professional Development	Delivery
					library; Students completed brief book review forms after reading each book, graded on details and persuasiveness by researcher			
					Traditional Writing Instruction plus Frequent Practice: Students required to write 8 essays of varying content and genres; Essays graded impressionistically by researcher			
					Best math assignments, reviews, and essays displayed and commented on publicly every 3 weeks			

(Continued)

	Sample			Intervention				
Study	N	Grade	Language Status Definition	Duration & Routine	Instructional Practices	Materials	Professional Development	Delivery
Reading to Children								
Hancock, 2002	77	K	Monolingual Spanish- and English-speaking children	1 semester (75 days)

Daily

Home-based

Individual | Teachers sent home a book each day

The treatment group received Spanish language books, while controls received English language books

Instructions in same language as book sent home asking parents to read the book to their child | Families Read Every Day (FRED) books

30 new Spanish-language FRED books distributed to each classroom | Parents asked to read a short paragraph aloud in either Spanish or English during parent/teacher conference

Paragraph emphasized benefits of reading aloud to children | Instructor: Parent or guardian

Fidelity: Parents asked to note their reading in a log kept in each book |
| Hastings-Góngora, 1993 | 11 | K | Bilingual Spanish-dominant students in a bilingual classroom | 5 weeks

*

Home-based | Parents encouraged to read aloud to children at home

Packets of children's | Packets of 7 Spanish-language children's books | 12-hour training workshop for parents and their children | Instructor: Parents

Fidelity: Parents given |

(Continued)

Study	Sample		Intervention		Instructional Practices	Materials	Professional Development	Delivery
	N	Grade	Language Status Definition	Duration & Routine				
			(degree of proficiency unclear)	One-on-one	books with a book-reading log sent home to two groups of parents: one group received training in reading aloud, the other did not	Spanish-language article on importance of reading to children (Trelease, 1992)	Bilingual teacher modeled reading aloud to children, shared and discussed an article on the benefits of parents reading to children, and provided a practice opportunity and feedback	a book-reading log
Ulanoff et al., 1999	60	3	English learners for whom Spanish was their first language	1 day

1 session (session length uncertain) | 3 instructional groups

Preview/Review: Teacher built background | Children's book: The Napping House (Wood & Wood, 1984) | * | Instructor: Classroom teacher

Fidelity: * |

(Continued)

| | Sample | | | Intervention | | | | |
Study	N	Grade	Language Status Definition	Duration & Routine	Instructional Practices	Materials	Professional Development	Delivery
				In-class	knowledge and previewed difficult vocabulary in Spanish, then children listened to teacher read book aloud in English, and teacher reviewed the story in Spanish			
				Whole group				
					Translation: Children listened to teacher read book aloud in English and concurrently translate the story into Spanish			
					Control: Students listened to teacher read book aloud in English with no intervention or discussion of story			

(Continued)

| | Sample | | | Intervention | | | | |
Study	N	Grade	Language Status Definition	Duration & Routine	Instructional Practices	Materials	Professional Development	Delivery
Tutoring and Remediation								
Escamilla 1994	46	1	Spanish-dominant students receiving initial reading instruction in Spanish and scoring low on 2 Spanish-language literacy measures (Spanish dominance determined using Home Language Survey and Language Assessment Scales)	12–16 weeks 30 minutes daily Pull-out One-on-one	Descubriendo la Lectura: Spanish version of Reading Recovery; Students receive short-term, individualized tutoring in becoming independent readers and writers; Activities are not prescribed, but include guided reading, problem solving, and daily writing; Instruction often builds on student writing	300 Spanish-language children's books at 28 levels of difficulty Spanish Observation Survey	1 year of training in Descubriendo la Lectura	Instructor: Descubriendo la Lectura teachers

(Continued)

	Sample			Intervention					
Study	N	Grade	Language Status Definition	Duration & Routine	Instructional Practices	Materials	Professional Development	Delivery
Syvanen, 1997	16	4–5	Intermediate ESL students	19 weeks 70–80 minutes, twice weekly In-class Whole group, individual	Students met with a reading buddy/tutee in kindergarten or first grade twice a week for 30 minutes Each tutoring session preceded by 20–30 minutes of preparation and training and 20 minutes of writing reflectively about and sharing experience Preparation and training included demonstrations of oral reading techniques, choosing appropriate books, and giving positive feedback	Children's books Reflective journals	*	Instructor: Classroom teachers Fidelity: *

(Continued)

Study	Sample		Language Status Definition	Intervention Duration & Routine	Instructional Practices	Materials	Professional Development	Delivery
	N	Grade						
Other Investigations								
Calderón et al., 1998	222	2–3	Bilingual students enrolled in transitional bilingual program	2 years 2 hours daily In-class (and pull-out) Whole group and small group	2 instructional groups using same basal materials (see Materials column) Traditional basal group: 90 minutes of largely whole group reading language arts instruction and 30 minutes pull-out ESL class; Activities included round-robin reading and workbook practice; Spanish basal used all year; English text introduced midyear and alternated daily with Spanish basal	Spanish basal reading series: Campanitas de Oro (Long & Tinajero, 1989) English transitional text: Transitional Reading Program (Tinajero, Long, Calderón, Castagha, & Maldonaldo-Colón, 1989)	Teachers of BCIRC students received extensive professional development and collaborated with researchers; Training in integration of first- and second-language development and transition principles, theories, and practices, as	Instructor: Classroom teachers Fidelity: *

(Continued)

Study	Sample			Intervention				
	N	Grade	Language Status Definition	Duration & Routine	Instructional Practices	Materials	Professional Development	Delivery
					Bilingual Cooperative Integrated Reading and Composition (BCIRC): 120 minutes direct instruction in reading comprehension and integrated writing and language arts, supplemented by worksheets; Each activity introduced by teacher to whole group and practiced in small groups and individually; Spanish basal used all year; English text introduced midyear and alternated every 2 weeks with Spanish basal		well as student-centered, constructivist philosophy	

(Continued)

Study	Sample			Intervention			Professional Development	Delivery
	N	Grade	Language Status Definition	Duration & Routine	Instructional Practices	Materials		
Cohen et al., 1980	150	1	Bilingual Mexican-American students competent enough in spoken English to handle English-language reading instruction (monolingual Spanish students excluded)	4 weeks 90 45-minute daily lessons In-class Whole group and/or small groups	2 instructional method using same basal series (see Materials column) High Intensity Learning: Students pretested and placed at points in curriculum aligned to their performance; Students work individually at a self-directed pace until they demonstrate mastery in workbook before progressing to reading from reader; Reading occurs individually or in small teacher-led groups	The Reading House Comprehension and Vocabulary (Lime) Series (Cohen & Hyman, 1977), which included taped lessons, 200-page workbook with 5 lessons on 18 instructional objectives, pre and post criterion-referenced tests, and a reader with a reading selection for each objective	All teachers received regular training provided by publisher in using the basal series, although teachers of two groups were trained separately Teachers using the Ramirez and Castaneda model additionally trained using the model's manual; Trainer selected by model authors	Instructor: Classroom teachers Fidelity: *

(Continued)

Study	Sample			Intervention				
	N	Grade	Language Status Definition	Duration & Routine	Instructional Practices	Materials	Professional Development	Delivery
					Ramirez and Castaneda Model (1974): Culturally-based instruction designed for Mexican-American students using whole and small groupings; Instruction is teacher-directed and sensitive to students' culture			
Golden-berg et al., 1992	10	K	Spanish-speaking students of Latin-American-born parents enrolled in Spanish-language kindergarten	1 year * Home-based One-on-one	2 instructional groups Reading Encouraged: New booklet sent home every 3 weeks; Parents encouraged to read aloud to children at home; Identical booklets used in classrooms	Set of 12 Spanish-language black-and-white booklets with simple plots and progressively more complex language	Teacher training unclear Parents in Reading Encouraged group told booklets would be sent home, encouraged to	Instructor: Parents Fidelity: Home observations conducted twice monthly

(Continued)

	Sample			Intervention				
Study	N	Grade	Language Status Definition	Duration & Routine	Instructional Practices	Materials	Professional Development	Delivery
					Phonics Worksheets: Packets of phonics worksheets sent home; Packets approximately same length as booklets; Packets aligned with classroom instruction	Phonics worksheets focused on developing letter and syllable knowledge through phonological activities and writing	treat them like any other children's book, and told not to teach word reading or decoding Training of parents in Phonics Worksheets group unclear	
Neuman et al., 1992	129	7–8	Students enrolled in various stages of transitional bilingual program	12 weeks 15–20 minute lessons, each lesson given twice weekly In-class	4 instructional groups Traditional TV: Students watched original versions of episodes after a one-sentence introduction; Lesson ended with a	Nine video segments of 3–2–1 Contact, a Children's Television Workshop science program;	*	Instructor: Classroom teachers Fidelity: Researchers monitored conditions via

(Continued)

220

Study	Sample			Intervention				
	N	Grade	Language Status Definition	Duration & Routine	Instructional Practices	Materials	Professional Development	Delivery
				Unspecified grouping	brief summary and no instruction of target vocabulary words Captioned TV: Students watched captioned versions of episodes after a one-sentence introduction; Lesson ended with a brief summary and no instruction of target vocabulary words Script: Students read and listened to other and read aloud a script of the captioned episodes Textbook: Regular science instruction;	Segments organized in 3 units of 3 segments each on survival, protection, and breathing Captioned version of video segments Texts with no pictures based on captioned versions of video segments		informal classroom visits and weekly teacher meetings

(Continued)

Study	N	Grade	Language Status Definition	Duration & Routine	Instructional Practices	Materials	Professional Development	Delivery
					Oral lessons in first language followed by reading from English-language textbooks; Topics differed from episodes			informal classroom visits and weekly teacher meetings
Saunders, 1999	125	2–5	Spanish-speaking LEP students enrolled in transitional bilingual program	4 years	Multi-year Transition Program: Comprehensive Language arts program with 12 components and 4 principles designed to transition students to	*	*	Instructor: Classroom teachers, who are members of a collaborative research team
				Daily (session length uncertain)				
				In-class	English instruction; 1st 2 years reading and writing instruction occurs in Spanish except for oral English language			Fidelity: *
				Unspecified grouping				

	(Continued)

	Sample			Intervention				
Study	N	Grade	Language Status Definition	Duration & Routine	Instructional Practices	Materials	Professional Development	Delivery
					development; 3rd year English reading and writing introduced, while Spanish reading and writing instruction continues; 4th and final year language arts instruction entirely in Spanish			
Saunders et al., 1999	116	4–5	Limited English proficient (LEP) students and fluent English-speaking students (both monolinguals and former LEPs)	4 days 90 minutes, daily In-class Small group	4 instructional groups All 4 within Multi-year Transition Program (see Saunders, 1999 above) and used rotating hetero-geneous small groups, with 2 seen each day for 45 minutes	Children's book: Louella's Song (Greenfield, 1993)	Teachers function as part of research team, which meets twice monthly to study instructional components, view videos	Instructor: Classroom teachers, who are members of a collaborative research team Fidelity: Researchers

(Continued)

223

Study	Sample			Intervention			Professional Development	Delivery
	N	Grade	Language Status Definition	Duration & Routine	Instructional Practices	Materials		
					Read + Study: Students worked independently on unrelated reading and writing activities		and demonstrations, plan units, and analyze student work	had daily contact with teachers
					Literature Logs (LL): Students prompted twice to write about experiences they have had that are similar to two of the protagonist's; Writing shared in two small group meetings with teacher		Teachers helped plan research	
					Instructional Conversation (IC): Students met twice with teacher in small			

(Continued)

Study	Sample		Language Status Definition	Intervention		Instructional Practices	Materials	Professional Development	Delivery
	N	Grade		Duration & Routine					
						groups to discuss the factual content and abstract concepts in the story			had daily contact with teachers
						LL + IC: Students met with teacher 4 times in small groups and completed all activities the LL and IC groups did			
Tharp, 1982	204	1	Bidialectical students speaking Hawaiian Creole English and standard English and "other" students (from a wide	1 year Daily (session length uncertain) In-class Small groups		KEEP Comprehension Program: Comprehension dominates reading curriculum; Students alternately read and discuss what they read with the teacher; Teachers guides	*	"Brief" training with follow-up supervision in KEEP comprehension approach	Instructor: Classroom teachers Fidelity: Follow-up supervision

(Continued)

Study	Sample			Intervention				
	N	Grade	Language Status Definition	Duration & Routine	Instructional Practices	Materials	Professional Development	Delivery
			variety of linguistic and cultural background and unclear linguistic proficiency)		discussions to promote connections with students' experiences and generate engagement in reading; Phonics, decoding, and vocabulary also taught, but within context of material also being read for comprehension			
Waxman et al., 1994	88 52	1–5 1–5	Hispanic LEP students with low achievement as identified by the district	6 months 15 3-hour sessions In-class Whole group	4 instructional groups Each group was taught by a teacher trained in 1 of 4 ways (see Professional Development column)	*	ESL in Content Areas (Chamot & O'Malley, 1986; 1987): Model builds English-language and content	Instructor: Classroom teachers Fidelity: *

(Continued)

	Sample			*Intervention*				
Study	*N*	*Grade*	*Language Status Definition*	*Duration & Routine*	*Instructional Practices*	*Materials*	*Professional Development*	*Delivery*
							knowledge through context-embedded problem solving; Concepts, problem-solving skills, and cognitive and metacognitive techniques (e.g., graphic mapping) taught in science, math, and reading using Spanish and English; Training	

(Contined)

Study	Sample			Intervention			Professional Development	Delivery
	N	Grade	Language Status Definition	Duration & Routine	Instructional Practices	Materials		
							focuses on verbalization, problem solving, imagery, and other cognitive heuristics, as well as cognitive and metacognitive learning strategies	
							Effective Use of Time (Stallings, 1980; 1986): Model focuses on using classroom time effectively; Its four steps are	

(Continued)

Study	Sample			Intervention				
	N	Grade	Language Status Definition	Duration & Routine	Instructional Practices	Materials	Professional Development	Delivery
							pre-testing, informing, organizing instruction through guided practice, and post-testing	
							Combination: Training time split equally between the ESL in Content Areas and Effective Use of Time models	
							Control: No training	

(Continued)

Sample				Intervention				Delivery
Study	N	Grade	Language Status Definition	Duration & Routine	Instructional Practices	Materials	Professional Development	

Success for All

Dianda et al., 1995	147	K-1	Spanish-dominant students, Spanish ESL students, and "other" ESL students	2 years	Comprehensive school reform program that focuses on prevention, early intervention, and long-term professional development	Exito para Todos (Spanish language) materials Success for All materials	*	Instructor: * Fidelity: *
Slavin et al., 1998:AZ	138	1	Spanish-dominant students	1 year Reading period: 90 minutes daily, in-class, whole group Tutoring: 20 minutes, uncertain frequency, pull-out, individual	Homogeneous reading groups of 15 students in which oral reading, story structure and comprehension, and integrated reading and writing are emphasized Beginning reading instruction also addresses phonological	Exito Para Todos (Spanish language) materials	Teachers received detailed teacher manuals and 2 days of in-service training at beginning of year Several follow-up in-service sessions during the year	Instructor: Spanish-English bilingual classroom teachers Fidelity: On-site program facilitator visited classes and tutoring sessions frequently

(Continued)

	Sample			Intervention				
Study	N	Grade	Language Status Definition	Duration & Routine	Instructional Practices	Materials	Professional Development	Delivery
					awareness, letter-sound correspondence, and decoding		reviewed classroom management, instructional pacing, and curriculum implementation	
Slavin et al., 1998: Fairhill	50	1–3	Limited English Proficient Hispanic students, as defined by district criteria	2 years	Student progress assessed every 8 weeks, at which point students may move to different reading groups	Success for All materials	Teachers received detailed teacher manuals and 2 days of in-service training at beginning of year	Instructor: Classroom teachers and ESL teachers
				Reading period: 90 minutes daily, in-class, whole group				Fidelity: On-site program facilitator visited classes and tutoring sessions frequently
				Tutoring: 20 minutes, uncertain frequency, pull-out, individual	One-on-one tutoring for students having difficulty keeping up with their homogeneous reading group		Several follow-up in-service sessions during the year	

(Continued)

Study	Sample			Intervention				
	N	Grade	Language Status Definition	Duration & Routine	Instructional Practices	Materials	Professional Development	Delivery
							reviewed classroom management, instructional pacing, and curriculum implementation	

* Insufficient information provided in the article to allow determination.

APPENDIX 6.D: STUDY SAMPLES AND METHODS USED TO IDENTIFY THE SAMPLES

Author	Study Sample	Methods Used to Identify Study Sample
Ruiz, 1995	A bilingual (Spanish–English) self-contained classroom for students identified as language learning disabled.	Not described here—see Ruiz (1988) for the complete ethnographic investigation of this classroom.
Wolf, 1993	Three limited-English-proficient third- and fourth-grade students.	Not described, but author indicates the boys had all received a Resource Specialist Program label that caused retention and special classroom placement throughout their careers.
Hughes, Vaughn, & Schumm, 1999	80 language-minority Hispanic parents.	Forty of the parents were selected based on their children having been identified by the school district as learning disabled (LD). School district criteria for LD identification included a discrepancy of one or more standard deviations between IQ and an academic score in reading, writing, arithmetic, or spelling; evidence of a disorder in one or more of the basic psychological processes; LD not due to second-language learning or other exclusionary criteria.
Perozzi, 1985[5]	Three English-speaking (ES) and three Spanish-speaking (SS) preschool children;	The diagnosis of the Spanish-speaking subjects was based on the clinical impression of the

(Continued)

[5] Although they were administered standardized scales of language functioning, details of the scores are not presented, making it difficult to understand the nature and degree of their deficit.

Author	Study Sample	Methods Used to Identify Study Sample
	one SS student was diagnosed as having mild language delay, one as being language disordered, and one as having normal language. One ES student was diagnosed as having mild language delay and two as having normal language.	diagnostician using the pooled information described below. The diagnoses for the English-speaking children were substantiated by scores on the Test of Language Development (TOLD).

A bilingual/bicultural American Speech-Language-Hearing Association (ASHA) certified speech-language pathologist with 10 years' experience working with communicatively handicapped bilingual children conducted an extensive interview with the parents of the subjects wherein a case history was obtained and a determination of the subjects' native language was made. A language-use matrix, which assesses the language of interaction between a child and parents, siblings, and others in the home environment, was used. Subjects were designated as Spanish speakers if only Spanish was used in the home and as English speakers if only English was used. If both languages were used, the subjects were dropped from the study.

Diagnosis of level of language functioning was conducted in Spanish for the SS children and |

(Continued)

Author	Study Sample	Methods Used to Identify Study Sample
		in English for the ES children. SS subjects were administered a locally translated Spanish adaptation of the Assessment of Children's Language Comprehension (ACLC) (Foster, Giddan, & Stark, 1973). ES children were administered the standard (English) version of the ACLC and TOLD (Newcomer & Hammill, 1977). An expressive language sample was obtained by the diagnostician for all six subjects in two contexts—child–clinician and child–parent conversations. Mean length of utterance, semantic content categories, and morphosyntactic forms were described and analyzed for each sample.
Echevarria, 1995, 1996[6]	The subjects in the study were classified as Learning Handicapped and had been placed in a self-contained special education classroom, Special Day Class (SDC)	Brigance, a criterion-referenced test to measure decoding and comprehension, was used to identify children who had poor decoding and comprehension.

Eligibility statements from Individualized Education Program (IEP) data indicate the following:[7] |

(Continued)

[6]Specific details regarding identification have not been provided.
[7]Information about the assessments used to provide the IEP data is not provided.

Author	Study Sample	Methods Used to Identify Study Sample
		1. Elena is eligible for special education due to learning disabilities in auditory memory, visual motor integration, and attention deficits affecting her educational performance in reading and written language.
		2. Fernanda has multiple handicaps, concomitant impairment, mental retardation, and orthopedic impairment, the combination of which causes such educational problems that she cannot be accommodated in a program solely for the impairments.
		3. Juan qualifies for special education due to a significant discrepancy between demonstrated ability and current academic performance in reading and language as related to auditory processing deficits and visual motor integration.
		4. Laura is eligible for special education services based on a discrepancy between her low average ability and achievement in the areas of reading and written language due to auditory sequential memory deficits and visual processing.
		5. Salvador is eligible for special education based on learning disabilities in the area of auditory processing and memory. These deficits affect his academic performance in all areas.

(Continued)

Author	Study Sample	Methods Used to Identify Study Sample
Bos, Allen, & Scanlon, 1989	Forty-two fourth- to sixth grade students with learning disabilities whose first language was Spanish and who spoke Spanish at home.	"Learning disabilities were identified according to a school district criteria including a discrepancy between intellectual ability and reading achievement" (p. 174).
Jiménez, 1997	Five Latino middle school students who were reading up to four grade levels below their current Grade 7 placement when the study began. Students' low levels of reading ability held true regardless of whether their dominant language was English or Spanish. Three students were drawn from a self-contained special education classroom and two from a self-contained at-risk bilingual education classroom.	Students in the special education class were administered the Total Reading Battery for the Metropolitan Achievement Test (MAT 6, Form L, 1986); Woodcock Spanish Psycho-Educational Battery (Form A, 1986); Receptive and Expressive One-Word Picture Vocabulary Tests (ROWPVX EOWPVT-R). Students in the self-contained at-risk bilingual education class had been identified by school personnel as at risk for referral to special education. One had taken the Spanish language academic achievement test, La Prueba Riverside de Realización en Español, Form A, Level 12.
Rohena, Jitendra, & Browder, 2002	Four Puerto Rican middle school students (two girls and two boys) with moderate mental retardation.	Each participant met the state criteria for mental retardation and district eligibility criteria for placement in life skills classrooms. Eligibility criteria included evidence of "impaired mental

(Continued)

Author	Study Sample	Methods Used to Identify Study Sample
		development which adversely affects the educational performance of a person. The term includes a person who exhibits a significantly impaired adaptive behavior in learning, maturation, or social adjustment as a result of subaverage intellectual functioning. The term does not include persons with IQ scores of 80" (Special Education Standards and Regulations of the Pennsylvania Department of Education, 1990, § 342). This determination was made through a full assessment and comprehensive report by a certified school psychologist. Determination of mental retardation was based on formal measures of intelligence, such as the Wechsler Intelligence Scale for Children, Third Edition (WISC–III; Wechsler, 1991) or the Stanford-Binet Intelligence Scale (Thorndike, Hagen, & Sattler, 1986), and of adaptive behavior, such as the Vineland Adaptive Behavior Scales (Sparrow, Balla, & Cichetti, 1984).
Rousseau, Tam, & Ramnarain, 1993[8]	Five Hispanic students, two males and three females, ages 11 years, 10 months to	All students attended the same special education class for language-minority students with speech

(Continued)

---

[8]The School Board did not allow specific scores for the children to be released. Thus, no information is presented on the actual test scores of the children, although they were tested in both English and Spanish (if Spanish was their first language). It would be interesting and important to know more about these children because it is not clear how the diagnosis of learning disability was made.

Author	Study Sample	Methods Used to Identify Study Sample
	12 years, 3 months (mean age = 12 years, 0 months) with speech and language deficits.	and language therapy three times per week. Diagnosis of speech and language deficits was made by a bilingual speech and language therapist using a test battery consisting of the Goldman-Fristoe Test of Articulation Skills (Goldman & Fristoe, 1986), the Clinical Evaluation of Language Fundamentals-Revised (Semel, Wiig, & Secord, 1987), and the Language Processing Test (Richard & Hanner, 1985). Additional diagnostic evaluation included the Degrees of Reading Power (DRP; Touchstone Applied Science Associates, 1990), administered annually to all elementary school students in Grades 3 through 6, and subtests of the Brigance Diagnostic Comprehensive Inventory (Brigance, 1983); the Kaufman Test of Educational Achievement (Kaufman & Kaufman, 1985), and the Woodcock-Johnson Psycho-Educational Battery-Revised (Woodcock & Johnson, 1989).
Graves, Valles, & Rueda, 2000	Four volunteers from a pool of 10 interns in the Bilingual Personnel Preparation Program in Special Education at San Diego State University, each working as a teacher intern, and their students.	All students were English-language learners with a learning disability, according to specific school district labeling processes. All students were tested in both Spanish and English and labeled because of a significant lag in both languages. All students had specific individualized education program goals in written expression.

(Continued)

Author	Study Sample	Methods Used to Identify Study Sample
VanWagenen, Williams, & McLaughlin, 1994[9]	Three Spanish-speaking students—one 12-year-old girl from Colombia, one 12-year-old boy from El Salvador, and one 12-year-old boy from Mexico—assigned to the special education teacher because of the need for intensive instruction on word recognition and meaning and pronunciation drill, with instruction in and application of grammatical structures.	Woodcock Reading Mastery Test Form A (Woodcock, 1973).
Fawcett & Lynch, 2000[10]	Children in their first year at a mixed-ability comprehensive school in Sheffield. Although the two English-language learners were identified as needing intensive literacy support because of reading and spelling performance 4 years behind their chronological age, it is not clear that their deficits were due to a learning disability.	Wechsler Objective Reading Dimension (WORD; Psychological Corporation, 1993) reading and spelling tests; the Dyslexia Screening Test (Fawcett & Nicolson, 1996); the British Picture Vocabulary Scale (BPVS; Dunn, Dunn, Whetton, & Pintillie, 1982).

(Continued)

[9]The diagnosis of reading difficulties was based on the Woodcock Reading Mastery Test. However, the scores of the children are not presented, so it is difficult to know the nature and extent of their reading difficulties.
[10]The Dyslexia Screening Test has poor validity.

Author	Study Sample	Methods Used to Identify Study Sample
Klingner & Vaughn, 1996[11]	The sample included 26 seventh- and eighth-grade students with learning disabilities.	Students selected to participate met the the following criteria: a significant discrepancy of at least 1.5 standard deviations between standard scores on an intelligence test and an achievement test (both administered in English) and evidence that their learning disabilities were not due to other conditions (e.g., English language learning, sensory handicap, physical handicap); Spanish spoken as their first language; English decoding skills at least at the second grade level; scores at least 2 years below grade level on the Woodcock-Johnson passage comprehension subtest.

---

[11]The diagnosis of learning disabled is especially problematic in this study because the researchers used the discrepancy between IQ and reading to identify students with learning disabilities; the use of the IQ test with language-minority children is inappropriate. In addition, the discrepancy definition should not be used to diagnose learning

REFERENCES

Alvarez, J. (1975). Comparison of academic aspirations and achievement in bilingual versus monolingual classrooms. Unpublished doctoral dissertation, University of Texas, Austin.

American Educational Research Association. (2005, Summer). Teaching teachers: Professional development to improve student achievement. *Research Points*, 3, 1–24.

Araujo, L. (2002). The literacy development of kindergarten English-language learners. *Journal of Research in Childhood Education*, 16, 232–247.

Au, K. H., & Carroll, J. H. (1997). Improving literacy achievement through a constructivist approach: The KEEP demonstration classroom project. *Elementary School Journal*, 97, 203–221.

Barik, H., & Swain, M. (1978). Evaluation of a bilingual education program in Canada: The Elgin study through grade six. *Bulletin CILA*, 27, 31–58.

Bean, T. W. (1982). Second language learners' comprehension of an ESL prose selection. *Journal of the Linguistic Association of the Southwest*, 4, 376–386.

Borenstein, M. (n.d.). Comprehensive meta-analysis: Study database analyser. Retrieved September 22, 2005, from http://www.assess.com/Software/Meta-Analysis.htm

Bos, C. S., Allen, A. A., & Scanlon, D. J. (1989). Vocabulary instruction and reading comprehension with bilingual learning disabled students. *Yearbook of the National Reading Conference*, 38, 173–179.

Brigance, A. H. (1983). Brigance Diagnostic Comprehensive Inventory of Basic Skills. North Billerica. MA: Curriculum Associates.

Browne, D. B., & Bordeaux, L. (1991). How South Dakota teachers see learning style differences. *Tribal College*, 2(4), 24–26.

Calderón, M., & Marsh, D. (1988, Winter). Applying research on effective bilingual instruction in a multi-district inservice teacher training program. *NABE Journal*, 133–152.

Calderón, M., & Minaya-Rowe, L. (2003). *Designing and implementing two-way bilingual programs*. Thousand Oaks, CA: Corwin.

Calderón, M., Hertz-Lazarowitz, R., & Slavin, R. E. (1998). Effects of Bilingual Cooperative Integrated Reading and Composition on students making the transition from Spanish to English reading. *Elementary School Journal*, 99, 153–165.

Campeau, P. L., Roberts, A., Oscar, H., Bowers, J. E., Austin, M., & Roberts, S. J. (1975). *The identification and description of exemplary bilingual education programs*. Palo Alto, CA: American Institutes for Research.

Carlo, M. S., August, D., McLaughlin, B., Snow, C. E., Dressler, C., Lippman, D., Lively, T., & White, C. (2004). Closing the gap: Addressing the vocabulary needs of English language learners in bilingual and mainstream classrooms. *Reading Research Quarterly*, 39, 188–215.

Cazden, C. (1992). *Language minority education in the United States: Implications of the Ramírez report*. Santa Cruz, CA, and Washington, DC: National Center for Research on Cultural Diversity and Second Language Learning. Available at www.ncbe.gwu.edu/miscpubs/ncrcdsll/epr3/

Chamot, A., & O'Malley, J. (1986). *A cognitive academic language learning approach: An ESL content-based curriculum*. Wheaton, MD: National Clearinghouse for Bilingual Education.

Chamot, A., & O'Malley, J. (1987). The cognitive academic language learning approach: A bridge to the mainstream. *TESOL Quarterly*, 21, 227–249.

Clark, C. M., & Peterson, P. L. (1986). Teachers' thought processes. In M. C. Wittrock (Ed.), *Handbook of research on teaching* (pp. 255–296). New York: Macmillan.

Cohen, A. D., Fathman, A. K., & Merino, B. (1976). *The Redwood City bilingual education report, 1971–1974: Spanish and English proficiency, mathematics, and language use over time.* Toronto: Ontario Institute for Studies in Education.

Cohen, S. A., & Hyman, J. S. (1977). *The reading house comprehension and vocabulary (lime) series.* New York: Random House.

Cohen, S. A., & Rodríquez, S. (1980). Experimental results that question the Ramírez-Castaneda model for teaching reading to first grade Mexican Americans. *Reading Teacher, 34,* 12–18.

Coleman, J., Campbell, E. Q., Hobson, C. J., McPartland, J., Mood, A. M., Weinfeld, F. D., & York, R. L. (1966). *Equality of educational opportunity.* Office of Education, U.S. Department of Health, Education, and Welfare. Washington, DC: U.S. Government Printing Office.

Covey, D. D. (1973). An analytical study of secondary freshmen bilingual education and its effects on academic achievement and attitudes of Mexican American students. Unpublished doctoral dissertation, Arizona State University.

Curran, C. A. (1972). *Counseling-learning: A whole-person model for education.* New York: Grune & Stratton.

Danoff, M. N., Coles, G. J., McLaughlin, D. H., & Reynolds, D. J. (1978). *Evaluation of the impact of ESEA Title VII Spanish/English bilingual education programs: Vol. I. Study design and interim findings: Vol. III. Year two impact data, educational process, and in-depth analyses.* Palo Alto, CA: American Institutes for Research.

De la Colina, M. G., Parker, R. I., Hasbrouck, J. E., & Lara-Alecio, R. (2001). Intensive intervention in reading fluency for at-risk beginning Spanish readers. *Bilingual Research Journal, 25,* 503–538.

De la Garza, V. J., & Medina, M., Jr. (1985). Academic achievement as influenced by bilingual instruction for Spanish-dominant Mexican American children. *Hispanic Journal of Behavioral Sciences, 7,* 247–259.

Denton, C. A. (2000). The efficacy of two English reading interventions in a bilingual education program. Unpublished doctoral dissertation, Texas A&M University, College Station.

Dianda, M. R., & Flaherty, J. F. (1995). *Report on workstation uses: Effects of Success for All on the reading achievement of first graders in California bilingual program.* (No. 91002006). Los Alamitos, CA: Southwest Regional Laboratory (ERIC Document Reproduction Service No. ED394327).

Doebler, L. K., & Mardis, L. J. (1980–81). Effects of a bilingual education program for Native American children. *NABE Journal, 5*(2), 23–28.

Dunn, L. M., Dunn, L. M., Whetton, C., & Pintillie, D. (1982). *The British Picture Vocabulary Scale (BPVS).* Berks, UK: National Foundation of Educational Research–Nelson.

Echevarría, J. (1995). Interactive reading instruction: A comparison of proximal and distal effects of instructional conversations. *Exceptional Children, 61,* 536–552.

Echevarría, J. (1996). The effects of instructional conversations on the language and concept development of Latino students with learning disabilities. *Bilingual Research Journal, 20,* 339–363.

Edmonds, R. (1979). Effective schools for the urban poor. *Educational Leadership, 37*(1), 15–24.

Elley, W. B. (1991). Acquiring literacy in a second language: The effect of book-based programs. *Language Learning, 41,* 375–411.

Engelmann, S., & Bruner, E. C. (1988). *Reading mastery.* Chicago, IL: Science Research Associates.

Engelmann, S., Carnine, L., & Johnson, G. (1988). *Corrective reading: Word-attack basics.* Teacher presentation book decoding A. Chicago, IL: Science Research Associates.

Escamilla, K. (1994). Descubriendo la lectura: An early intervention literacy program in Spanish. *Literacy Teaching and Learning, 1,* 57–70.

Escamilla, K., & Andrade, A. (1992). Descubriendo la lectura: An application of reading recovery in Spanish. *Education and Urban Society*, 24, 212–226.

Fawcett, A. J., & Lynch, L. (2000). Systematic identification and approach for reading difficulty: Case studies of children with EAL. *Dyslexia*, 6, 57–71.

Fawcett, A. J., & Nicolson, R. I. (1996). *The Dyslexia Screening Test*. London: The Psychological Corporation.

Fitzgerald, J. (1995a). English as a second language instruction in the United States: A research review. *Journal of Reading Behavior*, 27, 115–152.

Fitzgerald, J. (1995b). English-as-a-second-language learners' cognitive reading processes: A review of research in the United States. *Review of Educational Research*, 65, 145–190.

Fitzgerald, J., & Noblit, G. W. (1999). About hopes, aspirations, and uncertainty: First-grade English language learners' emergent reading. *Journal of Literacy Research*, 31, 133–182.

Fitzgerald, J., & Noblit, G. (2000). Balance in the making: Learning to read in an ethnically diverse first-grade classroom. *Journal of Educational Psychology*, 92, 3–22.

Flores, J., Guzmán, A., Long, S., Macías, R., Somoza, E., & Tinajero, J. (1987). *Lima, naranja, limón. Student's book*. New York: Macmillan.

Foster, R., Giddan, J. J., & Stark, J. (1973). *Assessment of children's language comprehension*. Palo Alto, CA: Consulting Psychologists Press.

Franken, M., & Haslett, S. J. (1999). Quantifying the effect of peer interaction on second language students' written argument texts. *New Zealand Journal of Educational Studies*, 34, 281–293.

Frith, U., Landerl, K., & Frith, C. (1995). Dyslexia and verbal fluency: More evidence for a phonological deficit. *Dyslexia*, 1, 2–11.

Genesee, F., Sheiner, E., Tucker, G. R., & Lambert, W. E. (1976). An experiment in trilingual education. *Canadian Modern Language Review*, 32, 115–128.

Genishi, C., Stires, S. E., & Yung-Chan, D. (2001). Writing in an integrated curriculum: Prekindergarten English language learners as symbol makers. *Elementary School Journal*, 101, 399–416.

Gersten, R., & Baker, S. (2000). What we know about effective instructional practices for English language learners. *Exceptional Children*, 66, 454–470.

Gersten, R., & Jiménez, R. T. (1994). A delicate balance: Enhancing literature instruction for students of English as a second language. *Reading Teacher*, 47, 438–449.

Gersten, R., & Woodward, J. (1995). A longitudinal study of transitional and immersion bilingual education programs in one district. *Elementary School Journal*, 95, 223–239.

Goldenberg, C., & Gallimore, R. (1991). Local knowledge, research knowledge, and educational change: A case study of early Spanish reading improvement. *Educational Researcher*, 20, 2–14.

Goldenberg, C., Reese, L., & Gallimore, R. (1992). Effects of literacy materials from school on Latino children's home experiences and early reading achievement. *American Journal of Education*, 100(4), 497–536.

Goldman, R., & Fristoe, M. (1986). *Goldman–Fristoe Test of Articulation Skills*. Circle Pines, MN: American Guidance Service.

Gómez, R., Jr., Parker, R., Lara-Alecio, R., & Gómez, L. (1996). Process versus product writing with limited English proficient students. *Bilingual Research Journal*, 20, 209–233.

Graham, S., & Perin, D. (in press). A meta-analysis of writing instruction for adolescent students. *Journal of Educational Psychology*.

Graves, A. W., Valles, E. C., & Rueda, R. (2000). Variations in interactive writing instruction: A study in four bilingual special education settings. *Learning Disabilities Research & Practice*, 15, 1–9.

Greene, J. P. (1997). A meta-analysis of the Rossell and Baker review of bilingual education research. *Bilingual Research Journal*, 21, 1–22.

Greenfield, E. (1993). Louella's song. In J. Pikulski (Sr. Author), *Dinosauring* (4th grade reader, pp. 430–436). Boston, MA: Houghton-Mifflin.

Gunn, B., Biglan, A., Smolkowski, K., & Ary, D. (2000). The efficacy of supplemental instruction in decoding skills for Hispanic and non-Hispanic students in early elementary school. *Journal of Special Education, 34*, 90–103.

Gunn, B., Smolkowski, K., Biglan, A., & Black, C. (2002). Supplemental instruction in decoding skills for Hispanic and non-Hispanic students in early elementary school: A follow-up. *Journal of Special Education, 36*, 69–79

Haager, D., & Windmueller, M. P. (2001). Early reading approach for English language learners at-risk for learning disabilities: Student and teacher outcomes in an urban school. *Learning Disability Quarterly, 24*, 235–249.

Hancock, D. R. (2002). The effects of native language books on the pre-literacy skill development of language minority kindergartners. *Journal of Research in Childhood Education, 17*, 62–68.

Hastings-Góngora, B. (1993). The effects of reading aloud on vocabulary development: Teacher insights. *Bilingual Research Journal, 17*, 135–138.

Hedges, L. V. (1981). Distribution theory for Glass's estimator of effect size and related estimators. *Journal of Educational Statistics, 6*, 107–128.

Hernández, J. S. (1991). Assisted performance in reading comprehension strategies with non- English proficient students. *Journal of Educational Issues of Language Minority Students, 8*, 91–112.

Hoffman, J. V., Roser, N. L., & Farest, C. (1988). Literature-sharing strategies in classrooms serving students from economically disadvantaged and language different home environments. *Yearbook of the National Reading Conference, 37*, 331–337.

Holdaway, D. (1979). *Foundations of literacy.* Sydney, New South Wales: Ashton Scholastic.

Hughes, M. T., Vaughn, S., & Schumm, J. S. (1999). Home literacy activities: Perceptions and practices of Hispanic parents of children with learning disabilities. *Learning Disability Quarterly, 22*, 224–235.

Hus, Y. (2001). Early reading for low-SES minority language children: An attempt to "catch them before they fall." *Folia Phoniatrica et Logopedica, 53*, 178–182.

Huzar, H. (1973). The effects of an English–Spanish primary grade reading program on second and third grade students. Unpublished master's thesis, Rutgers University.

Ihnot, C. (1992, 1997). *Read naturally.* St. Paul, MN: Read Naturally.

Jencks, C. M., Ackland, H., Bane, M. J., Cohen, D., Ginitis, H., Heyns, B., & Michelson, (1972). *Inequality: A reassessment of the effect of family and schooling in America.* New York: Harper & Row.

Jiménez, R. T. (1997). The strategic reading abilities and potential of five low-literacy Latina/o readers in middle school. *Reading Research Quarterly, 32*, 224–243.

Jiménez, R. T., & Gersten, R. (1999). Lessons and dilemmas derived from the literacy instruction of two Latina/o teachers. *American Educational Research Journal, 36*, 265–301.

Johnson, K. E. (1992). The relationship between teachers' beliefs and practices during literacy instruction for non-native speakers of English. *Journal of Reading Behavior, 24*, 83–108.

Kaufman, A. S., & Kaufman, N. L. (1985). *Kaufman Test of Educational Achievement.* Circle Pines, MN: American Guidance Service.

Kaufman, M. (1968). Will instruction in reading Spanish affect ability in reading English? *Journal of Reading, 11*, 521–527.

Kenner, C. (1999). Children's understandings of text in a multilingual nursery. *Language and Education, 13*, 1–16.

Kernan, D. (1983). *Steps to English Vocabulary Cue Cards #1–7.* New York: McGraw-Hill.

Kernan, D. (1983). *Steps to English, Teacher's Manual, Level One.* New York: McGraw-Hill.

Klingner, J. K., & Vaughn, S. (1996). Reciprocal teaching of reading comprehension strategies for students with learning disabilities who use English as a second language. *Elementary School Journal, 96,* 275–293.

Klingner, J. K., & Vaughn, S. (2000). The helping behaviors of fifth graders while using collaborative strategic reading during ESL content classes. *TESOL Quarterly, 34,* 69–98.

Kramer, V. R., Schell, L. M., & Rubison, R. M. (1983). Auditory discrimination training in English of Spanish-speaking children. *Reading Improvement, 20,* 162–168.

Kreuger, E., & Townshend, N. (1997). Reading clubs boost second-language first graders' reading achievement. *Reading Teacher, 51,* 122–127.

Kuball, Y. E., & Peck, S. (1997). The effects of whole language instruction on the writing development of Spanish-speaking and English-speaking kindergartners. *Bilingual Research Journal, 21,* 213–231.

Kucer, S. B. (1992). Six bilingual Mexican-American students' and their teacher's interpretations of cloze literacy lessons. *Elementary School Journal, 92,* 557–572.

Kucer, S. B. (1995). Guiding bilingual students through the literacy process. *Language Arts, 72,* 20–29.

Kucer, S. B. (1999). Two students' responses to, and literacy growth in, a whole language curriculum. *Reading Research & Instruction, 38,* 233–253.

Kucer, S. B., & Silva, C. (1999). The English literacy development of bilingual students within a transitional whole language curriculum. *Bilingual Research Journal, 23*(4), 347–371.

Lampman, H. P. (1973). *Southeastern New Mexico Bilingual Program: Final report.* Artesia, NM: Artesia Public Schools.

Larson, J. C. (1996). Impact of phonemic awareness training in Spanish and English on Puerto Rican firstgrade Chapter I students. Unpublished doctoral dissertation, Temple University, Philadelphia, PA.

Li, D., & Nes, S. (2001). Using paired reading to help ESL students become fluent and accurate readers. *Reading Improvement, 38,* 50–61.

Lloyd, S. (1992). *The phonics handbook.* UK: Jolly Learning.

Long, S. & Tinajero, J. (1989). *Campanitas de oro.* New York: Macmillan.

Maldonado, J. A. (1994). Bilingual special education: Specific learning disabilities in language and reading. *Journal of Education Issues of Language Minority Students, 14,* 127–147.

Maldonado, J. R. (1977). The effect of the ESEA Title VII program on the cognitive development of Mexican American students. Unpublished doctoral dissertation, University of Houston, Houston, TX.

Mangano, N., & Allen, J. (1986). Teachers' beliefs about language arts and their effects on students' beliefs and instruction. In J. Niles & R. Lalik (Eds.), *Solving problems in literacy: Learners, teachers, and researchers.* Thirty-fifth yearbook of the National Reading Conference (pp. 136–142). Rochester, NY: National Reading Conference.

Martínez-Roldan, C. M., & López-Robertson, J. M. (2000). Initiating literature circles in a first-grade bilingual classroom. *Reading Teacher, 53,* 270–281.

Miami Linguistic Readers, (1966). Lexington, MA: D. C. Heath.

Morgan, J. C. (1971). The effects of bilingual instruction of the English language arts achievement of first grade children. Unpublished doctoral dissertation, Northwestern State University of Louisiana.

National Institute of Child Health and Human Development. (2000). *Report of the National Reading Panel. Teaching children to read: An evidence-based assessment of the scientific research literature on reading and its implications for reading instruction* (NIH Publication No. 00–4769). Washington, DC: U.S. Government Printing Office.

Neufeld, P., & Fitzgerald, J. (2001). Early English reading development: Latino English learners in the "low" reading group. *Research in the Teaching of English, 36,* 64–109.

Neuman, S. B., & Koskinen, P. (1992). Captioned television as comprehensible input: Effects of incidental word learning from context for language minority students. *Reading Research Quarterly, 27,* 94–106.

Newcomer, P. L., & Hammill, D. D. (1977). *Test of Language Development-2 Primary* (TOLD-2). Austin, TX: Pro-Ed.

Orellana, M. F. (1995). Literacy as a gendered social practice: Tasks, texts, talk, and take-up. *Reading Research Quarterly, 30,* 674–708.

Padrón, Y. N. (1992). The effect of strategy instruction on bilingual students' cognitive strategy use in reading. *Bilingual Research Journal, 16,* 35–51.

Padrón, Y. N. (1994). Comparing reading instruction in Hispanic/limited-English-proficient schools and other inner-city schools. *Bilingual Research Journal, 18,* 49–66.

Palincsar, A. D., & Brown, A. L. (1984). Reciprocal teaching of comprehension-fostering and comprehension-monitoring activities. *Cognition and Instruction, 1,* 117–175.

Palincsar, A. D., & Brown, A. L. (1985). *Reciprocal teaching of comprehension strategies: A natural history of one program for enhancing learning* (Technical Report No. 334). Urbana: University of Illinois Center for the Study of Reading.

Paris, S. G., Cross, D. R., & Lipson, M. Y. (1984). Informed strategies for learning: A program to improve children's reading awareness and comprehension. *Journal of Educational Psychology, 76,* 1239–1252.

Pérez, E. (1981). Oral language competence improves reading skills of Mexican American third graders. *Reading Teacher, 35,* 24–27.

Pérez, B. (1994). Spanish literacy development: A descriptive study of four bilingual whole-language classrooms. *Journal of Reading Behavior, 26,* 75–94.

Perozzi, J. A. (1985). A pilot study of language facilitation for bilingual, language-handicapped children: Theoretical and approach implications. *Journal of Speech & Hearing Disorders, 50,* 403–406.

Pilgreen, J. K., & Krashen, S. (1983). Sustained silent reading with English as a second language high school students: Influence on reading comprehension, reading frequency, and reading enjoyment. *School Library Media Quarterly, 22,* 21–23.

Plante, A. J. (1976). *A study of effectiveness of the Connecticut "Pairing" model of bilingual/bicultural education.* Hamden, CT: Connecticut Staff Development Cooperative.

Prater, D. L., & Bermúdez, A. B. (1993). Using peer response groups with limited English proficient writers. *Bilingual Research Journal, 17,* 99–116.

Psychological Corporation (1993). *Wechser Objective Reading Dimension.* Sidcup: Psychological Corporation.

Purkey, S., & Smith, M. (1983). Research on effective schools: A review. *Elementary School Journal, 83,* 427–452.

Ramírez, J., Pasta, D. J., Yuen, S., Billings, D. K., & Ramey, D. R. (1991). *Final report: Longitudinal study of structural immersion strategy, early-exit, and late-exit transitional bilingual education programs for language-minority children* (Report to the U.S. Department of Education). San Mateo, CA: Aguirre International.

Ramírez, M., III, & Castaneda, A. (1974). *Cultural democracy, bi-cognitive development, and education.* San Francisco, CA: Academic.

Ramos, F., & Krashen, S. (1998). The influence of one trip to the public library: Making books available may be the best incentive for reading (Rapid Research Report). *Reading Teacher, 51,* 614–615.

Reyes, M. D. L. L. (1991). A process approach to literacy using dialogue journals and literature logs with second language learners. *Research in the Teaching of English, 25,* 292–313.

Richard, G., & Hanner, M. (1985). *Language Processing Test.* East Moline, IL: Linguisystems.

Rohena, E. I., Jitendra, A. K., & Browder, D. M. (2002). Comparison of the effects of Spanish and English constant time delay instruction on sight word reading by Hispanic learners with mental retardation. *Journal of Special Education, 36*, 169–184.

Rossell, C. H., & Baker, K. (1996). The educational effectiveness of bilingual education. *Research in the Teaching of English, 30*, 7–69.

Rousseau, M. K., Tam, B. K. Y., & Ramnarain, R. (1993). Increasing reading proficiency of languageminority students with speech and language impairments. *Education and Treatment of Children, 16*, 254–271.

Rueda, R., & García, E. (1996). Teachers' perspectives on literacy assessment and instruction with language-minority students: A comparative study. *Elementary School Journal, 96*, 311–332.

Ruiz, N. T. (1988). Language for learning in a bilingual special education classroom. Unpublished doctoral dissertation, Stanford University.

Ruiz, N. T. (1995). The social construction of ability and disability: II. Optimal and at-risk lessons in a bilingual special education classroom. *Journal of Learning Disabilities, 28*, 491–502.

Ruiz, N. T., Rueda, R., Figueroa, R. A., & Boothroyd, M. (1995). Bilingual special education teachers' shifting paradigms: Complex responses to educational reform. *Journal of Learning Disabilities, 28*, 622–635.

Saldate, M., Mishra, S. P., & Medina, M. (1985). Bilingual instruction and academic achievement: A longitudinal study. *Journal of Instructional Psychology, 12*, 24–30.

Sanders, W. L., & Horn, S. P. (1998). Research from the Tennessee Value-Added Assessment System (TVAAS) database: Implications for educational research and evaluation. *Journal of Personnel Evaluation in Education, 12*, 247–256.

Saunders, W. M. (1999). Improving literacy achievement for English learners in transitional bilingual programs. *Educational Research & Evaluation (An International Journal on Theory & Practice), 5*, 345–381.

Saunders, W. M., & Goldenberg, C. (1996). Four primary teachers work to define constructivism and teacher-directed learning: Implications for teacher assessment. *Elementary School Journal, 97*, 139–161.

Saunders, W. M., & Goldenberg, C. (1999). Effects of instructional conversations and literature logs on limited- and fluent-English proficient students' story comprehension and thematic understanding. *Elementary School Journal, 99*, 277–301.

Saville-Troike, M. (1984). What really matters in second language learning for academic achievement? *TESOL Quarterly, 18*, 199–219.

Schon, I., Hopkins, K. D., & Davis, W. A. (1982). The effects of books in Spanish and free reading time on Hispanic students' reading abilities and attitudes. *NABE: The Journal for the National Association for Bilingual Education, 7*, 13–20.

Schon, I., Hopkins, K. D., & Vojir, C. (1984). The effects of Spanish reading emphasis on the English and Spanish reading abilities of Hispanic high school students. *The Bilingual Review, 11*, 33–39.

Schon, I., Hopkins, K. D., & Vojir, C. (1985). The effects of special reading time in Spanish on the reading abilities and attitudes of Hispanic junior high school students. *Journal of Psycholinguistic Research, 14*, 57–65.

Semel, E., Wiig, E., & Secord, W. (1987). *Clinical evaluation of language fundamentals— revised*. San Antonio, TX: Psychological Corporation.

Sengupta, S. (2000). An investigation into the effects of revision strategy instruction on L2 secondary school learners. *System, 28*, 97–113.

Shames, R. (1998). The effects of a community language learning/comprehension processing strategies model on second language reading comprehension. Unpublished doctoral dissertation, Florida Atlantic University, Boca Raton.

Short, D. J. (1994). Expanding middle school horizons: Integrating language, culture, and social studies. *TESOL Quarterly, 28*, 581–608.

Siegel, J. (1992). Teaching initial literacy in a pidgin language: A preliminary evaluation. *Australian Review of Applied Linguistics*, 12, 53–65.

Siegel, L. S. (1989). IQ is irrelevant to the definition of learning disabilities. *Journal of Learning Disabilities*, 22, 469–478, 486.

Sindelar, P. R., Rosenburg, M. S., & Wilson, R. J. (1985). An adapted alternating treatments design for instructional research. *Education and Treatment of Children*, 8, 67–76.

Slavin, R. E., & Cheung, A. (2004). *A synthesis of research on language of reading instruction for English language learners*. Baltimore, MD: Johns Hopkins University.

Slavin, R. E., & Madden, N. A. (1998). *Success for All/Éxito Para Todos: Effects on the reading achievement of students acquiring English* (Report No. 19). Baltimore, MD: The Johns Hopkins University, Center for Research on the Education of Students Placed at Risk.

Sparrow, S., Balla, D., & Cichetti, D. (1984). *Vineland Adaptive Behavior Scales*. Circle Pines, MN: American Guidance Service.

Spivey, N.N. (1997). *The construction metaphor: Reading, writing, and the making of meaning.* San Diego: Academic Press.

Sprick, M. M., Howard, L. M. & Fidanque, A (1998), *Read well: Critical foundations in primary reading*. Longmont, CO: Sopris West.

Stallings, J. (1980). Effective use of time program. Unpublished training manual. Houston, TX: University of Houston.

Stallings, J. (1986). Using time effectively: A self-analytic approach. In K. Zimwalt (Ed.), *Improving teaching* (pp. 15–27). Alexandria, VA: Association for Supervision and Curriculum Development.

Stuart, M. (1999). Getting ready for reading: Early phoneme awareness and phonics teaching improves reading and spelling in inner-city second language learners. *British Journal of Educational Psychology*, 69, 587–605.

Swicegood, M. A. (1990). The effects of metacognitive reading strategy training on the reading performance and student reading analysis strategies of third grade Spanish-dominant students. Unpublished doctoral dissertation, Texas A&M University, College Station.

Syvanen, C. (1997). English as a second language students as cross-age tutors. *ORTESOL Journal*, 18, 33–41.

Tharp, R. G. (1982). The effective instruction of comprehension: Results and descriptions of the Kamehameha Early Education Program. *Reading Research Quarterly*, 17, 503–527.

Thorndike, R. L., Hagen, E. P., & Sattler, J. M. (1986). *Stanford-Binet Intelligence Scale* (4th ed.). Itasca, IL: Riverside.

Tierney, R. J., & Shanahan, T. (1992). Research on the reading–writing relationship: Interactions, transactions, and outcomes. In R. Barr, M. L. Kamil, P. Mosenthal, & P. D. Pearson (Eds.), *Handbook of reading research* (Vol. II, pp. 246–280). Mahwah, NJ: Lawrence Erlbaum Associates.

Tinajero, J., Long, S., Calderón, M., Castagha, C., & Maldonado-Colón, E. (1989). *Transitional reading program*. New York: Macmillan.

Touchstone Applied Science Associates. (1990). *Degrees of reading power*. Brewster, NY: Author.

Trelease, J. (1992). Léeme un cuento. *Ser Padres*, 8, 18–23.

Tsang, W. K. (1996). Comparing the effects of reading and writing on writing performance. *Applied Linguistics*, 17, 210–233.

Tudor, I., & Hafiz, F. (1989). Extensive reading as a means of input to L2 learning. *Journal of Research in Reading*, 12, 164–178.

Ulanoff, S. H., & Pucci, S. L. (1999). Learning words from books: The effects of read-aloud on second language vocabulary acquisition. *Bilingual Research Journal*, 23, 409–422.

Valladolid, L. A. (1991). The effects of bilingual education of students' academic achievement as they progress through a bilingual program. Unpublished doctoral dissertation, United States International University.

VanWagenen, M. A., Williams, R. L., & McLaughlin, T. F. (1994). Use of assisted reading to improve reading rate, word accuracy, and comprehension with ESL Spanish-speaking students. *Perceptual and Motor Skills, 79,* 227–230.

Vaughn-Shavuo, F. (1990). Using story grammar and language experience for improving recall and comprehension in the teaching of ESL to Spanish-dominant first-graders. Unpublished doctoral dissertation, Hofstra University, Hempstead.

Vygotsky, L. S. (1978). *Mind and society: The development of higher mental processes.* Cambridge, MA: Harvard University Press.

Waxman, H. C., Walker de Felix, J., Martínez, A., Knight, S. L., & Padrón, Y. (1994). Effects of implementing classroom instructional models on English language learners' cognitive and affective outcomes. *Bilingual Research Journal, 18,* 1–22.

Weaver, B., & Sawyer, D. J. (1984). Promoting language and reading development for two Vietnamese children. *Reading Horizons, 24,* 111–118.

Wechsler, D. (1991). *Wechsler Intelligence Scale for Children, Third Edition.* San Antonio, TX: Psychological Corporation.

Willig, A. (1985). A meta-analysis of selected studies on the effectiveness of bilingual education. *Review of Educational Research, 55,* 269–317.

Wolf, S. A. (1993). What's in a name? Labels and literacy in Readers Theatre. *Reading Teacher, 46,* 540–545.

Wood, D., & Wood, A. (1984). *The napping house.* San Diego, CA: Harcourt Brace, Jovanovich.

Woodcock, R. W. (1973). *Woodcock Reading Mastery Test.* Circle Pines, MN: American Guidance Service.

Woodcock, R. W. & Johnson, M. B. (1989). *Woodcock-Johnson Psycho-Educational Battery-Revised.* Allen, TX: Developmental Learning Materials

Wright, L. (1997). Enhancing ESL reading through reader strategy training. *Prospect, 12,* 15–28.

7

Language and Literacy Assessment

Georgia Earnest García, Gail McKoon, and Diane August

The literature on language and literacy assessment reviewed in this chapter covers a broad variety of measures that are used to evaluate language-minority students' oral language, reading, and writing performance—some employed as national, state, district, and classroom assessments to assess student performance and others developed for research purposes.

The following research questions are addressed in this chapter:

1. What assessments do states and school districts use with language-minority students for identification, program placement, and reclassification purposes? Are the assessments used for these purposes useful and appropriate?
2. What do we know about alternative assessments of oral English proficiency and literacy?
3. What first- and second-language vocabulary and wide-scale literacy assessments for language-minority students have been investigated? What does the research tell us about accommodations for language-minority students taking these assessments?
4. Are the assessments currently used to predict the literacy performance of language-minority students (including those with reading disabilities) useful and appropriate?
5. What do we know about language and literacy measures

developed for the identification of language-minority students eligible for special education services?

6. What standardized and researcher-developed oral proficiency, literacy, and literacy-related assessments have been used in the research?

Appropriate, valid, and reliable language and literacy assessments are key to understanding the literacy development of language-minority students, to improving classroom instruction, and for policy and research purposes.

We begin this chapter by presenting pertinent background information. We then describe the methodology of our review. Next, we describe methodological issues with the research and summarize the findings of the literature on the research questions addressed by our review. We close the chapter with recommendations for research in this area.

BACKGROUND

A myriad of concerns have been raised by educators and researchers about the use of language and literacy assessments with language-minority students. A major concern is that the validity and reliability of assessments administered in English to language-minority students may be seriously compromised when the students are not sufficiently proficient in English (American Educational Research Association, American Psychological Association, & National Council on Measurement in Education, 1999; Durán, 1989). As background, we discuss concerns related to possible linguistic and cultural biases and the validity and reliability of tests used with language-minority students. In addition, because of the influence of the No Child Left Behind (NCLB) Act on district and state policy, the provisions of the law that relate to the assessment of English-language learners are described.

Linguistic and Cultural Bias

Assessments developed for monolingual populations generally do not take into account issues related to English-language learners' second-language status (García, 1994; García & Pearson, 1994; Valdés & Figueroa, 1994). For example, as a result of differences in receptive and productive development in the second language, English-language learners may comprehend more than they can demonstrate when their test responses are in the second language (Lee, 1986). Second-language learners may need more time than monolingual students to complete written tests because they tend to process text in a second language more slowly (Mestre, 1984). They may know different vocabulary items in each of their languages, making it difficult to assess their total vocabulary knowledge with an assessment in only one of the languages (García, 1994; García & Pearson, 1994). They may have well-developed cognitive skills that underlie comprehension, such as integrating background knowledge with textual knowledge or drawing inferences across propositions, but may not be able to apply these skills to English text because their limited English proficiency interferes with their accessing enough of the text's meaning to apply the skills. Similarly, assessments developed for and/or normed on the dominant group in a society may pose issues of cultural bias for language-minority students from different ethnic, racial, or national groups and socioeconomic classes (García & Pearson, 1994; Mercer, 1979; Samuda, 1975).

Validity and Reliability

Knowing when English-language learners are proficient enough in English to participate in English assessments is an issue that still needs to be addressed (Figueroa, 1989; Hakuta & Beatty, 2000). When English-language learners are in the process of acquiring English, written tests in English may pose reading challenges that interfere with the assessment of the content (e.g., mathematics) they have learned, making their test scores invalid as indicators of content knowledge or achievement (Butler & Stevens, 2001). One response to this concern has been the use of testing accommodations with English-language learners. As reported in a recent National Academy of Sciences report (Koenig & Bachman, 2004), a review of research on the effects of accommodations on the wide-scale test performance of English-language learners (Sireci & Scarpati, 2003) found that "the most common accommodations studied were linguistic modification, provision of a dictionary or bilingual dictionary, provision of dual-language booklets, extended time, and oral administration. Most studies examined the effects of multiple accommodations" (p. 89).

It has been claimed that linguistic modification is the most effective method for reducing the score gap on content assessments (such as, mathematics) between English-language learners and native English speakers (Abedi, Hofstetter, Baker, & Lord, 2001). However, Sireci and Scarpati (2003) point out that in the Abedi et al. study, "the gap was narrowed because native-English speakers scored worse on the linguistically modified test, not because the English-language learners performed substantially better" (p. 65). In another study (Abedi, 2002), significant but small gains were noted for eighth-grade but not for fourth-grade students. Sireci and Scarpati indicate that Abedi explains this finding by hypothesizing that, "with an increase in grade level, more complex language may interfere with content-based assessment" (p. 13), and "in earlier grades, language may not be as great a hurdle as it is in the later grades" (p. 14). With regard to research on other accommodations provided for English-language learners, Sireci *et al.* note that providing English-language learners with customized dictionaries or glossaries appeared to improve their performance (e.g., Abedi, Lord, Boscardin, & Miyoshi, 2001). Two studies available on dual-language test booklets revealed no gains (Anderson, Liu, Swierzbin, Thurlow, & Bielinski, 2000).

Another issue is the appropriateness of testing English-language learners with standardized tests normed on monolingual populations (Butler & Stevens, 2001; García & Pearson, 1994; Mercer, 1979; Valdés & Figueroa, 1994). Few English-language learners are included in the norming samples for standardized tests developed in English (Butler & Stevens, 2001; García & Pearson, 1994). According to the Standards for Educational and Psychological Testing (American Education Research Association, American Psychological Association, & National Council on Measurement in Education, 1999), serious test bias occurs when measures normed on native English speakers are used with English-language learners:

> Test norms based on native speakers of English either should not be used with individuals whose first language is not English or such individuals' test results should be interpreted as reflecting in part current level of English proficiency rather than ability, potential, aptitude, or personality characteristics or symptomatology (p. 91).

The standards further state that when a test is

> administered in the same language to all examinees in a linguistically diverse population, the test user should investigate the validity of the score interpretations for test takers believed to have limited proficiency in the language of the test [because] the achievement, abilities, and traits of examinees who do not speak the language of the test as their primary language may be seriously mismeasured by the test (p. 118).

Unfortunately, native-language assessments may not have appropriate norming samples either (American Educational Research Association, American Psychological Association, & National Council on Measurement in Education, 1999; August & Hakuta, 1997). For example, a standardized test in Spanish normed on students from Mexico City or on Cuban American students from Miami may not be appropriate for Mexican American students in the United States.

Assessment of English-language learners in their native language raises other issues as well. Hakuta and Beatty (2000) note that assessing a student in the native language may mean providing the student with a parallel version of the English assessment or providing an assessment in the native language that focuses on the "same or closely related constructs as the original English version" of the test (p. 25). However, developing native-language assessments that are equivalent to English assessments is not an easy task (American Educational Research Association, American Psychological Association, & National Council on Measurement in Education, 1999; August & Hakuta, 1997; García & Pearson, 1994). Vocabulary items may differ in their word frequency or difficulty from the original items and "may exhibit psychometric properties substantially different from those of the original English items" (Olmeda, 1981, p. 1083). Deciding which English-language learners should take a particular assessment in the native language is also tricky because it is difficult to determine language dominance, and English-language learners may acquire some concepts in one language and others in the other language (García & Pearson, 1994). Some states address these concerns by providing side-by-side versions of tests in English and the native language, a technique used successfully for math assessment in Oregon (Durán, Brown, & McCall, 2002).

A final validity issue relates to language proficiency measures (August & Hakuta, 1997; Durán, 1989; García, 1994). Language proficiency measures typically sample students' knowledge and use of a particular language. They often include skills considered necessary for oral language proficiency, such as those related to phonology, morphology, syntax, and lexicon. However, they do not necessarily measure students' ability to use the language in real-life settings or for academic purposes. Moreover, many language proficiency measures were developed to determine the appropriate placement for English-language learners, rather than to track their progress in component skills over time. In recent years, researchers and policymakers have called for language proficiency measures that assess how well students can perform and learn in academic settings where instruction is conducted in English as well as for language proficiency measures that allow for assessing development over time.

Assessment and Educational Policy

The standards-based accountability reform movement, with its emphasis on high academic standards and high expectations for all students and the use of assessments to measure students' attainment of such standards, has led to mandates to include English-language learners in assessments sooner and more broadly than in the past. In the policy context when this research review was undertaken, the NCLB Act holds states and school districts accountable for all students by requiring

English-language learners to be assessed and assessment data to be disaggregated to show how well specific groups of students, including English-language learners, are meeting state and district standards. Testing requirements under Title I and Title III of NCLB require school districts and states to provide for an annual assessment of English proficiency in the four domains of reading, writing, speaking, and listening. Title III also requires the assessment of comprehension. The Title III integrated system of standards and assessments requires that language proficiency assessments be aligned with state language proficiency standards, which in turn are aligned with challenging state academic content and achievement standards. In addition, Title I stipulates that all students take an academic content assessment in reading/language arts and math in grades 3–8 and one time in high school. This includes students identified as English-language learners. Title I also stipulates that:

> States may not exempt [limited English proficient] students from participating in the State assessment system, in the grades the assessment is given, in their first three years of attending schools in the United States. Inclusion in the State academic assessment system must immediately begin when the student enrolls in school. [However, see exemption clause below for recent arrivals.] No exemptions are permitted based on level of English proficiency.
> (U.S. Department of Education, 2003, p. 19)

English-language learners who have been in U.S. schools fewer than 3 years may take the academic content assessment in language arts/reading and math in their native language or in English with the use of linguistically appropriate accommodations. Just as the content assessments in core content areas developed in English must be aligned to the content standards, the native language assessment must also be aligned with the state content and achievement standards. English-language learners who have attended schools in the United States for at least 3 consecutive years (except those living in Puerto Rico) are subject to the same types of assessments, including literacy assessments, in English as native-English-speaking students.

In specific situations, districts may use an assessment in a language other than English for up to 2 additional years. Moreover, schools are required to show adequate yearly progress (AYP) in making sure that all students achieve academic proficiency in order to close the achievement gap by 2014. NCLB requires states to include the academic achievement results of all students, including English-language learners, in school and state AYP calculations.

In 2004, then Secretary of Education Paige announced two new policies related to the implementation of NCLB. The new policies allow limited

English proficient (LEP) students who are new arrivals to U.S. public schools during their first year of enrollment in U.S. schools to have the option of not taking the reading/language arts content assessment in addition to the English-language proficiency assessment. Previously, they were required to take both assessments. They are required to take the mathematics assessment, with accommodations as appropriate. In addition, states are now permitted to exclude for 1 year or one occasion the results from the mathematics and, if given, the reading/language arts content assessments in AYP calculations. The other new policy change allows states, for the purpose of AYP calculations for up to 2 years, to include in the LEP subgroup students who have attained English proficiency and who no longer are considered LEP according to the district/state's definition. According to the press release (U.S. Department of Education, 2004), the intent of this change is to "give states the flexibility to allow schools and local education agencies (LEAs) to get credit for improving English language proficiency from year to year" (p. 1).

METHODS

Our review of the literature on student assessment includes studies that evaluate and measure students' listening and speaking, as well as their reading and writing proficiencies. The focus of this chapter is on language minority students acquiring English as a second language. Nevertheless, we include studies on the assessment of first-language oral proficiency and literacy in this population of students. In most cases, the first language studied is Spanish. In addition to the electronic search for studies, we also identified relevant technical reports by contacting the National Center for Research on Evaluation, Standards, and Student Testing; examined the references cited in studies already included in our database; and reviewed the references cited in key syntheses and theoretical works on the assessment of language-minority children. Finally, we performed a manual search of articles on assessment in the *National Reading Conference Yearbook*.

The initial search resulted in a total of 115 peer-reviewed journal articles and technical reports. Of these, 38 studies were included in the review (the rest failed to meet the various selection criteria established by the Panel, including that they had to analyze data relevant to our review questions). This number of studies is remarkably small given the importance of assessing language-minority children's language and literacy achievement.

We conducted a qualitative analysis of the empirical literature. The 38 studies do not lend themselves to meta-analysis because there were not sufficient numbers of studies on any conceptual issue to combine statistical data across studies.

SUMMARY OF EMPIRICAL FINDINGS

Our review of research on the assessment of literacy with language-minority students was organized into six topics.

Assessments to Identify, Place, and Reclassify Language-Minority Students

Although educators rely on assessment data to evaluate English proficiency, research conducted on the assessments used to identify, place, and reclassify students is extremely limited. Only one national survey reports on the assessments used for these purposes (Kindler, 2002). According to Kindler, 94% of the states and other governing bodies (e.g., Guam) indicated that they used a commercial language proficiency test in English to help identify limited English proficient students eligible for bilingual education or ESL services. The most commonly used were the *Language Assessment Scales* (LAS, 85%: De Avila & Duncan, 1990; Duncan & De Avila, 1988), *IDEA Language Proficiency Tests* (IPT, 70%: IDEA, 1978, 1994), and *Woodcock-Muñoz Language Survey* (52%: Woodcock & Muñoz-Sandoval, 1993). More than 75% of the states indicated that they used other sources of information as well, including home language surveys, information from parents, teacher observations, student records, teacher interviews, referrals by educational personnel, student grades, language samples, or other commercial achievement tests. More than one third of the states reported taking into account students' performance on a criterion-referenced achievement test, although no one such test was used by a majority of the states. These summary data do not reveal how states or local education agencies combine this information in order to place or reclassify students; similarly, they do not capture the nuances of practice at the local education agency level. It is also important to note that these data were collected prior to the No Child Left Behind (NCLB) Act, which resulted in dramatic changes in states' assessment activities.

Two groups of researchers concluded that the *Language Assessment Scales* (LAS: De Avila & Duncan, 1990; Duncan & De Avila, 1988), a commonly used language proficiency measure, should not be used to determine the academic language proficiency of English-language learners because it did not adequately predict how well the students performed on a standardized reading test or content area assessment in English (Laesch & Van Kleeck, 1987; Stevens, Butler, & Castellón-Wellington, 2000). Additionally, in a study that examined the placement and reclassification of Spanish-speaking students in a K-3 bilingual education program, Nadeau & Miramontes (1988) reported moderately high correlations among the students' academic and reading test performance in Spanish, their oral English performance, and academic and reading test performance in English. The teachers' determination of students' readiness for reclassification also positively correlated with the students' performance on academic measures, in which higher performing students were recommended for reclassification. The authors conclude that Spanish-speaking students' academic and reading test performance in Spanish, oral English performance, and teacher judgments should be taken into account when reclassification decisions are made. However, given the small number of studies conducted on the use of assessments for reclassification purposes, considerably more research is needed to validate the above methods.

Alternative Assessments of Oral Language Proficiency and Literacy

Many commercial oral language proficiency tests have been criticized because they do not assess students' actual use of the language to communicate in social or academic contexts. Most research related to alternative assessments of oral proficiency (Brown, 1983; Gómez, Parker, Lara-Alecio, Ochoa, & Gómez, 1996) used cloze tests for this purpose. Brown found that the correlation between students' performance on conversational cloze tests and their participation in two 5-minute oral interviews was .80. Although he concludes that the conversational cloze test had the potential to provide a useful estimate of students' oral communication, that estimate appeared to be limited to conversational English within a narrow social context. No detailed information is available about the choice of the cloze items or the content of the interviews. Another group of researchers (Gómez et al., 1996) developed and tested a language observation procedure for assessing bilingual fifth graders' actual use of language to communicate while solving problems in mathematics in an academic setting. The authors report that their instrument allowed them to observe and evaluate seven social language attributes based on Hatch's (1992) definition of *social language* in terms of cognitive, linguistic, and social facets. Although their results correlate with those from the *IDEA Language Proficiency Tests*, the practicality of their instrument for classroom use and its generalizability are issues that need to be considered.

Alternative measures of literacy emphasized the development of low-cost alternatives (cloze tests, curriculum-based measures, and sentence verification tests) that could be used by educational personnel in lieu of time-consuming standardized tests (Baker & Good, 1995; Baldauf,

Dawson, Prior, & Propst, 1980; Laesch & Van Kleeck, 1987; Ozete, 1980; Royer & Carlo, 1991; Royer, Carlo, Carlisle, & Furman, 1991). Findings indicate these alternative assessments are promising but additional research is needed because the limited number of studies on these procedures has not yet answered critical questions on validity or reliability.

Vocabulary and Wide-Scale Literacy Assessments

Four sets of researchers investigated the use of both the English (PPVT, PPVT–R: Dunn & Dunn, 1981) and Spanish (Test de Vocabulario en Imágenes Peabody [TVIP]–H: Dunn, Padilla, Lugo, & Dunn, 1986) versions of the *Peabody Picture Vocabulary Test* (PPVT) with samples of language-minority children in the United States who spoke Spanish and Native American languages (Argulewicz & Abel, 1984; Fernández, Pearson, Umbel, Oller, & Molinet-Molina, 1992; Sattler & Altes, 1984; Scruggs, Mastropieri, & Argulewicz, 1983). In all four studies, the language-minority children scored lower than corresponding samples of native-English-speaking children on the PPVT. In a Canadian study (Geva, Yaghoub-Zadeh, & Schuster, 2000), English-language learners also performed lower on the PPVT–R. However, a limitation of the PPVT is that the "standardization sample did not include individuals [showing] evidence of . . . limited ability in English" (Bessai, 2001, p. 909), Current assessment standards call for piloting and norming assessments on the relevant populations.

What the PPVT and TVIP actually measure in terms of language-minority students' conceptual and vocabulary knowledge has been a major concern. Three groups of researchers identified test bias issues related to using the PPVT or word frequency tests in English and Spanish with Spanish-speaking students (Fernández *et al.*, 1992; Sattler & Altes, 1984; Tamayo, 1987). For example, two studies (Fernández *et al.*, 1992; Tamayo, 1987) suggest that the basic test procedures of the PPVT and the TVIP–H, which emphasize increasingly difficult and less frequent words and stopping the test after a student misses a certain number of words in a row, may constitute a bias since the order of word presentation is not based upon frequency measures drawn from the student's first language or cultural group. Fernández *et al.* also report that assessing bilingual preschoolers' vocabulary knowledge in each language, and not across both languages, can result in a serious underestimation of their vocabulary when students know vocabulary concepts in one language, but not in the other.

Although Sattler and Altes (1984) warn that the PPVT-R "should not be used to assess the intellectual capacities of Hispanic children" (p. 315), it may appropriately estimate how well language-minority children's recognition of "mainstream" English vocabulary matches that of native-English-speaking students (Geva *et al.*, 2000). Two sets of researchers also reported that when they tested the English version of the PPVT with small samples of Spanish speakers, psychometric properties, such as temporal stability (Scruggs *et al.*, 1983) and internal item consistency (Argulewicz & Abel, 1984), indicated that the measure was reliable.

Other studies focus on the use of wide-scale reading tests in English with language-minority students in the United States (Abedi, 2002; Davidson, 1994; García, 1991) and the use of a state-level, standards-based reading test with this population (Pomplun & Omar, 2001). Additional studies investigate how the second-language status of language-minority students affects their performance on content area assessments in mathematics, science, or social studies (Abedi, 2002; Davies, 1991; Stevens *et al.*, 2000). Although federal policy allows the use of testing accommodations with English-language learners with limited English proficiency, only one study (Hannon & McNally, 1986) looked specifically at such accommodations, and its focus was on a reading test not commonly used in the United States.

Findings from this group of studies indicate that when traditional psychometric properties are examined relative to the reliability of wide-scale English reading tests used with language-minority students, the tests typically are found to be reliable. However, the studies reported in this section also substantiate Messick's (1994) concern "that language factors may be a source of construct-irrelevant variance in standardized achievement tests, affecting the construct validity of the tests themselves" (Abedi, 2002, p. 232). In addition, García (1991) identified a number of test bias factors that adversely affected the standardized reading test performance of Spanish-speaking Hispanic students as compared to that of native-English-speaking Anglo students. These included too little time to complete the test, less familiarity with the test vocabulary and passage topics, and lower performance on test questions that required the integration of background information with test information. When students were given the opportunity to respond to test questions in Spanish or when the test questions were read to them in Spanish, then they revealed much greater comprehension of the English passages and test items than their original test scores had indicated.

Assessments Used to Predict the Literacy Performance of Language-Minority Students

A number of researchers tested how well early reading measures designed for native English speakers predicted the early reading performance of language-minority students (Chiappe, Siegel, & Gottardo, 2002; Everatt, Smythe, Adams, & Ocampo, 2000; Geva *et al.*, 2000; Stage,

Sheppard, Davidson, & Browning, 2001). The studies found that various measures of phonological and grapho-phonological processing, including letter naming, letter-naming fluency, rapid letter naming, and phonological awareness, were good predictors of English word recognition, oral reading fluency, and early reading test performance for English-language learners in kindergarten, first, and/or second grade. These researchers concluded that the above measures could differentiate low performers from average or high performers, identifying students with possible reading disabilities. However, some of the findings must be qualified because the researchers did not control for students' oral English proficiency or examine their native literacy development or performance on the same measures. Nonetheless, the fact that Geva *et al.* (2000) obtained similar results with English measures adapted for English-language learners suggests that other researchers should test these findings, taking into account students' oral English proficiency and native-language literacy development.

The findings of a longitudinal study (Jansky, Hoffman, Layton, & Sugar, 1989) question whether commercial test batteries that accurately identify native-English-speaking first graders who later are at risk for reading failure in grades 2–6 can be used with English-language learners. Jansky *et al.* found that many Hispanic students identified as at risk for reading failure in first grade, due to low pre-literacy skills in English, later substantially improved their reading performance. Their findings suggest that additional longitudinal studies are needed to test the predictors against language-minority students' actual reading performance.

Two sets of researchers examined the role of teacher judgments. In a study with first- and second-grade English-language learners and native English speakers, Limbos and Geva (2001) found that teacher nominations and ratings of academic skills were better individual predictors of reading disabilities, as determined by standardized reading test scores, than teachers' spontaneous expressions of concern. When teacher nominations and ratings of academic skills were combined, then all of the students with reading disabilities were identified. When teachers made errors in determining English-language learners' reading performance, it usually was because they over-relied on the students' oral language proficiency in English in making this determination.

Another approach to screening is to have teachers' attempt to identify potential drop outs (Frontera & Horowitz, 1995). As with the previous studies, teachers were found to be more reliable with this kind of prediction when they were asked to respond to specific criteria, rather than to express their opinions spontaneously. Because teacher judgment plays a significant role in the education of language-minority students, additional research is needed to explore its use as an assessment tool.

Measures and Methods Used to Identify Students Eligible for Special Services

Another important issue is the accurate identification of language-minority students with language and learning difficulties. Studies addressing this issue have focused on the types of language proficiency assessments school psychologists have used for the placement of language-minority children in special education, the identification of language-minority children with language disorders, and the identification of learning disabilities in older language-minority children. Consistent with Public Law 94–142, the Education for All Handicapped Children Act, which states that an oral proficiency assessment in the home/native language is required before language-minority students are identified as eligible for special education services, three of the studies on speech and language disorders emphasized the importance of conducting assessments in the children's home language (Ambert, 1986; Holm, Dodd, Stow, & Pert, 1999; Restrepo, 1998).

Studies that surveyed the assessment practices of school psychologists or speech and language pathologists indicated that both groups tended to emphasize assessments that provided a limited view of students' language development. For example, Ochoa, Galarza, and González (1996) surveyed the types of language proficiency assessments used in special education placement decisions by 859 school psychologists from eight different states. They voiced concerns that the most frequent measure that the school psychologists reported using was a measure of receptive vocabulary acquisition. In a survey of the types of assessments used by a small sample of speech and language pathologists in California, Langdon (1989) reported that even though the speech and language pathologists said that they collected language samples in students' two languages, they still placed the most importance on students' discrete-point proficiency test scores.

In contrast to the limited assessments emphasized in the surveys, Restrepo (1998) found that parents' report of a speech-language problem, the length of student clauses and the number of errors that a student makes in spontaneous speech, and a family history of speech-language problems significantly differentiated a small sample of Spanish speakers with and without severe to moderate language impairments. Although Restrepo does not present a protocol that could be used by speech and language pathologists, his findings suggest that such a protocol could be developed.

Two sets of researchers reported that it was not useful to compare the language development of English-language learners or bilingual learners with that of monolingual native English speakers. Quinn (2001) questioned the validity of using language measures developed for monolingual English speakers to screen English-language learners for special programs because the receptive and expressive developmental patterns of the English-language learners were substantially different from those of native-English-speaking students

The complexity of the measurement problem is also well illustrated in the study of Holm *et al.* (1999). Their goal was to identify bilingual language-minority children with speech disorders in language production. To this end, the children's language production abilities were compared with those of normal children, both bilingual and monolingual, in both their first language and English. The comparison was carried out with a test in which the children were asked to name pictured objects aloud. A full comparison required that the words to be spoken capture a range of similarities and differences in the phonological and word structures of the first language and English, so the word lists were constructed only after a careful linguistic investigation of the similarities and differences in fluent adult speech. The resulting list of words was pilot tested and refined to ensure that the test givers who worked with the children could score their pronunciations accurately.

The results of this study show the importance of measuring language structures in both the native language and English and comparing them with the structures of fluent monolingual children. The distributions of the speech errors made by the bilingual children were different in the two languages. When speaking English, for example, the most frequent error the children made involved cluster reduction; when speaking their native language, the most frequent error involved voicing. Moreover, the frequency orderings of errors for these children speaking English were different from those for monolingual children speaking English, and they were different for the bilingual children speaking their native language and monolingual children speaking the native language. These differences demonstrate that the bilingual children had a different structure of phonology for their first language than for English, and that both of these structures differed from those of monolingual children.

Only two studies investigated the identification of older language-minority students with learning difficulties (Goldstein, Harris, & Klein, 1993; Miramontes, 1987). Weak story-retelling schema may be one way to identify language-minority students with learning disabilities; however, students' low performance may be associated with low English proficiency rather than a learning disability (Goldstein, Harris, & Klein, 1993). Miramontes (1987) also found that the limited English proficiency of middle school students in her sample resulted in the over-identification of these students as learning disabled. She concludes that "a process-oriented assessment procedure conducted in each language might be a more useful way to determine students with learning disabilities because students' strengths and weaknesses could then be compared in each language to provide a more accurate view of reading proficiency" (p. 631).

Assessments Used in the Research Included in This Volume

To aid future research on English-language learners, this volume describes the assessments used in the research reviewed in the report. Table 7.1 provides the frequencies of use of literacy assessments by literacy component. Across all the studies included in Chapters 3 to 7, the greatest number of measures focused on reading comprehension (79). This was followed by phonemic and phonological awareness (77) and vocabulary (51). The fewest measures addressed pragmatics (1), morphology (3), and discourse (2). Interestingly, with regard to frequency of use, there were more researcher-developed assessments (240 English measures, 55 Spanish measures) than standardized/commercial measures (103 in English, 41 in Spanish); many studies relied solely on researcher-developed measures. Research infrequently used any of the state standards/accountability measures in either Spanish (10) or English (28). Unfortunately, few researchers reported information on the validity or reliability of the measures they had developed, making them unsuitable for making decisions about students and leaving their study findings open to question.

METHODOLOGICAL ISSUES

A major concern is the limited number of studies that address any given research question. For example, only four studies examined whether a measure used for placement or reclassification decisions was useful or appropriate. None of these studies was of sufficient magnitude to allow sound conclusions to be drawn.

In addition, the studies do not represent sufficiently high-quality research to permit firm conclusions about the validity of specific assessments for language-minority children, the reliability of those instruments, or their contextual or cultural appropriateness. First, many of the 38 studies reviewed are pilot efforts, the number of subjects or the number of items being too small to provide generalizable findings. Second, the data for some of the studies are reported in summary forms that do not allow scrutiny of essential features. Third, in many studies, the assessment items are not reported, so that independent evaluation of the instruments is not possible. Overall, there has been little effort to achieve replicability, an essential aspect of high-quality research. For example, researchers have not typically included in their studies the measures used by other researchers addressing similar research questions. It is

TABLE 7.1

Frequencies of Standardized/Commercial, Researcher-Developed, and State-Standards/Accountability Measures by Literacy Component

Literacy Component	Total Measures of		Standardized/Commercial		Standardized/Commercial		Researcher-Developed Measures-English		Researcher-Developed Measures-Spanish		State Standards/Accountability-English		State Standards/Accountability-Spanish	
	Freq	Studies	Freq	Studies	Freq	Studies	Freq	Studies	Freq	Studies	Freq	Studies	Freq	Studies
Print concepts	8	(7)	2	(2)	1	(1)	4	(3)	2	(2)	0	(0)	0	(0)
Letter identification	23	(24)	6	(8)	1	(1)	12	(11)	3	(3)	1	(1)	0	(0)
Word or pseudoword reading	47	(59)	12	(21)	6	(17)	23	(15)	5	(5)	1	(1)	0	(0)
Oral reading fluency	20	(17)	2	(2)	3	(3)	12	(9)	2	(2)	1	(1)	0	(0)
Reading comprehension	79	(71)	21	(25)	7	(11)	34	(22)	12	(8)	4	(4)	1	(1)
Reading broadly defined	42	(50)	14	(18)	7	(10)	9	(9)	4	(5)	6	(6)	2	(2)
Reading unspecified	30	(39)	14	(19)	4	(9)	5	(5)	0	(0)	5	(4)	2	(2)
Vocabulary	51	(69)	16	(33)	6	(12)	12	(9)	9	(7)	5	(5)	3	(3)
Spelling	31	(28)	2	(4)	1	(3)	24	(17)	1	(1)	2	(2)	1	(1)
Writing proficiency	39	(30)	4	(4)	2	(2)	25	(16)	5	(5)	2	(2)	1	(1)
Phonemic/phonological awareness	77	(35)	9	(10)	0	(0)	55	(18)	13	(7)	0	(0)	0	(0)
Morphology	3	(3)	1	(1)	1	(1)	1	(1)	0	(0)	0	(0)	0	(0)
Syntax	40	(34)	7	(7)	2	(3)	22	(19)	8	(4)	1	(1)	0	(0)
Discourse	2	(2)	0	(0)	0	(0)	1	(1)	1	(1)	0	(0)	0	(0)
Pragmatics	1	(1)	0	(0)	0	(0)	1	(1)	0	(0)	0	(0)	0	(0)

Note. The numbers of studies in the database that measured the literacy component are in parentheses.

only with such efforts that the construction of a base of high-quality research is possible and the systematic development of a body of research findings advanced.

RECOMMENDATIONS FOR FUTURE RESEARCH

Substantive Recommendations for Improving the Research Base

In research on assessment, it is essential to address two different but related goals: (a) the use of assessments to understand the development of first- and second-language oral proficiency and literacy, and (b) the use of assessments for making placement and policy decisions, such as choice of learning environment. With regard to the former, research should provide an array of demonstrably valid and reliable measures that characterize exactly what a language-minority child knows and can do—including knowledge of all facets of English, from oral proficiency through orthographic, phonological, morphological, and lexical knowledge to sentence and discourse comprehension—with an appropriate range of developmental points. The measures should also be designed to measure English proficiency within academic contexts. Such measures would provide the information needed to monitor students' development, assess instructional techniques, and conduct sound research. The development effort would benefit from replication across minority languages. Wherever possible, it would be beneficial to explore what existing measures allow accurate, practical decisions about language and literacy development. A searchable database, which describes the assessments used in this review, is available with the longer volume (August & Shanahan, 2006) and is a good starting place to locate some of these assessments. In the following sections, we outline some of the requirements and considerations that would define a research agenda in this area. A second area of research is how such assessments should be used to make placement and policy decisions.

Assessing Language Proficiency and Literacy. To assess a language-minority child's language, literacy, and content knowledge, we need to understand the linguistic and psychological structures he or she has in both the minority and majority languages and how they interact. We also need understand how and to what degree the linguistic and psychological structures differ for fluent bilingual and fluent monolingual speakers. Interactions can take place at many levels—from the specific constructs of languages (e.g., phonemes, words) to abstract linguistic structures to metacognitive processes. See Chapter 3 of this volume for a discussion of literacy development, and see Chapter 4 for a discussion of cross-language relationships. We also need to understand the influence of culture. The studies reported in Chapter 5 make a modest case for the proposition that language-minority students' literacy achievement improves when they read or otherwise use culturally familiar materials.

Even a simple task such as assessing children's ability to read a list of individual words aloud requires knowing enough about the similarities and differences between the two languages to take into account, for example, which English words will be especially difficult for a child acquiring English and how this compares with fluent monolinguals. Moreover, accurate understanding of the similarities and differences between the two languages and between bilingual and monolingual language processing is essential if lists of words that will assess the whole range of the child's ability are to be constructed.

Vocabulary is an important component of oral language proficiency and literacy for second-language learners and is crucial to reading comprehension. For vocabulary tests normed on monolingual populations, the frequency-ordering of words may be different for second-language learners than for the norming population. Whether or how language-minority children's performance on vocabulary tests can be mapped to monolingual academic literacy performance is an important question. There have been no studies of sufficient breadth to address these issues convincingly.

Language comprehension is not a unidimensional construct. Advances in theory have come to depend on several structural dimensions. One is the distinction among what a reader or listener brings to the comprehension process, what the text or discourse brings, and what the reader or listener takes away. Another is the distinction between the processes in which the reader or listener engages during comprehension and the products of those processes that can be remembered later. Still another is the distinction among various levels of information that a reader or listener may comprehend, including the words in which information was expressed, the ideas embodied in those words, and a mental model of how those ideas could combine into a real-life situation. We assume that the goal of educating language-minority children is for them to comprehend the second language as effectively as a fluent speaker does. The inferences and signals needed to connect information across text may differ between second and first languages. Outcomes on measures of comprehension are certainly influenced by first- and second-language proficiency and literacy. Thus, in developing robust comprehension tests for second-language literacy, contributions from cognitive psychology, education, linguistics, and disciplines that examine sociocultural aspects of learning are needed.

Assessment for Making Placement and Policy Decisions.   More research is needed to document and evaluate methods used at the district level to classify, track, and reclassify English-language learners as well as assess them for accountability. What types of assessments do districts use, singly or in combination, to place students in bilingual education or ESL instruction? What types of assessments do they use to identify language-minority students eligible for services, such as Title I and special education? How do they determine when students are ready to be placed in all-English instruction without special support? What methods and standards are used to determine whether English-language learners are retained, can graduate, or can be tested solely in English? Are the instruments used valid and reliable across the range of types of students with whom they are used? How well do the assessments currently employed actually predict the literacy performance of language-minority students?

Experts, for example, often warn that data from oral language proficiency measures in English should not be the only basis for exit decisions (August & Hakuta, 1997; Collier, 1995; Cummins, 1984). They recommend that decisions about reclassification and assessment policies be based on measures of students' academic language proficiency in English. Considerable future research is needed to develop valid and reliable measures for this purpose. Especially important is the question of whether any single measure can provide sufficient information about all the component skills needed by an English-language learner to do well in an unsupported English classroom or on assessment without accommodations. We stress that research must examine the relationship between any measure used for placement decisions or policy decisions and the performance of children who are assessed on the basis of that measure.

One goal of assessing English-language learners' literacy performance is the identification of students who have special needs in learning to read beyond those imposed by learning a second language. Identification of such problems as dyslexia is difficult when assessments are administered in English and English-language learners' preliteracy skills in that language are minimal or nonexistent. Educators are required by law to assess these children in their first language, but there have been no longitudinal studies to determine what first-language assessments are effective for diagnosing various kinds of impairments. Although several studies explored this issue by examining whether specific measures or indices adequately predict which children will have difficulty, all were limited in their sample of students and the measures chosen for investigation. In future research, a wide range of measures needs to be examined across a broad spectrum of abilities (in English and in the first language), and the predictive validity of these measures must be examined longitudinally.

Methodological Recommendations for Improving the Research Base

Our first recommendation is that future empirical investigations of language and literacy assessments for language-minority students incorporate necessary expertise from a range of disciplines: linguistics, cognitive psychology, education, and psychometrics. Linguists are necessary because of the importance of assessing language-minority children's knowledge of aspects of first and second languages adequately and accurately. For example, the phonology and word structures of English and how they map to those of other languages are complex issues that have been the subject of considerable research in linguistics. In turn, whether and how these structures are projected in the human lexicon has been the subject of a great deal of research in psychology. In cases where the assessments are used to assess instruction and development within classroom contexts, educators can help ensure that they will be useful and easy to administer. Psychometric expertise helps ensure that the assessments are valid and reliable.

The second recommendation is that, when reporting on their studies, researchers publish an appendix containing the items used in the assessment measures they investigated, or otherwise make them accessible. Researcher-constructed measures need to provide appropriate reliability and validity information. Without complete knowledge of the assessments used in a study, other researchers cannot evaluate the study findings, nor carry out replications essential for building a strong body of empirical knowledge.

Our third recommendation is that researchers make every effort to include in their research designs at least some of the same measures used by other researchers to investigate similar questions and found to be valid and reliable with language-minority students. For example, if earlier work on reading comprehension used a particular assessment, future research should include it along with whatever other measures are important to the study. We reiterate here the necessity for a systematic, progressive accumulation of empirical findings.

REFERENCES

Abedi, J. (2002). Assessment and accommodations of English language learners: Issues, concerns, and recommendations. *Journal of School Improvement*, 3(1), 83–89.

Abedi, J., Hofstetter, C., Baker, E., & Lord, C. (2001). *NAEP math performance and test accommodations: Interactions with student language background* (Technical Report No. 536). Los Angeles: University of California, Center for the Study of Evaluation/National Center for Research on Evaluation, Standards, and Student Testing.

Abedi, J., Lord, C., Boscardin, C. K., & Miyoshi, J. (2001). *The effects of accommodations on the assessment of limited English proficient (LEP) students in the National Assessment of*

Educational Progress (NAEP) (Technical Report No. 537). Los Angeles: University of California, Center for the Study of Evaluation/National Center for Research on Evaluation, Standards, and Student Testing.

Ambert, A. N. (1986). Identifying language disorders in Spanish-speakers. *Journal of Reading, Writing, and Learning Disabilities International*, 2(1), 21–41.

American Educational Research Association, American Psychological Association, & National Council on Measurement in Education. (1999). *Standards for educational and psychological testing 1999*. Washington, DC: American Educational Research Association Publications.

Anderson, M., Liu, K., Swierzbin, B., Thurlow, M., & Bielinski, J. (2000). *Bilingual accommodations for limited English proficient students on statewide reading tests: Phase 2* (Minnesota Report No. 31). Minneapolis, MN: University of Minnesota, National Center on Educational Outcomes.

Argulewicz, E. N., & Abel, R. R. (1984). Internal evidence of bias in the PPVT–R for Anglo- American and Mexican-American children. *Journal of School Psychology*, 22(3), 299–303.

August, D. L., & Hakuta, K. (Eds.). (1997). *Improving schooling for language-minority learners*. Washington, DC: National Academy Press.

August, D. & Shanahan, T. (Eds.) (2006). *Developing literacy in second-language learners: Report of the National Literacy Panel on Language Minority Children and Youth*. Mahwah, NJ: Lawrence Erlbaum Associates.

Baker, S. K., & Good, R. (1995). Curriculum-based measurement reading with bilingual Hispanic students: A validation study with second-grade students. *School Psychology Review*, 24(4), 561–578.

Baldauf, R. B., Jr., Dawson, R. T., Prior, J., & Propst, I. K., Jr. (1980). Can matching cloze be used with secondary ESL pupils? *Journal of Reading*, 23(5), 435–440.

Bessai, F. (2001). *Review of the Peabody Picture Vocabulary Test–III*. Retrieved September 28, 2005, from http://www.unm.edu/~fv3003/shs533/ppvt%20III.doc

Brown, D. (1983). Conversational cloze tests and conversational ability. *ELT Journal*, 37(2), 158–161.

Butler, F. A., & Stevens, R. (2001). Standardized assessment of the content knowledge of English language learners K–12: Current trends and old dilemmas. *Language Testing*, 18(4), 409–427.

Chiappe, P., Siegel, L. S., & Gottardo, A. (2002). Reading-related skills of kindergartners from diverse linguistic backgrounds. *Applied Psycholinguistics*, 23(1), 95–116.

Collier, V. P. (1995). Acquiring a second language for school. *Directions in Language & Education*, 1(4), 1–12.

Cummins, J. (1984). *Bilingualism and special education: Issues in assessment and pedagogy*. Clevedon, UK: Multilingual Matters.

Davidson, F. (1994). Norms appropriacy of achievement tests: Spanish-speaking children and English children's norms. *Language Testing*, 11(1), 83–95.

Davies, A. (1991). *The native speaker in applied linguistics*. Edinburgh: Edinburgh University Press.

De Avila, E., & Duncan, S. (1990). *Language assessment scales – oral*. Monterey, CA: CTB McGraw-Hill.

Duncan, S., & De Avila, E. (1988). *Language assessment scales – reading and writing*. Monterey, CA: CTB McGraw-Hill.

Dunn, L. M., & Dunn, L. M. (1981). *Peabody picture vocabulary test*. Circle Pines, MN: American Guidance Service.

Dunn, L. M., Padilla, E. R., Lugo, D. E., & Dunn, L. M. (1986). *Test de vocabulario en imágenes Peabody*. Circle Pines, MN: American Guidance Service.

Durán, R. P. (1989). Testing of linguistic minorities. In R. L. Linn (Ed.), *Educational measurement* (3rd ed., pp. 573–587). New York: American Council on Education.

Durán, R. P., Brown, C., & McCall, M. (2002). Assessment of English-language learners in the Oregon statewide assessment system: National and state perspectives. In G. Tindal & T. M. Haladyna (Eds.), *Large-scale assessment programs for all students*. St. Paul, MN: Assessment Systems Corporation.

Everatt, J., Smythe, I., Adams, E., & Ocampo, D. (2000). Dyslexia screening measures and bilingualism. *Dyslexia*, 6(1), 42–56.

Fernández, M. C., Pearson, B. Z., Umbel, V. M., Oller, D. K., & Molinet-Molina, M. (1992). Bilingual receptive vocabulary in Hispanic preschool children. *Hispanic Journal of Behavioral Sciences*, 14(2), 268–276.

Figueroa, R. A. (1989). Best practices in the assessment of bilingual children. In A. Thomas & J. Grimes (Eds.), *Best practices in school psychology* (pp. 93–106). Washington, DC: National Association of School Psychologists.

Frontera, L. S., & Horowitz, R. (1995). Reading and study behaviors of fourth-grade Hispanics: Can teachers assess risk? *Hispanic Journal of Behavioral Sciences*, 17(1), 100–120.

García, G. E. (1991). Factors influencing the English reading test performance of Spanish-speaking Hispanic children. *Reading Research Quarterly*, 26(4), 371–392.

García, E. (1994). *Understanding and meeting the challenge of student cultural diversity*. Boston, MA: Houghton-Mifflin.

García, G. E., & Pearson, P. D. (1994). Assessment and diversity. In L. Darling-Hammond (Ed.), *Review of research in education* (Vol. 20, pp. 337–392). Washington, DC: American Educational Research Association.

Geva, E., Yaghoub-Zadeh, Z., & Schuster, B. (2000). Part IV: Reading and foreign language learning: Understanding individual differences in word recognition skills of ESL children. *Annals of Dyslexia*, 50, 121–154.

Goldstein, B. C., Harris, K. C., & Klein, M. D. (1993). Assessment of oral storytelling abilities of Latino junior high school students with learning handicaps. *Journal of Learning Disabilities*, 26(2), 138–132.

Gómez, L., Parker, R., Lara-Alecio, R., Ochoa, S. H., & Gómez, R., Jr. (1996). Naturalistic language assessment of LEP students in classroom interactions. *Bilingual Research Journal*, 20(1), 69–92.

Hakuta, K., & Beatty, A. (2000). *Testing English language learners in U. S. schools*. Washington, DC: National Academy Press.

Hannon, P., & McNally, J. (1986). Children's understanding and cultural factors in reading test performance. *Educational Review*, 38(3), 237–246.

Hatch, E. (1992). *Discourse and language education*. New York: Cambridge University Press.

Holm, A., Dodd, B., Stow, C., & Pert, S. (1999). Identification and differential diagnosis of phonological disorder in bilingual children. *Language Testing*, 16(3), 271–292.

IDEA language proficiency tests. (1978, 1994). Brea, CA: Ballard & Tighe.

Jansky, J. J., Hoffman, M. J., Layton, J., & Sugar, F. (1989). Prediction: A six-year follow-up. *Annals of Dyslexia*, 39, 227–246.

Kindler, A. L. (2002). *Survey of the states' limited English proficient students and available educational programs and services, 2000–2001 summary report*. Washington, DC: National Clearinghouse for English Language Acquisition and Language Instruction Educational Programs.

Koenig, J. A., & Bachman, L. F. (2004). *Keeping score for all: The effects of inclusion and accommodation policies on large-scale educational assessment*. Washington, DC: National Academy Press.

Laesch, K. B., & Van Kleeck, A. (1987). The cloze test as an alternative measure of language proficiency of children considered for exit from bilingual education programs. *Language Learning*, 37(2), 171–189.

Langdon, H. W. (1989). Language disorder or difference? Assessing the language skills of Hispanic students. *Exceptional Children*, 56(2), 160–167.

Lee, J. F. (1986). Background knowledge and L2 reading. *Modern Language Journal*, 70, 350–354.

Limbos, M., & Geva, E. (2001). Accuracy of teacher assessments of second-language students at risk for reading disability. *Journal of Learning Disabilities*, 34(2), 136–151.

Mercer, J. R. (1979). In defense of racially and culturally nondiscriminatory assessment. *School Psychology Digest*, 8, 89–115.

Messick, S. (1994). The interplay of evidence and consequences in the validation of performance assessments. *Educational Researcher*, 23(2), 13–23.

Mestre, J. P. (1984, Fall). The problem with problems: Hispanic students and math. *Bilingual Journal*, pp. 15–20.

Miramontes, O. B. (1987). Oral reading miscues of Hispanic students: Implications for assessment of learning disabilities. *Journal of Learning Disabilities*, 20(10), 627–632.

Nadeau, A., & Miramontes, O. (1988). The reclassification of limited English proficient students: Assessing the inter-relationship of selected variables. *NABE: The Journal for the National Association for Bilingual Education*, 12(3), 219–242.

Ochoa, S. H., Galarza, A., & González, D. (1996). An investigation of school psychologists' assessment practices of language proficiency with bilingual and limited-English-proficient students. *Diagnostique*, 21(4), 17–36.

Olmeda, E. L. (1981). Testing linguistic minorities. *American Psychologist*, 36, 1078–1085.

Ozete, O. (1980). Modified cloze and cloze testing in Spanish. *Bilingual Review/Revista Bilingue*, 7(3), 203–211.

Pomplun, M., & Omar, M. H. (2001). The factorial invariance of a test of reading comprehension across groups of limited English proficient students. *Applied Measurement in Education*, 14(3), 261–283.

Quinn, C. (2001). The developmental acquisition of English grammar as an additional language. *International Journal of Language & Communication Disorders*, 36(Suppl.), 309–314.

Restrepo, M. A. (1998). Identifiers of predominantly Spanish-speaking children with language impairment. *Journal of Speech, Language, and Hearing Research*, 41(6), 1398–1411.

Royer, J. M., & Carlo, M. S. (1991). Assessing the language acquisition progress of limited English proficient students: Problems and a new alternative. *Applied Measurement in Education*, 4(2), 85–113.

Royer, J. M., Carlo, M. S., Carlisle, J. F., & Furman, G. A. (1991). A new procedure for assessing progress in transitional bilingual education programs. *Bilingual Review/Revista Bilingue*, 16(1), 3–14.

Samuda, R. J. (1975). *Psychological testing of American minorities*. New York: Dodd Mead.

Sattler, J. M., & Altes, L. M. (1984). Performance of bilingual and monolingual Hispanic children on the Peabody Picture Vocabulary Test–Revised and the McCarthy Perceptual Performance Scale. *Psychology in the Schools*, 21(3), 313–316.

Scruggs, T. E., Mastropieri, M. A., & Argulewicz, E. N. (1983). Stability of performance on the PPVT–R for three ethnic groups attending a bilingual kindergarten. *Psychology in the Schools*, 20(4), 433–435.

Sireci, S., Li, S., & Scarpati, S. (2003). *The effects of test accommodation on test performance: A review of the literature* (Center for Educational Assessment Research Report No. 485). Amherst, MA: School of Education, University of Massachusetts.

Stage, S. A., Sheppard, J., Davidson, M. M., & Browning, M. M. (2001). Prediction of first-graders' growth in oral reading fluency using kindergarten letter fluency. *Journal of School Psychology*, 39(3), 225–237.

Stevens, R. A., Butler, F. A., & Castellón-Wellington, M. (2000). *Academic language and content assessment: Measuring the progress of English-language learners* (CSE Technical Report No. 552). Los Angeles: University of California, National Center for Research on Evaluation, Standards, and Student Testing.

Tamayo, J. M. (1987). Frequency of use as a measure of word difficulty in bilingual vocabulary test construction and translation. *Educational and Psychological Measurement, 47*(4), 893–902.

U.S. Department of Education. (2003). *Title I, Standards and assessment, non-regulatory draft guidance.* Retrieved September 28, 2005, from http://www.ed.gov/policy/speced/guid/nclb/standassguidance03.pdf

U.S. Department of Education. (2004, February 19). Secretary Paige announces new policies to help English language learners (Press release). Retrieved September 28, 2005, from http://www.ed.gov/news/pressreleases/2004/02/02192004.html

Valdés, G., & Figueroa, R. (1994). *Bilingualism and testing: A special case of bias.* Norwood, NJ: Ablex.

Woodcock, R., & Muñoz-Sandoval, A. (1993). *Woodcock–Muñoz language survey.* Itasca, IL: Riverside.

8

Cross-Cutting Themes and Future Research Directions

Catherine Snow

Summarizing research on a topic as complex as second-language literacy is a Herculean task. The complexity of the Panel's work is revealed in the topic-based organization and in the richness of the individual chapters in this volume. Understanding the development of second-language literacy skills requires at the following subtasks:

- Understanding the complexity of the reading process. The contributions to successful reading made by accuracy and fluency in word reading, control over the requisite language skills (vocabulary, syntax, discourse structures), and world knowledge have all been richly documented for monolingual readers. Although the reading process is complex for all students, the individual differences among second-language learners greatly increase the complexity of the task of understanding the reading process for these students.
- Understanding individual differences. Any learner brings certain strengths and weaknesses to the task of learning to read. However, second-language learners are more variable by far in the kinds of knowledge they bring to the literacy classroom than are monolingual children. Some second-language learners know how to read in their first language and some do not. Second-language learners are also likely, for example, to fall below the range of monolingual children on measures of second-language knowledge, and some may fall below that range on knowledge of the

second-language alphabet and other aspects of second-language orthography.

- Understanding development. Dynamic models of development view the acquisition of any complex skill as successive restructurings, not just accretions of knowledge. There is good evidence that children adopt, abandon, and reformulate their theories of how a second language is spelled and read as they develop from novice to skilled readers.
- Understanding the context in which second-language learners develop reading. Second-language learners vary tremendously in their conditions of learning—classrooms where almost everyone else is a monolingual speaker of the second language; mixed first-language classrooms learning exclusively in a second language; and bilingual classrooms, where the first language may be used a little or a lot. Their home environments are also varied with regard to language use (i.e., monolingual first language or bilingual) and literacy practices. Even describing these many variations is a massive task, let alone understanding how they interact with literacy outcomes.

The Panel reviewed information relevant to each of these four dimensions of second-language literacy. We start this concluding chapter by presenting those propositions that, according to the research reviews in the preceding chapters, could be defended with the available evidence. Associated with each of those propositions, we note a set of claims we would like to be able to make that are not yet sufficiently supported by the available evidence.

We highlight what appears to be the most important subset of true knowledge gaps—areas that simply have not received enough research attention. Many of the suggestions for future research presented in this chapter—both in areas in which we have partial knowledge and areas that have thus far been largely ignored—come directly from the preceding chapters. A list of all the valuable suggestions for future research formulated by the authors of those chapters would, unfortunately, be much longer than the list of propositions for which we have reasonably convincing research evidence. Therefore, we limit our suggestions here to the most salient of those made previously.

In the next section, we delineate themes that cut across the preceding chapters, noting how the findings presented in one chapter illuminate those discussed in others. We argue for the need to use data from all the chapters in an integrated fashion in an effort to understand the complexities of literacy development in a second language. In the process, we bring into the discussion a few studies outside the scope of those reviewed by the Panel that we would argue are highly relevant to our charge. This is not to criticize the scope of the Panel's work, but to highlight the inherently multidisciplinary nature of work on second-language literacy. The Panel focused for the most part on research related to the literacy development of language-minority children and youth that had been published in peer-reviewed journals and included literacy outcomes. But data of relevance to understanding the issues addressed in this volume also come from anthropological, linguistic, discourse-analytic, and applied linguistic work that may have appeared in books rather than journals and that reflect different perspectives on literacy development. In addition to studies discussed later in this chapter, the huge literature on foreign-language teaching, whose roots predate the interest in second-language literacy acquisition, is of considerable potential relevance and yet fell largely outside the Panel's purview.

WHAT WE KNOW

The research reviewed in previous chapters has yielded a number of conclusions on second-language reading about which we can have a fair degree of certainty. These conclusions are presented in this section, together with some indication of the major limitations on how far we can take them.

Domains of Achievement

Second-language readers are more likely to achieve adequate performance (defined as performance that either is equivalent to that of monolinguals or meets local educational standards) on measures of word recognition and spelling than on measures of reading vocabulary, comprehension, and writing. Adequate performance on word-level skills in the second language can be achieved either through bilingual instruction or instruction exclusively in the target language. Obviously, excellent instruction (systematic, intensive, differentiated) is more likely than poor instruction to generate expected levels of performance on word-level skills. But instruction good enough to produce expected levels of second-language performance on word-level skills does not ensure expected levels of performance on text-level skills. The research reviewed in this volume provides few descriptions or evaluations of programs that have generated expected levels of performance on comprehension or writing for the majority of second-language learners studied.

In all, there were only three experimental studies that focused on vocabulary, three that examined methods to improve comprehension, and four that focused on writing. These small numbers contrast mark-edly with the National Reading Panel's summary of research (National Institute of Child Health and Human Development, 2000) on literacy instruction for monolinguals, which had available approximately 45 experimental studies focused on vocabulary and 205 experimental studies focused on comprehension.

Although the capacity of English-language learners to achieve adequate word reading may be the most robust conclusion identified by the Panel, it is important to note that almost all the available studies of word reading were carried out with elementary school learners who are typically asked to read only relatively short, regular, and frequent words. Despite the clear strengths in word reading displayed by English-language learners, for example, in many cases we do not know how fluently they read, nor do we know how they perform when expected to read novel, multisyllabic, technical vocabulary in the middle and secondary grades.

Findings from studies on reading comprehension paint a different picture from the one that emerges from studies focused on word reading and spelling. The few available studies on the development of reading comprehension, many carried out in the Netherlands, yielded highly consistent results, indicating that the reading comprehension perform-ance of language-minority students falls well below that of their native-speaking peers. Of the 17 experimental studies focused on developing components of literacy in language minority children (see Chapter 6), only 6 employed comprehension measures. When comprehension was measured, the studies often found no significant improvement in that outcome due to the instruction (e.g., Denton, 2000); when such improvement was observed, it was less pronounced than was the case for other measures (e.g., Gunn, Biglan et al., 2000; Gunn, Smolkowski et al., 2002). Studies of comprehension have similarly been limited largely to students in the elementary and middle grades, leaving open the pos-sibility that English-language learners take longer to catch up on com-prehension, but eventually do arrive at the levels of native speakers. This optimistic conclusion, unfortunately, is not supported by the National Assessment of Educational Progress (NAEP) data or available research on older second-language readers. For example, Barnitz and Speaker (1991) found that intermediate-level English-as-a-second-language (ESL) university students and secondary-level English-language learners failed to draw even fairly obvious inferences when reading a poem rich in figurative language, although their literal comprehension was adequate; advanced-level ESL university students drew some inferences, but not to a degree that would be considered satisfactory in a literature class.

Factors Influencing Literacy: The Same and Maybe Some More

The same societal, familial, and individual factors that predict good literacy outcomes for monolingual readers do so for second-language readers as well:

- Societal/cultural factors related to literacy outcomes for both first- and second-language readers include supportive communities, stable economic prospects, effective schools, high educational standards, high teacher expectations for student performance, and good instruction.
- Familial/cultural factors include socioeconomic status (SES), parental education and literacy levels, and home support for literacy development.
- Individual factors include school readiness skills, phonological processing skills, oral language proficiency (including vocabulary), and use of comprehension strategies.

It is widely assumed that additional societal, familial, and individual factors not relevant to the literacy development of monolingual readers may come into play in predicting literacy outcomes for second-language readers. Indeed, the greater complexity of predicting outcomes for the latter readers is one reason they are the focus of research. Unfortunately, strong research evidence does not exist to support the impact of many societal/familial factors that one might predict would be related to second- but not first-language outcomes. The weak evidence concerning certain societal/familial factors and the stronger evidence concerning individual factors that are particularly relevant to predicting second-language outcomes are briefly summarized here.

- One might expect societal factors, both institutional and cultural, to influence second-language outcomes, but evidence supporting this expectation is scarce. For example, research has not demonstrated an impact of such factors as the history of the second-language group's immigration (voluntary or forced, economically or politically motivated), the status of the first-language group in the second-language setting (e.g., Koreans have high status in the United States, but low status in Japan), and the history and nature of literacy within the first language (Chinese has a long and revered literacy tradition, whereas Hmong does not). One fairly consistent finding across studies is that language-minority students' reading comprehension improves when they read culturally familiar materials. However, the language of the text is a stronger influence on reading performance: Students perform better when they read or use material in the language they know better. Although the general hypothesis that the sociocultural context influences literacy outcomes remains highly plausible, limitations in the design, systematicity, instrumentation, and, most important, theoretical grounding of the available research limit the strength of the basis for this interpretation. Moreover, students' cultural affiliations are frequently confounded with SES, for which there is strong evidence of an impact on literacy outcomes, rendering interpretation even more problematic.

- Familial factors, like societal factors, incorporate economic, legal, and cultural influences. Remarkably, there is little evidence of influence of such likely determinants of child outcomes as immigration status (documented or not), commitment to maintaining the first language as a home language, parental literacy in either the first or second language, capacity and opportunity to select educational programs for the child, and presence in the home of highly proficient first-language (e.g., grandparents) and second-language (e.g., older siblings schooled in the United States) speakers.

- Individual factors relevant to second-language reading include, in addition to school readiness and emergent literacy skills, level of language and literacy knowledge in the first language, background knowledge, metacognitive capacity to treat those first-language skills as resources in learning the second language, strategies to approach text comprehension, and motivation to succeed academically and socially in the second-language setting. Age of onset of second-language learning is widely thought to influence second-language outcomes, but its influence cannot be easily disentangled from the impact of factors that happen to correlate with age, such as motivation, access to social contacts, commitment to maintaining the first language, and grade-level task demands.

The Sorry State of Assessment

Our review of assessments used with English-language learners in Chapter 7 clearly reveals the need for more research. The lack of diagnostic assessments in the domain of reading comprehension (see Snow, 2003) is particularly poignant for second-language readers, whose sources of difficulty with comprehension may be different from those of monolingual readers. The state of the art of oral proficiency and academic-language assessment is far behind that of phonological awareness, word reading accuracy, and fluency assessment. Finally, little research has focused on identifying older English-language learners with learning disabilities. Serious attention to these issues is prerequisite to making real progress in understanding second-language literacy development and in helping teachers monitor and improve instructional outcomes for second-language learners.

Transfer Cannot Be Ruled Out

The concept of transfer from a first to a second language or from a first to a second literacy system has an honored, but contested, place in thinking about language learning. The classic definition of transfer, derived from the tradition of behaviorist psychology and contrastive analysis (Lado, 1964), suggests that strongly developed first-language habits are hardest to overcome in a second language—in other words, transfer is considered to be mostly negative in its impact. In contrast, the potential for transfer is a major plank in many arguments favoring bilingual over purely second-language education. A somewhat moderated potential for transfer is a central claim in Cummins' (1979) influential notions about the threshold hypothesis.

It is thus striking that there has been so little research speaking directly and unequivocally to the existence, role, or strength of transfer in second-language literacy development. Much of the evidence reviewed in Chapter 4 is consistent with the transfer of knowledge from the first to the second language in specific domains. However, few of the research findings unequivocally support the conclusion that transfer exists because alternative explanations are not systematically ruled out.

The evidence does show that:

- Word reading in the second language correlates with that in the first language, but to a greater or lesser extent, depending on the orthographic relationships between the first and second languages.
- Spelling in the second language shows the influence of first-language orthographic knowledge at the early stages of second-language development if second-language orthographic knowledge is limited.
- Vocabulary knowledge in the second language can be enhanced by the use of vocabulary knowledge from the first language in cases where etymological relationships between the first and second languages exist, with positive consequences for second-language reading comprehension. At the later stages of second-language development, however, the enhancement is more powerful for metalinguistic aspects of word knowledge and often requires mediation through first-language literacy.
- Reading comprehension in the second language correlates with that in the first language, but perhaps more strongly at later grades, when comprehension tasks are more challenging.
- Use of reading strategies in the first language correlates with their

use in the second language once second-language reading has developed sufficiently so such strategies can be used.

- Strategic aspects of writing are closely related in the first and second languages, although again probably only after some threshold of second-language knowledge has been achieved.

Overall, correlations across languages in performance on particular tasks certainly are consistent with the claim that there is transfer from the first to the second language, but they hardly constitute strong proof of any causal relation implicating transfer. Perhaps performance in both languages is accounted for by some third factor, such as intelligence, speed of processing, visual memory, phonological sensitivity, or metalinguistic skill. In fact, there is good evidence (reviewed in Chapter 4) that phonological recoding, phonological memory, and phonological awareness are strongly related across languages, suggesting that such tasks draw on the same abilities no matter the language in which they are performed. Perhaps the impact of instruction in the second language changes the nature of processing in the first language, a phenomenon that might be seen as transfer, but not of the type in which most researchers or educators are interested.

Conversely, the conditional nature of most of these documented transfer candidates could be regarded as support for the claim that these are true examples of transfer. We would hardly expect transfer of word reading skill from Chinese to English to be as strong as that from Spanish to English. It makes sense that transfer of vocabulary knowledge from Spanish to English is mediated by literacy knowledge in Spanish because Spanish–English cognates are more similar in written than in spoken form. It also makes sense that more metalinguistic tasks constitute sites for transfer. Following Bialystok and Bouchard Ryan (1985), we define metalinguistic as encompassing two dimensions: control of processing and analysis of knowledge. Control of processing is not a specifically linguistic capacity, and thus should be equally available across languages. Analysis skills, similarly, are language neutral; the knowledge to be analyzed, in contrast, is highly language specific, so we cannot expect that analysis of knowledge tasks will show transfer until there is some second-language knowledge to which analysis skills can be applied. This is precisely the pattern that has been documented for transfer in the domains of lexicon and reading comprehension. But the case remains somewhat circumstantial.

What would constitute stronger proof of transfer? Unequivocal proof of transfer would come from intervention studies in which some fairly specific skill was taught in the first language to one group of learners and their performance in the second language on some related skill was compared with that of another group not receiving the first-language instruction. Yet designing such a study would require having a theory of what may transfer and to what, of how language and literacy skills relate to one another, and of what aspects of first-language knowledge may be usable for the second language. It is not certain that we have a sufficiently well-developed theory to test a full array of specific hypotheses in this domain.

To take a simple example, we might hypothesize that learning to spell in Spanish will generate skills that transfer to English. Thus, we would provide a group of learners with systematic Spanish spelling instruction and then assess their English spelling. Evidence reviewed in Chapter 4 indeed suggests that the students would make many errors influenced by Spanish spelling and pronunciation—for example, "Guen mi mami smail her aic ar beri briti" ("When my mommy smiles her eyes are very pretty"). This would constitute presumptive evidence of transfer, especially if the comparison group made few such errors, and the transfer would appear to be entirely negative. But what if the two groups of learners were assessed on phonological analysis of words—for example, were asked to count phonemes? On that task, the children who had been taught to spell in Spanish might well perform better than those who had not because they would be relying much less on memorized spellings (sight words are a big part of early literacy instruction in English) or visual memory, and because they would have had instruction that systematically linked letters to sounds. Does this situation provide evidence in support of positive or negative transfer?

To take another example based on real but perplexing data, most studies of immigrant children growing up bilingual show negative correlations between first- and second-language vocabulary. On the face of it, those negative correlations appear to exclude the possibility of positive transfer. However, classroom teachers are unanimous in noting that children who arrive in the United States with strong first-language vocabularies have little difficulty acquiring English words. The mechanism widely suggested for this phenomenon is that knowledge of the concepts need not be reacquired; all that is needed is new labels for those known concepts. In other words, conceptual knowledge is available in the first language and facilitates vocabulary acquisition in the second language. Is this evidence of transfer from the first to the second language, or is the conceptual knowledge nonlinguistic? If the availability of conceptual knowledge promotes second-language acquisition for older learners, why does the same not hold true for younger children growing up bilingual? Or is the more rapid second-language acquisition of children with large first-language vocabularies simply a reflection of the fact that they are more likely to have had excellent first-language schooling? Finally, it may be that the assessments used to measure vocabulary do not adequately represent children's real vocabulary knowledge in their first or second language in part because they were normed on monolingual populations.

The intriguing lack of a documented relationship in the studies reviewed in this volume between oral language proficiency in the first language and second-language literacy suggests the value of a double-dissociation design for identifying cases of true transfer. If one teaches Skill X in the first language as part of a study designed to test for transfer, perhaps one should be required to predict not just what second-language skill will be influenced, but also what second-language skill will not be influenced. Returning to the earlier Spanish spelling example, we would interpret findings such as those we have imagined to be a demonstration of positive transfer from Spanish spelling to English phonological analysis, possibly mediated by Spanish phonological analysis. But if the children who had received Spanish spelling instruction also showed greater improvement than controls on English oral language proficiency, it would be difficult to attribute these changes to any well-specified transfer mechanism. Such findings would appear to suggest a prima facie case that the effects in English resulted from something other than pure transfer because no hypothesized mechanism links Spanish spelling to English oral proficiency.

In short, then, on the basis of the available evidence, transfer cannot be ruled out as a factor in second-language literacy development, but neither is the evidence demonstrating its impact strong or unequivocal. Most discouraging, despite the recurrent invocation of transfer as an argument for bilingual instruction and the long history of its use as a central theoretical concept, there is still remarkably little clarity about how to define transfer operationally, what evidence would count as demonstrating its existence, or the range of phenomena for which it might be expected to operate.

We Have to Believe Instruction Is Important

The literature we reviewed reveals remarkably little about the effectiveness of different aspects of instruction, and it provides only limited guidance about how good instruction for second-language speakers might differ from that for first-language speakers. Many of the instructional components known to be effective with monolingual English speakers—enhancing children's phonological awareness before or while teaching letter–sound relationships, teaching letter–sound relationships systematically, integrating letter–sound instruction with use of meaningful and engaging texts, providing extra help immediately to students who are falling behind—appear to be effective as well with English-language learners. Adapting instruction to specifics of the child's knowledge base (e.g., focusing phonological awareness instruction on phoneme distinctions not made in the child's first language, pointing out cognates, drawing contrasts between the first and second language in preferred discourse structures) has sometimes proved helpful, but English-language learners in heterogeneous classrooms where such first-language-specific help is unavailable can be successful if provided high-quality instruction in their second language. Some evidence exists concerning the value of specific instructional approaches to well-defined learning challenges (e.g., using more elaborated, context-enriched methods for teaching vocabulary; see Chapter 6). Although the qualitative studies suggest that high-quality comprehensive literacy programs promote second-language literacy development, there is limited quasi-experimental research on the value of these more comprehensively defined approaches to literacy instruction for second-language learners (e.g., Instructional Conversations, Success for All). Given the importance of concurrently developing a multitude of skills in second-language learners, much more research is needed in this area.

Most discouraging, the research we reviewed provides little basis for deciding whether or what kinds of accommodations or adaptations are most helpful to second-language learners. The research does suggest, however, that one kind of accommodation—developing English oral proficiency in the context of literacy instruction—would help. Chapter 6 indicates that effect sizes for English-language learners are lower and more variable than those for native-English-speaking students (except with vocabulary teaching), suggesting that the teaching of most component skills is likely to be necessary, but insufficient, for improving literacy achievement among the English-language learners, and the research in Chapter 3 indicates that second-language oral language proficiency influences text-level skills.

Just as the studies cited in Chapter 4 highlight cross-language relationships, the studies in Chapter 6 demonstrate that language-minority students instructed in their native language (primarily Spanish) as well as English perform, on average, better on English reading measures than language-minority students instructed only in their second language (English in this case). This is the case at both the elementary and secondary levels. The strongest evidence supporting this claim comes from the randomized studies that indicate a moderate effect in favor of bilingual instruction. Nonetheless, the advantage of bilingual over English-only instruction is moderate, so lower expectations for learners without access to native-language literacy instruction are unjustified. Obviously, if there is political or educational value attached to bilingualism and biliteracy, then bilingual programs are to be preferred even more strongly because there is no basis in the research findings to suggest that they are in any way disadvantageous to English academic outcomes.

A logical case could be made that factors shown to promote

monolingual children's literacy development, such as the capacity of the teacher to adapt instruction to the child's needs, are even more important to children learning to read in a second language. The quantitative data needed to support this statement are not directly available, however, and collecting them would require a complex study to test what is, in effect, an interaction hypothesis: Differentiation of instruction according to individual learner needs accounts for a larger proportion of the variance in reading outcomes for students learning to read in a second than in a first language. But if we accept that learning to read in a second language is more difficult than learning to read in a language one already speaks, it appears obvious that this is also a task whose outcome is more determined by quality of teaching. Thus, it is surprising that we do not have more robust findings concerning the relationship of high-quality instruction to good outcomes for second-language learners. A first step might be simply to expand the available database of descriptions of instruction demonstrated to be highly effective with second-language readers. The currently available descriptive studies of instruction (see Chapter 7) do not provide empirical warrants that the instruction described generates excellent outcomes for bilingual learners.

In Chapter 7, in addition to the experimental studies, we review studies offering rich descriptions of promising instructional practices. These descriptions can provide considerable guidance to educators about what kinds of practices might be used with second-language readers, even in the absence of incontrovertible evidence that these are the best possible practices. For example, both the experimental and qualitative studies indicate that students' English-language proficiency appears to interact with the instructional approach employed; accordingly, teachers may need to differentiate instruction depending on student proficiency levels. Use of student assessment data to focus instruction and collaboration between special education teachers and resource specialists was also deemed important in meeting student needs. It appears obvious that understanding something about cultural differences is important for educators working with such students; case studies of classroom practice (e.g., Au & Mason's [1981] study of the Kamehameha School) suggest that adapting instruction to the cultural and linguistic characteristics of learners has positive effects on students' level of engagement and participation during reading lessons. But the studies lack measures of literacy achievement or comprehension, or are not designed in ways that allow causal inferences attributing improvement in reading to cultural accommodations. Clearly, more research is needed in this area.

Some sparse evidence suggests that features of effective professional development are not specific to teachers of second-language learners. More specifically, it suggests that creating change in teachers is a time-consuming process that requires considerable investment on the part of the change agents as well as the teachers. Consistent with previous findings (Baker & Smith, 1999), teachers found the professional development to be most helpful when it provided hands-on practice opportunities with teaching techniques readily applicable to their classrooms or in-class demonstrations with their own or a colleague's students. In addition, teachers requested more personalized coaching—a time-tested method for improving teaching practices (Gersten, Morvant, & Brengelman, 1995). Unfortunately, large-scale evaluations of professional development that focus on issues specific to English-language learners are not available. However, many features of good instruction are as useful to teachers of English-language learners as to teachers of monolingual children, and of course many classrooms contain both types of students. Thus, professional development that attends to the need for differentiated instruction should be available to all teachers in U.S. schools, and issues of second-language acquisition and second-language reading should not be restricted to professional development for ESL or bilingual teachers.

THE KEY GAPS

In the preceding section, we note not just what we know about various topics, but also where conclusions are limited or where research has thus far failed to confirm expectations. In this section, we focus on the true gaps—the topics that have been neglected almost entirely.

Whole Chunks of Development

It is striking how little systematic attention has been paid to school readiness, the course of emergent literacy skills, or the design of optimal preschool programs for English-language learners. Prevention has become a slogan for good literacy practice, and it is widely acknowledged that prevention is most effective if begun during the preschool period. Yet it appears that the field is ignoring the needs of a group that is at high risk of literacy difficulties by failing to focus on efforts to understand or enhance their development during the preschool years. The topic of simultaneous bilingual development is frequently visited in the field of child language; it has generated dozens of case studies and some small-group analyses. A smaller number of studies have addressed the development of incipiently bilingual children in the preschool period (see Tabors & Snow, 1994, 2001, for reviews), but those studies for the most part have not addressed questions related to designing optimal preschool environments for these second-language learners.

The vast majority of the studies reviewed in this volume focus on kindergarten through fifth-grade students. Middle- and secondary-grade students are not included in most of the studies reviewed. Hence, research has paid far too little attention to issues that become increasingly important in those grades: vocabulary development, oral language proficiency, comprehension of challenging texts, instruction for dealing with academic text structures, interactions between reading comprehension and content area learning, writing and so on.

The topic of age differences in second-language learning and the related topic of the impact of varying levels of first-language literacy cannot be addressed systematically without more studies providing comparable cross-age data. Questions about the existence of and explanations for age differences in second-language/second-literacy acquisition have generated an extensive literature (see Marinova-Todd, Marshall, & Snow, 2000, for a highly partial review). Although much of that literature might be regarded as tangential to issues of literacy development, a little probing makes clear that literacy in the first and second languages interacts with age in complex ways. Jia and Aaronson (2003), for example, showed that Chinese immigrant children under the ages of 10 and 11 switched toward dominance in English relatively quickly, in part, because their access to literacy in Chinese was still quite limited. Slightly older immigrants who had mastered full literacy in Chinese and who had more autonomy selected Chinese-focused activities at a much higher rate, choosing to read Chinese books and magazines, listen to Chinese music, view Chinese videos, and associate with Chinese-speaking peers. Needless to say, their progress in English was slower than that of the younger immigrants, but their maintenance of Chinese was much greater. Greater attention to age differences is consistent with the dynamic, developmental dimension of the model that provides the framework for this volume. Such an emphasis also has enormous importance for practice if the evidence suggests that younger and older English-language learners benefit from different emphases in instruction.

Practitioners are desperate for information about how best to serve older immigrant students, particularly those who have experienced poor or interrupted schooling, whose first-language academic skills are low or indeterminate, and who come from language and schooling backgrounds about which little is known. A much greater focus on postprimary second-language learners is needed to provide a research basis for improved practice in the middle and secondary grades.

Aspects of Literacy

New instructional topics would emerge into sharper focus with greater research attention to older learners, including the challenges of comprehension, learning from text, understanding and producing academic language, genre differentiation, and academic writing. These tasks receive little attention in the early grades, where word reading and initial vocabulary learning dominate the instructional agenda. Yet they are the key challenges for later arrivals, who must tackle them simultaneously with learning basic vocabulary and the basics of reading words in a second language.

Questions about factors that influence the development of academic language skills and the possibility of transfer of these skills from the first to the second language need to take into account cultural differences, individual differences, home language influences, and educational settings and goals.

There is actually a good deal of information available about the production and comprehension of extended discourse by second-language learners. Much of this information comes from the ESL or foreign-language field, and thus deals mainly with students outside the 3- to 18-year age range on which we focus in this volume. Nonetheless, this work holds considerable relevance for understanding the reading development of older English-language learners. For example, Maeno (2000, 2004) found that college-age Japanese second-language speakers learned relatively quickly some key rules for successful Japanese narrative discourse (e.g., to avoid excessive detail), but did not appear to notice other rules adhered to by native speakers (e.g., that information is typically organized in stanzas of three lines). Kang (2003) found that Korean college students writing English narratives tended to underuse orientation and character delineation (by native English speakers' standards) and were much more likely than native English speakers to draw explicit morals from each narrative. Hu-Chou (2000) found that advanced foreign-language students of Chinese failed to organize information in the way expected by Chinese readers when writing academic essays. These examples (all taken from recent Harvard dissertations; dozens more such studies could be cited with a broader and more systematic search) offer some indication of contrasts in textual or extended-discourse rules that could well interfere with comprehension, as well as with the evaluation of students' written output, thereby suggesting some specific targets for instruction.

The impacts of such variations in cultural schemata on second-language reading comprehension and writing have been documented repeatedly since the work of Kintsch and Greene (1978), Kaplan (1966), and Carrell (1983; see also Barnitz, 1986; Devine, Carrell, & Eskey, 1987, for reviews). Much of that work, however, has been published in journals devoted primarily to adult second- and foreign-language learning (*Language Learning, Studies in Second Language Acquisition*), in which learning to read is viewed as a secondary goal or inevitable consequence of language learning, rather than a major task in its own right.

There is also a small body of work on the acquisition of features of academic or distanced discourse among second-language learners. This work is important because of evidence showing that control over academic discourse features relates to reading comprehension (Snow, 1990; Velasco, 1989). In the areas of development and instruction, the Panel limited its review to studies in which reading and writing were outcomes, but a broader definition of literacy could defensibly encompass the oral language skills that relate closely to reading. Velasco (1989), for example, showed that poor readers were less likely than good readers to produce formal word definitions (i.e., ones that included a superordinate) and provided less differentiating information about target words both in Spanish (their first language) and English (the language they were learning).

One can also see the use of language skills in distanced communication as requiring metalinguistic skill—in particular, control of processing skills (Snow, Cancino, De Temple, & Schley, 1991), in which case metalinguistic skill is a possible site for transfer from the first language. In giving definitions, one must suppress the natural, narrative mode and provide information that appears obvious (e.g., "A cat is a small animal that purrs" rather than "I have a cat and she likes to eat cucumbers") to satisfy the task demands. In providing picture descriptions, children are often asked to describe the picture to an imagined listener/reader who cannot see it, thus requiring them to anticipate the communicative needs of a distant audience. The general picture that can be gleaned from this work is that second-language speakers, like first-language speakers, differentiate face-to-face from distanced communication; even in the early grades, second-language learners understand both the need to adapt and the kinds of adaptations that may be helpful. For example, Rodino and Snow (1997) found that Spanish–English bilingual fifth graders in mainstream classrooms produced more words, different words, clarificatory markers, adjectives, specific locatives, and references to internal states when describing a picture to a distant rather than a present audience; these differences held across languages, but were much stronger in English, as was performance overall, suggesting that these learners were forgetting their Spanish. A similar group of learners still in bilingual classrooms showed poorer performance in English, but better performance in Spanish on these measures. Comparable adjustments were made in the content of picture descriptions produced in English (De Temple, Wu, & Snow, 1991) and French (Wu, De Temple, Herman, & Snow, 1994) by elementary students in an international school. In English, the longest and most detailed descriptions were produced orally for the distant audience; in French, the written descriptions were longer and more specific, even when the instructions did not mention the need for distanced communication.

Home exposure to English had limited effects on the quantity or quality of picture descriptions among these students (Ricard & Snow, 1990), about one third of whom came from non-English-speaking homes. Home exposure related more strongly to the quality of formal definitions. Students who spoke French at home produced longer and more complex picture descriptions in French than those who did not, but not more specific or adapted descriptions and not better formal definitions, suggesting indeed that control of processing is independent of language proficiency.

Cross-language correlations in performance on academic language tasks have been found to be quite high in some cases (Davidson, Kline, & Snow, 1986; Velasco, 1989), but rather low in the international-school students studied by other researchers (De Temple *et al.*, 1991; Snow, 1990; Wu *et al.*, 1994). That disparity may be related to the different educational settings of these two groups of students: The first set of studies examined students in truly bilingual programs attempting to promote literacy and academic language use in both languages, whereas the international school, which was the site of the second set of studies, used English as the medium of instruction, offered instruction in English as a second language to students low in English proficiency, and taught French as a foreign language.

Attrition and Bilingualism

Given our focus on English literacy outcomes, it is not surprising that the Panel paid little attention to studies of first-language attrition and the limits on bilingualism under different educational and societal conditions. Language attrition is a complex field in its own right, and one that would not have been easy to incorporate into this review. It is relevant, however, as an aspect of thinking about the value of first-language support in instructional settings and about transfer. After all, if the system from which transfer is meant to occur is withering, what are the implications for the possibility of optimizing transfer effects?

Understanding Where They Start

Reading research conducted in North America has paid remarkably little attention to the reading processes of monolingual readers in other languages. Yet understanding the word- and text-level processing in which both skilled and developing readers of Chinese, Japanese, Arabic, Hindi, Spanish, and other languages engage appears crucial if we are to develop explicit theories of transfer and of universal versus particular processes involved in literacy development. Every orthography poses its own challenges and offers unique mechanisms for representing words graphically, and every language similarly creates specific challenges and offers its own preferred mechanisms for organizing information into literate structures. Research has focused on the psycholinguistic processes involved in reading Chinese (e.g., Chen & Shu, 2001; Perfetti & Tan, 1998), and European researchers have exploited variation in orthographic depth in the study of word-reading development (e.g., Goswami & Bryant, 1990). However, the implications of this work for second-language reading development have been underemphasized.

In addition to arguing for systematic exploitation of what we know about early reading development in other languages, we would argue for much more cross-linguistic analysis that incorporates attention to grammar and discourse as well as orthography. One might argue that proponents of contrastive analysis conducted all the cross-linguistic analysis ever needed. Yet their analyses could be better characterized as cross-language than cross-linguistic; that is, their work was not sufficiently informed by a sophisticated understanding of linguistic systems.

A lesson to be learned from studying first-language acquisition across a wide range of languages is that each language has a domain of relative elaboration or complexity: Spanish has its multiple verb forms, Russian nouns must be marked simultaneously for one of six cases in a way that differs in each of four declensions, Hebrew marks gender on all nouns and on verbs that agree with them, and so on. To the foreign-language learner of any of these languages, these systems seem impossibly complex, and the naive prediction is that they will be acquired late and with difficulty by the young first-language learner. Yet nothing could be further from the truth; children are more likely to make errors with verbs in English than in Spanish and take longer to learn pronominal cases in English than noun cases in Russian. The complexity of the target system becomes a spur to the learner, rather than an obstacle: It defines a problem space that children learning a language encounter early and thus work on diligently.

Our understanding of literacy acquisition can be informed by these findings from cross-linguistic studies of language acquisition. The task of learning to read in any language is defined by the orthographic system of that language. To learn to read in Chinese, one must solve the presenting problem of visual discrimination and visual memory, and all the evidence suggests that Chinese children do so rather efficiently. To learn to read in Arabic, one must solve the presenting problem of selecting from among a small set of possible pronunciations of the written form by using syntactic and meaning cues. To learn to read in English, one must solve the presenting problem of orthographic depth and the identification of both phonological and morphological units. A successful course of acquisition is driven by the nature of the skilled processes needed. This is the insight provided by truly cross-linguistic analyses.

Thus, it is not surprising that the individual skills that predict good reading outcomes for English-learning versus monolingual English readers are so similar—they are the skills that help children solve the particular challenges of reading English. Nor is it surprising that features of instruction that work well for English monolingual children also work for English-learning children, who must learn the same skills because they are ultimately faced with the same task. These understandings would be more accessible if the research being done on second-language reading were informed more systematically by the linguistic and orthographic challenges of the target language.

This same argument, of course, should apply equally, although perhaps even more complexly, to the processes involved in comprehension. As discussed earlier, we know that there are language-specific rules for organizing information in text and differentiating genres. There are also culture-specific rules for what it means to comprehend—how much work is meant to be the responsibility of the reader versus the writer. These are systems that reveal themselves in differences among the narratives of Asian, Latino, and Anglo preschool children (McCabe, 1996; McCabe & Bliss, 2003), in school-age children's science reasoning (Ballenger, 1997; Hudicourt-Barnes, in press), and in extended written and oral discourses (Hu-Chou, 2000; Kang, 2003; Maeno, 2000, 2004). These systems need to be understood on their own terms before it becomes possible to see how any two of them contrast, where the potential for positive and negative transfer lies, and what aspects of the contrasts can be targeted most helpfully in instruction.

Finally, second-language literacy instruction ideally should be designed with some understanding of the literacy practices and preferences of second-language learners. For example, Rubinstein-Avila (2001) found that Dominican- and Mexican-origin Latino English-language-learning adolescents read, in both Spanish and English, materials that could have been used as a resource in their literacy instruction had their teachers known more about the students' preferred literacy activities. The students in Rubinstein-Avila's sample who read the most outside of school were also those whose mothers had higher educational levels and who defined themselves as better readers. Survey information from a wider range of second-language learners about their out-of-school literacy practices could be of great value in adapting literacy instruction to these students' needs and interests.

The complex model of influences on reading that informed the Panel's work notes the importance of having available data about both monolingual and fluent bilingual readers to allow for comparison with English-language learners learning to read in their first language, their second language, or both. Clearly, in this view, studies of literacy development in languages other than English constitute part of the research agenda for understanding second-language literacy development.

Learning to Read in a Second Language, the First Time or the Second?

Finally, a key issue that needs more attention in both research and theory on biliteracy is the difference between learning to read in a second language and learning to read a second language. Learning to read for the first time in a second language is arguably a difficult task, particularly for children who have limited oral skills in that language and limited emergent literacy skills in any language. For such children, the task of literacy development is unsupported by a well-developed understanding of the nature and purposes of literacy, and the potential for self-monitoring and self-teaching (Share, 1995) is absent because these processes presume access to meaning via decoding. Children with limited vocabulary knowledge who try to apply initial knowledge of letter–sound correspondences to printed forms will have little basis for knowing whether they are performing this task correctly, and thus they will be unable to progress without constant access to instructional guidance.

Weber and Longhi-Chirlin (2001) present case studies of two Spanish-speaking first graders in an English-only classroom. Both children were making slow progress in comprehending spoken English and in decoding and spelling in English. But they linked the words they were reading only minimally to their oral comprehension skills. Their reading was not informed by the expectation of meaning that is present among first-language readers, and thus the course of literacy development they experienced was quite different from (and likely to be slower and less successful than) that of English-only speakers learning to read in a language they already speak

THEMES THAT CUT ACROSS THE CHAPTERS OF THIS VOLUME

Inevitably in the process of trying to organize and synthesize a sprawling literature, it is necessary to put studies into categories, formulate specific questions, and in other ways simplify the task. The result is that studies that could inform one another sometimes end up being discussed in isolation.

In Chapter 6, we review experimental research suggesting that certain literacy instructional practices are quite effective with second- and first-language readers. But to understand those practices and how to avoid ones that are less effective, we must have information from the qualitative studies discussed in Chapter 7, including rich descriptions of what teachers actually do in classroom settings to engage learners, present lessons, organize the classroom to make differentiated instruction possible, and so on. Thus, there is value in linking studies of instructional effectiveness explicitly to rich descriptions of those effective strategies, rather than isolating impact studies from descriptive studies. In Chapter 3, it makes perfect sense as an organizational strategy to separate studies that identify the predictors of second-language oral proficiency from those that identify the predictors of second-language literacy. But this separation promotes the notion that second-language oral and literacy skills develop independently of one another—that they have separate ontogenies. In fact, language and literacy skills in either the first or second language have a transactional relationship with one another: The development of each depends on and contributes to the development of the other. Thus, it is useful to study first- and second-language oral proficiency and literacy skills together so that transactional links among them can be studied.

Most distorting, however, is the division of topics resulting in the presence in this volume of two chapters focused on the sociocultural context, separating the treatment of language and literacy development from the web of meaning in which it occurs. We would argue that this convenient and perhaps inevitable separation is particularly disorienting when discussing language minorities living in a traditionally monolingual society that is widely committed to monolingual schooling and places little value on bilingualism. The challenge of being, becoming, or remaining a bilingual has an entirely different character in the United States than in the highlands of Peru, in Stockholm, or in Riga; even within the United States, the challenge is quite different in National City, California, than it is in Des Moines, Iowa. We are failing to understand the phenomenon of biliteracy development if we do not integrate the sociocultural context with developmental and instructional data. Thus, it is important to connect the topic of sociocultural context to the treatment of language and literacy development, integrating data about the sociocultural context with developmental and instructional data.

Yet we do not believe we are misrepresenting the field by separating these topics, which tend to be treated in different bodies of work, approached with different methods, and even published in different journals. We are struck (and discouraged) by the degree to which research reports on the literacy development of bilingual children ignore the nature of the communities in which they live, the quality of the instruction they receive, the language-learning goals their parents hold for them, and the daily opportunities they experience to speak English or another tongue. We are equally troubled by how often we encounter descriptions of the context of second-language/literacy acquisition unaccompanied by data about the outcome of the acquisition process.

Building on the previous chapters that link language to literacy and on the synthesis that appears earlier in the present chapter, we discuss here a few further specific cases of the need for integration. In doing so, we explore in greater detail how integrating information across levels, disciplines, and settings—something seldom done because it requires a level of collaboration and cross-fertilization that goes beyond the capacity of most research—could lead to a comprehensive picture of second-language and second-literacy learning.

The Link Between English Proficiency and the First-Language Context

In one scenario, adolescent immigrants from China, the Dominican Republic, Mexico, and Haiti all arrive in the United States at about the same time, with parents who have immigrated for more or less the same reasons (Páez, 2001). They all attend similar sorts of schools, sometimes even the same schools. Yet four years later, there are significant differences in the levels of English spoken by members of the three language groups and in the degree to which they have maintained their home language. The Haitian adolescent immigrants speak English best, but are least likely to have maintained their parents' language. The Spanish speakers are most likely to continue to use Spanish regularly, but their skills in English fall far short of what we might expect. The Chinese adolescent immigrants' scores on a measure of oral English are, on average, slightly below those of the Haitians, but only in the Chinese group do any students score at a level indicating adequate English proficiency. In other words, the process of learning English is related to the likelihood of maintaining the home language, and that in turn is influenced by such factors as the history of literacy and education in the home language (which promote home language maintenance for Chinese immigrants) and the ease of travel to and continued political participation in the home country (which promote home language maintenance for Spanish-speaking immigrants).

The Link Between English Proficiency and the Second-Language Context

In another scenario, Spanish-speaking children are learning to read and write in English in a number of different settings: in English-only instructional settings in Seattle, Washington; in transitional bilingual programs in New York City; in two-way bilingual programs in Boston, Massachusetts; and in bilingual schools in Bogotá, Colombia. In the second and fourth cases, all the children in the class are native Spanish speakers, whereas in the first and third, half or fewer are. The children in Bogotá are probably more middle class than those in the other settings. The children in the three U.S. settings hear quite a lot of English outside of school, whereas the children in Bogotá rarely do. From one perspective, the tasks of learning to speak, understand, read, and write English are the same for all these children. All must grapple with the problem spaces defined by English vocabulary, phonology, grammar, and orthography.

From other perspectives, however, these learners have quite different tasks ahead of them. Spanish speakers in Seattle are a minority of the non-English speakers in the city's schools; the faster they learn English, the sooner they assert their dominance within the immigrant community. By fourth grade, most of these students are essentially monolingual English speakers, but many are still reading poorly in English. Spanish speakers in New York are given little support for Spanish literacy development, but they code mix Spanish and English daily with family members and neighbors, and they visit Puerto Rico or the Dominican Republic regularly; thus, their oral Spanish skills continue to develop even as they learn English. Furthermore, the variety of English they learn is heavily influenced by Spanish, just as their variety of Spanish is heavily influenced by English. The Spanish speakers in Boston have access to support for Spanish literacy development, but their opportunities for rich oral Spanish are constrained by the limited Spanish of their English-speaking classmates. By fourth grade, quite a lot of English is spoken by everyone in their classes, even during Spanish time. Several of the Spanish speakers are resisting returning to the bilingual fifth grade, saying they would rather go to a regular school. The children in Bogotá continue to speak Spanish with each other; by fourth grade, some of them are competent English readers, whereas others are still struggling in English, although they read well in Spanish. A few of the children have been pulled out of the school and placed in all-Spanish educational settings by their parents in response to their struggles.

Although they have been exposed to as much English instruction as the children in Boston, on average their English is much less developed. In contrast, the Spanish-speaking parents in Boston are worried that their children do not speak English well enough, whereas the parents in Bogotá are thrilled at their children's English skills.

All these children faced the same tasks from a purely psycholinguistic perspective, from a cross-linguistic perspective, and from an instructional perspective. But these perspectives are not enough. The political perspective that defines English as the national language of the United States and Spanish as the national language of Colombia cannot be ignored. Also relevant is the economic perspective—that immigrants must learn English to survive in the United States and gain little additional value from their home language, whereas Colombians must speak Spanish but gain an advantage in the labor market if they also speak English. The sociological perspective, which defines who interacts with whom and in what languages, must be considered as well because opportunities for interaction also constitute opportunities for language learning. Nor can the cultural perspective, from which derive the value of bilingualism to children and their families and their sense of connection to the ancestral land, be forgotten, although it can be trumped by other considerations. As the students in these four settings grow older, the forces of adolescent development, identity formation, personal preferences, talents, and motivation start to play a role in their pursuit of English, Spanish, or bilingual outcomes. Most clearly, however, if they have not also learned to read well in either or both languages, their futures will be severely imperiled.

REFERENCES

Au, K. H.-P., & Mason, J. M. (1981). Social organizational factors in learning to read: The balance of rights hypothesis. *Reading Research Quarterly, 17*(1), 115–152.

Baker, S., & Smith, S. (1999). Starting off on the right foot: The influence of four principles of professional development in improving literacy instruction in two kindergarten programs. *Learning Disabilities Research and Practice, 14*(4), 239–253.

Ballenger, C. (1997). Social identities, moral narratives, scientific argumentation: Science talk in a bilingual classroom. *Language and Education, 11*(1), 1–14.

Barnitz, J. (1986). Toward understanding the effects of cross-cultural schemata and discourse structure on second language reading comprehension. *Journal of Reading Behavior, 18*, 95–118.

Barnitz, J., & Speaker, R. (1991). Second language readers' comprehension of a poem: Exploring contextual and linguistic aspects. *World English, 10*, 197–209.

Bialystok, E., & Bouchard Ryan, E. (1985). Toward a definition of metalinguistic skill. *Merrill-Palmer Quarterly, 31*, 229–251.

Carrell, P. (1983). Three components of background knowledge in reading comprehension. *Language Learning, 33*, 183–207.

Chen, H.-C., & Shu, H. (2001). Lexical activation during the recognition of Chinese characters: Evidence against early phonological activation. *Psychonomic Bulletin and Review*, 8, 511–518.

Cummins, J. (1979). Linguistic interdependence and the educational development of bilingual children. *Review of Educational Research*, 49, 221–225.

Davidson, R., Kline, S., & Snow, C. E. (1986). Definitions and definite noun phrases: Indicators of children's decontextualized language skills. *Journal of Research in Childhood Education*, 1, 37–48.

De Temple, J., Wu, H. F., & Snow, C. E. (1991). Papa Pig just left for Pigtown: Children's oral and written picture descriptions under varying instructions. *Discourse Processes*, 14, 469–495.

Denton, C. A. (2000). The efficacy of two English reading interventions in a bilingual education program. Unpublished doctoral dissertation, Texas A&M University, College Station.

Devine, J., Carrell, P., & Eskey, D. (Eds.). (1987). *Research in reading in English as a second language*. Washington, DC: Teachers of English to Speakers of Other Languages.

Gersten, R., Morvant, M., & Brengleman, S. (1995). Close to the classroom is close to the bone: Coaching as a means to translate research into classroom practice. *Exceptional Children*, 52, 102–197.

Goswami, U., & Bryant, P. (1990). *Phonological skills and learning to read*. Hillsdale, NJ: Lawrence Erlbaum Associates.

Gunn, B., Biglan, A., Smolkowski, K., & Ary, D. (2000). The efficacy of supplemental instruction in decoding skills for Hispanic and non-Hispanic students in early elementary school. *Journal of Special Education*, 34(2), 90–103.

Gunn, B., Smolkowski, K., Biglan, A., & Black, C. (2002). Supplemental instruction in decoding skills for Hispanic and non-Hispanic students in early elementary school: A follow-up. *Journal of Special Education*, 36(2), 69–79.

Hu-Chou, H.-L. (2000). Toward an understanding of writing in a second language: Evidence and its implications from L2 writers of Chinese. Unpublished doctoral dissertation, Harvard Graduate School of Education.

Hudicourt-Barnes, J. (in press). Argumentation in Haitian Creole classrooms. *Harvard Educational Review*.

Jia, G., & Aaronson, D. (2003). A longitudinal study of Chinese children and adolescents learning English in the United States. *Applied Psycholinguistics*, 24, 131–161.

Kang, J. Y. (2003). On producing culturally and linguistically appropriate narratives in a foreign language: A discourse analysis of Korean EFL learners' written narratives. Unpublished doctoral dissertation, Harvard Graduate School of Education.

Kaplan, R. B. (1966). Cultural thought patterns in intercultural education. *Language Learning*, 16(1), 1–20.

Kintsch, W., & Greene, E. (1978). The role of culture-specific schemata in the comprehension and recall of stories. *Discourse Processes*, 1, 1–13.

Lado, R. (1964). *Language teaching: A scientific approach*, New York: McGraw-Hill.

Maeno, Y. (2000). Acquisition of Japanese oral narrative style by native English-speaking bilinguals. Unpublished doctoral dissertation, Harvard Graduate School of Education.

Maeno, Y. (2004). *The acquisition of the Japanese oral narrative style by native English-speaking bilinguals*. Lewiston, NY: Edwin Mellen.

Marinova-Todd, S., Marshall, D. B., & Snow, C. E. (2000). Three misconceptions about age and second-language learning. *TESOL Quarterly*, 34, 9–34.

McCabe, A. (1996). *Chameleon readers: Teaching children to appreciate all kinds of good stories*. New York: McGraw-Hill.

McCabe, A., & Bliss, L. (2003). *Patterns of narrative discourse: A multicultural, life span approach*. Boston, MA: Allyn & Bacon.

National Institute of Child Health and Human Development. (2000). *Report of the National Reading Panel. Teaching children to read: An evidence-based assessment of the scientific research literature on reading and its implications for reading instruction* (NIH Publication No. 00–4769). Washington, DC: U.S. Government Printing Office.

Páez, M. (2001). Language and the immigrant child: Predicting English language proficiency for Chinese, Dominican, and Haitian students. Unpublished doctoral dissertation, Harvard Graduate School of Education.

Perfetti, C., & Tan, L. H. (1998). The time course of graphic, phonological, and semantic activation in Chinese character identification. *Journal of Experimental Psychology: Learning, Memory, & Cognition, 24,* 101–118.

Ricard, R. J., & Snow, C. E. (1990). Language skills in and out of context: Evidence from children's picture descriptions. *Journal of Applied Developmental Psychology, 11,* 251–266.

Rodino, A. M., & Snow, C. E. (1997). "Y . . . no puedo decir mas nada": Distanced communication skills of Puerto Rican children. In G. Kasper & E. Kellerman (Eds.), *Communication strategies: Psycholinguistic and sociolinguistic perspectives* (pp. 168–191). London: Longman.

Rubinstein-Avila, E. (2001). From their points of view: Literacies among Latino immigrant students. Unpublished doctoral dissertation, Harvard Graduate School of Education.

Share, D. L. (1995). Phonological recoding and self-teaching: Sine qua non of reading acquisition. *Cognition, 55,* 151–218.

Snow, C. E. (1990). The development of definitional skill. *Journal of Child Language, 17,* 697–710.

Snow, C. E., Cancino, H., De Temple, J., & Schley, S. (1991). Giving formal definitions: A linguistic or metalinguistic skill? In E. Bialystok (Ed.), *Language processing and language awareness by bilingual children* (pp. 90–112). New York: Cambridge University Press.

Snow, C. E., (2003). Assessment of reading comprehension: Researchers and practitioners helping themselves and each other. In A. Sweet, & C. E. Snow, (Eds.). *Rethinking reading comprehension* (pp. 192–206). New York: The Guilford Press.

Tabors, P. O., & Snow, C. E. (1994). English as a second language in pre-school programs. In F. Genesee (Ed.), *Educating second language children* (pp. 103–125). New York: Cambridge University Press.

Tabors, P. O., & Snow, C. E. (2001). Young bilingual children and early literacy development. In S. Neuman & D. K. Dickinson (Eds.), *Handbook of early literacy research* (pp. 159–178). New York: Guilford.

Velasco, P. M. (1989). The relationship of oral decontextualized language and reading comprehension in bilingual children. Unpublished doctoral dissertation, Harvard Graduate School of Education.

Weber, R.-M., & Longhi-Chirlin, T. (2001). Beginning in English: The growth of linguistic and literate abilities in Spanish-speaking first graders. *Reading Research and Instruction, 41,* 19–50.

Wu, H. F., De Temple, J. M., Herman, J. A., & Snow, C. E. (1994). L'animal qui fait oink! oink!: Bilingual children's oral and written picture descriptions in English and French under varying circumstances. *Discourse Processes, 18,* 141–164.

Notes on Contributors

DIANE AUGUST, PRINCIPAL INVESTIGATOR

Dr. August is currently a Senior Research Scientist at the Center for Applied Linguistics, where she is directing a large study funded by the National Institute of Child Health and Human Development (NICHD) and the Institute of Education Sciences (IES), which investigates the development of literacy in English-language learners. She is also co-principal investigator on two IES-funded studies: The first is to develop, implement, and evaluate two models of instruction for language-minority children; and the second is to develop a diagnostic assessment of reading comprehension. She is also a co-principal investigator for the Department of Education-funded National Research and Development Center for English Language Learners. Dr. August has worked for many years as an educational consultant in the areas of literacy, program improvement, evaluation and testing, and federal and state education policy. She has been a Senior Program Officer at the National Academy of Sciences and study director for the Committee on Developing a Research Agenda on the Education of Limited English Proficient and Bilingual Students. For 10 years, she was a public school teacher in California, specializing in literacy programs for language minority children in Grades K to 8. Subsequently, she served as a legislative assistant in the area of education for a U.S. congressman from California, worked as a Grants Officer for Carnegie Corporation of New York, and was Director of Education for the Children's Defense Fund. Among her numerous publications are two volumes co-edited with Kenji Hakuta: *Educating English Language Learners* and *Improving Schooling for Language-Minority Children: A Research Agenda*.

TIMOTHY SHANAHAN, PANEL CHAIR

Dr. Shanahan is Professor of Urban Education at the University of Illinois at Chicago (UIC) and Director of the UIC Center for Literacy. He was President of the International Reading Association (IRA) in 2006–2007. He was Director of Reading for the Chicago Public Schools, the nation's third largest school district. Dr. Shanahan was a member of the National Reading Panel that advised the U.S. Congress on reading research, and he is Chair of the National Early Literacy Panel. He has published more than 150 books, articles, and chapters on reading education, and he received the Albert J. Harris Research Award for his work on reading disabilities. Professor Shanahan co-designed Project FLAME, a family literacy program for Latino immigrants, which has received an Academic Excellence designation from the U.S. Department of Education. He has been editor of the *Journal of Reading Behavior* and the *Yearbook of the National Reading Conference*. He serves on the Board of Directors of the National Family Literacy Center.

ISABEL L. BECK

Dr. Beck is Professor of Education in the School of Education and Senior Scientist at the Learning Research and Development Center, both at the University of Pittsburgh. She has engaged in extensive research on decoding, vocabulary, and comprehension, and she has published approximately 100 articles and book chapters, as well as several books. Most recently, she co-authored *Bringing Words to Life: Robust Vocabulary Instruction* (with M. McKeown and L. Kucan, Guilford). Dr. Beck's work has been acknowledged with such awards as the Oscar S. Causey Award for outstanding research from the National Reading Conference and the Contributing Researcher Award from the American Federation of Teachers for "bridging the gap between research and practice." She is also a member of the International Reading Association's Hall of Fame, and most recently she received that organization's William S. Gray Citation. Among the criteria for which she received the latter was "initiation and development of original ideas that have ... improved practices in reading."

MARGARITA CALDERÓN

Dr. Calderón, a native of Juárez, Mexico, is a Research Scientist at Johns Hopkins University's Center for Research on the Education of Students Placed at Risk (CRESPAR). She is co-principal investigator with Robert Slavin on the 5-year randomized evaluation of English immersion, transitional, and two-way bilingual programs, funded by the Institute of Education Sciences. Through a series of other grants from OERI/IES, the Texas Education Agency, the Texas Workforce Commission, and the Department of Labor, she is conducting longitudinal research and development projects in El Paso, Texas, regarding teachers' learning communities, bilingual staff development, and adult English-language learners. She conducts research on reading programs for the Success for All Foundation and is collaborating with the Center for Applied Linguistics in a longitudinal study investigating the development of literacy in English-language learners. She co-edited (with Robert Slavin) *Effective Programs for Latino Students*, co-authored (with Liliana Minaya-Rowe) *Implementing Two-Way Bilingual Programs*, and has published more than 100 articles, chapters, books, and teacher training manuals. Other professional activities include the research and development of the Bilingual Cooperative Integrated Reading and Composition (BCIRC) model and the Teachers' Learning Communities program.

CHERYL DRESSLER

Dr. Dressler is a literacy consultant. She was a teacher of English as a second language (ESOL) at the secondary level in Switzerland and at the primary and university levels in the United States. In 2002, Dr. Dressler received an EdD from the Harvard Graduate School of Education. During her doctoral study years, she assisted in a longitudinal, in-depth study of the vocabulary development of monolingual and bilingual fourth- and fifth-graders. Her doctoral thesis investigated the English spelling development of Spanish-speaking English-language learners. Dr. Dressler's current research interests include the development of vocabulary and word structure knowledge, including orthographic and morphological knowledge, both in children who are native English speakers and in English learners. She has published in *Reading Research Quarterly* and *Learning Disabilities Research & Practice*, and she recently authored a vocabulary program for students in kindergarten and first grade, *Wordly Wise 3000 Book K and Book 1, Junior* (Educators Publishing Service).

FREDERICK ERICKSON

Dr. Erickson is George F. Kneller Professor of Anthropology of Education at the University of California, Los Angeles, where he has also been director of research at the university's laboratory elementary school. Previously, he taught at the University of Illinois, Harvard University, Michigan State University, and the University of Pennsylvania. He has been involved in the development of theory and methods in contemporary ethnography, sociolinguistics, and discourse analysis, and he has been an innovator in video-based analysis of face-to-face interaction. His sponsored research includes support by the National Institute of Mental Health, the National Institute of Education, the Spencer Foundation, and the Ford Foundation, as well as grants from the Fulbright Commission and the British Council. He has published two books and numerous articles, including an essay on qualitative research on teaching for the third edition of the *Handbook of Research on Teaching*, and articles on ethnicity and ethnographic description in *Sociolinguistics: An International Handbook of the Science of Language and Society*. He has served on the editorial boards of several journals and was editor of *Anthropology and Education Quarterly*. He has been an officer of the American Anthropological Association, from which he received the George and Louise Spindler Award for outstanding scholarly contributions to educational anthropology, and of the American Educational Research Association (AERA), from which he received an award for distinguished research on minority issues in education. In 2000, he was elected a Fellow of the National Academy of Education. In 1998–1999, he was a Fellow at the Center for Advanced Study in the Behavioral Sciences in Stanford, California. He returned to the center as a Fellow in 2006–2007.

DAVID J. FRANCIS

Dr. Francis is Professor of Quantitative Methods and Chairman of the Department of Psychology at the University of Houston, where he also serves as Director of the Texas Institute for Measurement, Evaluation, and Statistics. He is a Fellow of Division 5 (Measurement, Evaluation, and Statistics) of the American Psychological Association and a member of the Technical Advisory Group of the What Works Clearinghouse. He has also served as Chairman of the Mental Retardation Research Subcommittee of the National Institute of Child Health and Human Development (NICHD) and the Advisory Council on Education Statistics. He is a member of national advisory panels for several federally funded projects, research centers, and state departments of education. He is also a recipient of the University of Houston Teaching Excellence Award. His areas of quantitative interest include multilevel and latent variable modeling, individual growth models, item response theory (IRT), and exploratory data analysis. Dr. Francis is currently the principal investigator on three major research projects funded by the Institute of Education Sciences and NICHD that focus on language and literacy acquisition of language-minority children. He has collaborated for many years in research on reading and reading disabilities, attention problems, and developmental consequences of brain injuries and birth defects.

GEORGIA EARNEST GARCÍA

Dr. García is a Professor in the Language and Literacy Division, Department of Curriculum and Instruction, University of Illinois at Urbana–Champaign. She also holds an appointment in the Department of Educational Policy Studies and is a faculty affiliate with the Latinas/ Latinos Studies Program. Dr. García was a Senior Research Scientist at the Center for the Study of Reading for 6 years and a Fellow in the Bureau of Educational Research from 1993 to 1996. She served on the Assessment Task Force, National Council on Education Standards and Testing and, most recently, was a member of the RAND Reading Study Group on Skillful Reading. She was named a College of Education Distinguished Scholar in 1997 and was awarded the Faculty Award for Excellence in Graduate Teaching, Advising, and Research by the Council of Graduate Students in Education in 1993. She was elected to the Board of Directors of the National Reading Conference from 1998 to 2000. Dr. García's research has been funded by the Office of Educational Research and Improvement (now the Institute of Education Sciences), the Office of Special Education Programs, and the Mellon Foundation. Her areas of research include the literacy development, instruction, and assessment of students from culturally and linguistically diverse backgrounds, with much of her current research focusing on bilingual reading and writing. She has published her work in the *American Educational Research Journal, Anthropology and Education Quarterly, Journal of Literacy Research/Reading Behavior, Reading Research Quarterly, Research in the Teaching of English*, and *Review of Research in Education*. She wrote the chapter on bilingual children's reading for the third volume of the *Handbook of Reading Research*, and she was co-guest editor for the themed issue on multicultural literacy research and practice for the *Journal of Literacy Research*.

FRED GENESEE

Dr. Genesee is a Professor in the Psychology Department at McGill University, Montreal, Canada. He is the author of nine books and numerous articles in scientific, professional, and popular journals and publications. He has carried out extensive research on alternative approaches to bilingual education, including second/foreign-language immersion programs for language-majority students and alternative forms of bilingual education for language-minority students. This work has systematically documented the longitudinal language development (oral and written) and academic achievement of students educated through the media of two languages. Along with Donna Christian and Elizabeth Howard, he has carried out a national longitudinal study of a number of two-way immersion programs in the United States. He has consulted with policy groups in Canada, Estonia, Germany, Hong Kong, Italy, Japan, Latvia, Russia, Spain, and the United States on issues related to second-language teaching and learning in school-age learners. Dr. Genesee's current research focuses on simultaneous acquisition of two languages during early infancy and childhood. His specific interests include language representation (lexical and syntactic) in early stages of bilingual acquisition, transfer in bilingual development, structural and functional characteristics of child bilingual code mixing, and communication skills in young bilingual children.

ESTHER GEVA

Dr. Geva is a Professor in the Department of Human Development and Applied Psychology at the Ontario Institute for Studies in Education of the University of Toronto. The bulk of Dr. Geva's research, publications, conference presentations, and workshops concerns issues in the development of second-language reading skills in children and adults from various linguistic backgrounds. In recent years, Dr. Geva's research interests have focused primarily on theoretical and clinical aspects of language and literacy development in primary-level English-language learning children. Her research is funded by the Social Sciences and Humanities Research Council of Canada, the Ontario Ministry of Education, and the National Center of Excellence. Recently, Dr. Geva obtained (with Michal Shany from Haifa University) a grant to study developmental and instructional issues in the literacy development of Ethiopian children in Israel. This grant, funded by the Israeli National Research Council, was awarded the Chief Scientist prize for the best research grant. Dr. Geva is a member of the Highly Qualified Personnel Committee of the Canadian Language and Literacy Research Network and has served on various U.S. and Canadian committees concerned with literacy development in minority children. She has edited (with Ludo Verhoeven) a special issue of *Reading and Writing: An Interdisciplinary Journal*, entitled Cross-Orthography Perspectives on Word Recognition, and co-edited a special issue of the *Journal of Scientific Studies of Reading*, entitled Basic Processes in Early Second Language Reading. Her clinical and research work with minority children resulted in the book *Interprofessional Practice With Diverse Populations: Cases in Point* (co-edited with A. Barsky and F. Westernoff). Her articles have appeared in journals such as *Annals of Dyslexia, Language Learning, Applied Psycholinguistics, Reading and Writing: An Interdisciplinary Journal*, and *Dyslexia*.

CLAUDE GOLDENBERG

Dr. Goldenberg, a native of Argentina, is Executive Director of the Center for Language Minority Education and Research (CLMER) and Associate Dean of the College of Education at California State University, Long Beach. His research has focused on Latino children's academic development, home–school connections to improve achievement, home and school factors in Latino children's academic achievement, and the processes and dynamics of school change. Dr. Goldenberg was a National Academy of Education Spencer Fellow, received a Research Recognition Award from the University of California Office of the President, and was co-recipient (with Ronald Gallimore) of the International Reading Association's Albert J. Harris Award. He was on the National Research Council's Head Start Research Roundtable and on the Council's Committee on the Prevention of Early Reading Difficulties in Young Children. He has been on the editorial boards of *Language Arts, The Elementary School Journal*, and *Literacy, Teaching and Learning*. He is the author of *Successful School Change: Creating Settings to Improve Teaching and Learning* (Teachers College Press, 2004), which describes a 5-year project to improve teaching and learning in a predominantly Hispanic school.

MICHAEL L. KAMIL

Dr. Kamil is Professor of Education at Stanford University. He is a member of the Psychological Studies in Education Committee and is on the faculty of the Learning Sciences and Technology Design Program. His research explores the effects of computer technologies on literacy and the acquisition of literacy in first and second languages. For the past several years, he has been researching the effects of recreational reading on reading achievement for English-language learner populations. His research is funded by the California Postsecondary Education Commission, Mid-Atlantic Regional Educational Laboratory, and Pacific Regional Educational Laboratory. Dr. Kamil has been editor of *Reading Research Quarterly, Journal of Reading Behavior*, and the *Yearbook of the National Reading Conference*. He currently serves on several editorial advisory boards for research journals. He was a member of the National Reading Panel and the RAND Reading Study Group. He was the lead editor of the *Handbook of Reading Research*, Volume III, and is the lead editor for Volume IV. He served as chair of the 2009 NAEP Reading Framework Committee for the National Assessment of Educational Progress. He serves as a member of the Advisory Panel for the National Evaluation of Educational Technology. In addition, he has edited, authored, or co-authored more than 100 books, chapters, and journal articles.

His recent publications include a co-edited volume on professional development for reading instruction (with Dorothy Strickland) and a monograph reviewing the research on adolescent literacy.

KEIKO KODA

Dr. Koda is Associate Professor in the Department of Modern Languages at Carnegie Mellon University. Her major research areas include second-language reading, biliteracy development, psycholinguistics, and foreign language pedagogy. She has been widely published in refereed journals and has authored a number of book chapters. She recently completed a monograph, *Insights Into Second Language Reading* (Cambridge University Press, 2004). She has been a member of the editorial boards of *TESOL Quarterly, Research in Second Language Learning, International Review of Applied Linguistics in Language Teaching,* and *The Modern Language Journal.* She is a consultant for the Educational Testing Service and the American Council on the Teaching of Foreign Languages in second-language reading and assessment. She also serves as a member of the Test of English as a Foreign Language (TOEFL) Committee of Examiners at the Educational Testing Service. Her work has appeared in *Applied Psycholinguistics, Cognition, The Modern Language Journal, Journal of Child Language, Journal of Psycholinguistic Research, Language Learning, Second Language Research,* and *Studies in Second Language Acquisition.* Currently, she is involved in ongoing projects on crosslinguistic variations in reading acquisition, which will be published in a forthcoming volume, *Learning to Read Across Languages* (Lawrence Erlbaum Associates, 2006).

NONIE K. LESAUX

Dr. Lesaux is Assistant Professor of Human Development and Psychology at the Harvard Graduate School of Education. Her research focuses on the reading development and developmental health of children who are at risk for learning difficulties. These children include children from language-minority backgrounds, children from low socioeconomic backgrounds, and children with difficulties in language processing and other skills that influence reading development. Her doctoral research (University of British Columbia, 2003) reported on the findings of a 5-year longitudinal study that examined the development of reading, from kindergarten through Grade 4, of language-minority learners who entered mainstream classrooms with little or no proficiency in English, compared with their native-speaking peers. Her current research projects are designed to continue to develop an understanding of reading development of language-minority learners, as well as to continue to examine the relationships among demographic, health, language, and reading-related variables in at-risk populations. Dr. Lesaux is currently principal investigator on a project funded by the NICHD that focuses on the relationship between Spanish and English oral language and literacy skills as they relate to reading comprehension for Spanish speakers developing literacy skills in English. In 2003, she was a finalist in the International Reading Association's Outstanding Dissertation Competition. Dr. Lesaux has published her work in *Developmental Psychology* and the *Journal of Learning Disabilities*, and she is a member of the International Academy for Research in Learning Disabilities, Society for the Scientific Study of Reading, and Society for Research in Child Development.

GAIL McKOON

Dr. McKoon is Professor of Psychology in the College of Social and Behavioral Sciences at Ohio State University. Her primary research interests are reading, human memory, and knowledge representation, and she is considered a leading expert in research on reading comprehension. She has served on advisory panels for the National Science Foundation and the National Institute of Mental Health, and she has published more than 80 articles in peer-reviewed journals. In 1985, she was designated by the Social Science Citation Indices as one of the 50 highest-impact authors in psychology, and in 2002, she was honored by election to the prestigious Society for Experimental Psychology.

ROBERT S. RUEDA

Dr. Rueda is Professor of Psychology in Education at the Rossier School of education at the University of Southern California. Dr. Rueda's research interests center on the sociocultural factors in learning and motivation, with a focus on reading and literacy in students in at-risk conditions, English-language learners, and students with mild learning disabilities. His recent work has been funded through the National Center for the Improvement of Early Reading Achievement, and the National Center for Research on Education, Diversity, and Excellence. His articles have appeared in journals such as the *Journal of Research in Education, Remedial and Special Education, Exceptional Children, Anthropology and Education Quarterly, Urban Education*, and *The Elementary School Journal*. Recently, in monographs and book chapters, he has collaborated with others in treating the sociocultural issues involved in the teaching of diverse learners. He has served as a reviewer for a wide variety of journals of education and psychology, and he has been a member of the editorial boards of *American Educational Research Journal, Journal of Literacy Research, NRC Yearbook, The California Reader, Review of Research in Education, Learning Disabilities Research and Practice, Exceptional Children,* and *Education and Training in Mental Retardation and Developmental Disabilities.* Dr. Rueda is a Fellow of the American Psychological Association.

LINDA S. SIEGEL

Dr. Siegel holds the Dorothy C. Lam Chair in the Department of Special Education and is Associate Dean for Graduate Studies and Research in the Faculty of Education at the University of British Columbia. She has published more than 130 peer-reviewed articles, as well as numerous other publications, on cognitive and language development (spanning oral language development as well as reading, writing, and spelling). She has received international recognition for her research in reading, learning disabilities (e.g., assessment and intelligence tests), bilingualism, ESOL, and language learning of French, Spanish, Chinese, Punjabi, Arabic, Italian, Portuguese, and other languages, and she has published articles in Italian, French, Spanish, and English. Dr. Siegel has been the Associate Editor of *Child Development* and the Editor of the *International Journal of Behavioral Development,* has served on the editorial boards of a number of journals, and has participated in research grant review panels in the United States, Canada, and Hong Kong. She is currently directing an English immersion program in Xian, China, and conducting research on English-language teaching in Hong Kong.

CATHERINE SNOW

Dr. Snow is the Henry Lee Shattuck Professor of Education at the Harvard Graduate School of Education. Her work focuses on language development in mono- and bilingual children, and on the role of language knowledge in literacy development. She has been a visiting professor or visiting scientist at several institutions, including the Universidad Autónoma de Madrid and New York University. She began her academic career in the Linguistics Institute at the University of Amsterdam. A leading authority in the field of reading and literacy, Dr. Snow has a list of publications that fills many pages. In 2001–2003 alone, she authored or co-authored more than a dozen articles and chapters and co-edited seven books. She chaired the Committee on the Prevention of Reading Difficulties in Young Children of the National Research Council and The RAND Reading Study Group, and currently chairs the Carnegie Corporation of New York's Advisory Council on Advancing Literacy.

Index

311

Greene, E. 289
Greene, J. P. 178–179*t*
Gregory, E. 112
Gunn, B. *et al.* 141, 142*t*, 184–185*t*
Guthrie, J. 33
Gutiérrez, K. D. 114

Haager, D. 164, 165, 166
Hacquebord, H. 41, 43
Hafiz, F. 147
Hakuta, K. 13, 253, 254–255, 269
Hancin-Bhatt, B. 76–77
Hancock, D. R. 109, 148*t*, 150, 211*t*
Hannon, P. 261
Hansen, D. A. 109
Hart, B. 33
Haslett, S. J. 145
Hastings-Góngora, B. 148*t*, 150, 211–212*t*
Hatch, E. 259
Hawkins, R. 66
Hernández, J. S. 79, 151, 152–153
Hoffman, J. V. *et al.* 164, 165
Holm, A. *et al.* 70, 263, 264
Horn, S. P. 167
Horowitz, R. 262
Hsia, S. 70
Hu-Chou, H.-L. 289, 293
Hudicourt-Barnes, J. 293
Huerta-Macías, A. 104, 114
Hughes, M. T. *et al.* 160, 164, 233*t*
Humphreys, G. W. 37, 72, 73
Hus, Y. 151, 152, 153
Huss, R. L. 112, 114
Huss-Keeler, R. L. 112, 114
Huzar, H. 137*t*, 139, 178*t*, 183*t*
Hyltenstam, K. 63

IDEA Language Proficiency Tests 258, 259
Ima, K. 101, 103
immigration 117–118
  generation status 103
  influence of circumstances 102–103, 279
  in other countries 24–25
individual differences 33, 275–276, 279, 280
instruction 131–177
  age differences 288
  and assessment 286
  background 132

complex approaches 147–151, 148–149*t*, 154–158, 205–232*t*
  contexts 20–21
  cross-cutting themes 167–172, 284–287, 295
  developing students' proficiency 168
  differentiation 33, 156, 169–170, 286
  effective classrooms and schools 158–159, 169
  effective literacy teaching 140–151, 153, 167–168
  findings 9–11, 133–167, 284–287
  future research recommendations 174–177, 288
  influence of native-language literacy 171, 293–294
  influence of second-language oral proficiency 171
  language of instruction 11, 132, 133–140, 136–137*t*, 138*t*, 178–179*t*, 180–183*t* 285
  literacy development 170–171
  methodological issues 53, 172–174, 175–176
  methodology of the review 132–133
  and professional development 157–158, 168–169, 286–287
  qualitative studies of practice 151–159, 172, 173–174, 175
  role of sociocultural context 105–107, 119–120, 171–172, 286
  school change 159, 169
  segregation 20–21
  special needs 160–164, 161*t* 286
  specific elements of literacy 141–147, 142–143*t*, 151–154, 184–204*t*
  teacher expectations 156–157
  see also teachers: beliefs
intelligence (IQ) tests 164
interdependence hypothesis 64–65, 68, 75, 281
interlanguage theories 66, 75, 76
intervention studies 87–88
Israel 24–25

Jackson, N. E. 45
Jackson, N. *et al.* 36
Jacobs, J. E. 79
James, C. 75–77
Jansky, J. J. *et al.* 262